D1429138

EDUCATION AND THE WORKING CLASS

Reports of
The Institute of Community Studies

EDUCATION AND THE WORKING CLASS

Some general themes raised by a study of
88 working-class children in a
northern industrial city

Brian Jackson
and
Dennis Marsden

LONDON
ROUTLEDGE AND KEGAN PAUL

First Published 1962
by Routledge & Kegan Paul Ltd
Broadway House, 68-74 Carter Lane
London, E.C.4

Printed in Great Britain
by Compton Printing Co. Ltd.
London, N.1

© *Institute of Community Studies 1962*

Second Impression, 1962
Third Impression, 1965

823408

CONTENTS

for Sheila

ACKNOWLEDGEMENTS

This study was financed out of a grant made to the Institute of Community Studies by the Joseph Rowntree Memorial Trust. We are especially grateful to the Trustees, not only for such fundamental support, but also for many small attentions to present progress and future hopes, too numerous to mention. Without their help the enquiry could hardly have been done in this way.

No doubt it was almost inevitable that we should, at some time, write a report like this. But it might have taken very many years yet, and then been done under considerable disabilities. The circumstance that changed this was a meeting in the summer of 1958 with Michael Young, and the beginning of his generous and often audacious support. A very special debt is also due to Richard Hoggart and Peter Townsend for making so free with a multiplying wealth of social insights, tips, and suggestions; and to our third partner in this venture, Sheila Jackson, we can only say thank you. Others who have helped in various, and often quite vital ways, include Mary Barclay, Douglas Brown, Gwen Burhouse, Ann Cartwright, Daphne Chandler, Tony Crowe, E. Darke, Howard Dickinson, Mary Hoggart, John Garbutt, H. Gray, A. H. Halsey, Robin Hammond, Pat Marsden, Peter Marris, Harold Mettrick, Simon Pratt, Jean Pledger, Jean Rowntree, Richard Titmuss, Ruth Townsend, Lewis Waddilove, William Wallace, Peter Willmott, Phyllis Willmott, the members of the Institute's Advisory Committee, and of course the teachers and former pupils of Marburton's schools.

Cambridge
May, 1961.

BRIAN JACKSON
DENNIS MARSDEN

ACKNOWLEDGEMENTS

PART ONE

I

INTRODUCTION

THIS book is about a city called Marburton. It is a study of the people who live there, their children, and the schools they attend. In particular it is a record of the impact of grammar school education on working-class life. But because the survey we are going to recount is so intimate and local in its detail, we have thought it best to cover our informants, and the places they speak of, with the screen of false names. Marburton is a real city in the north of England. It is the place where we were born ourselves, and the place where we grew up and where we went to school.

This must be declared first. We were formed by the grammar school world of Marburton, and for some years our natural line of interest has led to constant discussion around questions of social class and state education. To begin with there was our own experience. This was not much to build on, nor perhaps was it very reliable. But when we turned elsewhere, combing the libraries for fuller evidence, or when we hunted down the factual basis for the many opinions which shimmered around us, we could find very little. In 1959, 745,126 children were attending grammar schools in England and Wales. What kind of boys and girls they were, or what kind of men and women they became is a closed book. No one knows. The literature of the subject illustrates how complete is our theory of the essential grammar school, and how slender our practical knowledge of its social effects.

When we began this enquiry, we could have chosen as our centre, any city in the country. We chose Marburton. To have gone elsewhere would have strengthened our claims to 'distance' and 'objectivity'. And these are qualities which we value deeply and have tried to attain in this report. But against this there seemed so much to be gained by facing the paramount fact that we were dealing with people and not things; and that any 'objectivity' to

3

which we could lay claim must always conceal areas of 'relation-ship' which, though they might threaten to divert or swamp the social observer, were also, in potential, the richest source of vital understanding. No social observer can simply observe. His essential humanity compels him to feel, to 'belong'. We have therefore brought this unspoken assumption into the light, and on this occasion have stepped outside the conventions and not only chosen as a field one that is intimately linked with our own past lives, but so drawn our central sample that we ourselves would have fallen in it. The image is remote, but in some ways it is as if a Tahitian, trained in London, had returned to the South Seas as an anthropologist. His work would have its limitations, but who would doubt its peculiar rewards for the reader?

There is an essay by Malinowski[1] in which he says, 'The field worker in an exotic tribe has to attune himself as far as possible to the strange mode of behaviour of his human material .. In the study of kinship and marriage, of parenthood and reverence towards ancestors, the human or subjective element cannot be eliminated. The more the observer feels in sympathy with those under observation, the better will he be able to interpret psycho-logically the acts, ritual and personal, of his natives; the more conclusively will he be able to document the occurrence of typical sentiments within his community ... Speech, that is the verbal gestures related to the bodily state of the speakers is undoubtedly the principal clue to easy, intimate converse between observer and native ... To start fieldwork with the native vernacular ... is a handicap so serious that it makes full obser-vation well nigh impossible.' This basic flow of sympathy, which carries on its surface, information, and, in its deeper currents, understanding, has been our aim. In the following pages, we hope to present if not an 'exotic', then an absorbing people, and to present them as far as possible in their own words, 'in the native vernacular'. Two conventions of presentation require comment. We have tried to put down the actual language used by men and women, even when deviant from the Queen's English, because to retranslate it without losing shades and weightings of meaning would have been beyond our powers, and to 'correct' it, beyond our desires. Further, when we report the parents in our samples we have always styled them Mr.

[1] Malinowski, B., 'A Nation Wide Intelligence Service', p. 98

Briggs or Mrs. Hinchcliffe and only when we mention the children have we used Christian names (Peter Briggs or Alice Hinchcliffe) for greater clarity. These are simply conventions, and not meant to carry overtones of superiority or discourtesy.[1] Further than this we can only repeat the common caveat; that the limit of our powers is to report what people say, which is not necessarily always the same thing as what people think and do; and add an extra warning that the people we interview are drawing heavily on memory—and memory can be highly selective.[2]

Marburton

Marburton is a rich city. It claims to have more Rolls Royces per head than any other place on earth. Its unemployment problem is slight, and prosperity has flowed here in easy tides since the 1930's. It enjoys a protective variety of industries, being neither an engineering centre, nor a woollen city, nor a cotton town, nor a brewing capital. It is all these at once, and much more besides. Such distribution of work and wealth guards it from the lesser trade cycles that trouble neighbouring cities. It has its poor, its aged, its crippled, its sick, its unlucky; but these are not easily seen, and their presence, if not forgotten, is obscured by the general buoyancy.

The city has a population of 130,000. In 1800 it was just touching 7,000—for Marburton is one of the new cities of England, the cities bred out of the Industrial Revolution. Its population spiral follows Manchester, Liverpool, Birmingham. By 1820 that 7,000 had nearly doubled into 13,000; by 1840 it had almost doubled again to 25,000. By 1890 it had leapt to over 90,000. The railway had arrived; and after the great new railway station came the city's major public buildings—the new parish church, the post office of 1875, the town hall of 1879. The local historians trace all this back to the mediaeval hamlet of 'Marton',

---

[1] Peter Townsend cites from his experience of old people's homes that in the most humane establishments the members were given the full dignity of their surnames, (e.g. Mr. Rawson): in the poor ones the staff spoke *down* by using christian names (Albert); and in the slackest homes the patronising use of nicknames was common (Bertie).

[2] 'Just as the individual recall takes on a peculiar personal tinge, owing to the play of temperament and character; so that kind of recall which is directed and dominated by social conditions takes a colouring which is characteristic of the special social organisation concerned, owing to the play of preferred persistent tendencies in the group'. Bartlett, F. C. *Remembering*, p. 309.

or the Roman station 'Marcaster'. They point to Brigantine settlements on the surrounding hillsides, or Saxon ruins along one of the far valleys. They drag up shields and coats of arms, and all the rich drapery of the mediaeval past. But Marburton as a society has no such history. The Romans and the Normans merely travelled over the same stretch of earth, and handed nothing down. Marburton begins with the industrial revolution.

It sucked in the population of the surrounding countryside, and with them something of their culture. But the 'culture' of Marburton is the submerged culture of the industrial working class. It is now settled and stylized into a pattern of living, but it was bred in the long working hours of the mills, the rapid spread of overcrowded streets, the tangles of the master-man relationship, the personal cycle of poverty (childhood/marriage/ age) crossing the national waves of work or hunger. Such a style of living, and fashioned by such conditions, radiates today from the close centres of family life into that whole web of ties— kinship, friendship, the shared childhood or working life, the formal groupings of club, band, choir, union, chapel—all the many strands of 'neighbourhood' that reach out to attain 'community'. The expectations, dues, refusals, irritations, rights and assurances that family and neighbourhood arouse and inherit play all through this report. For the working-class culture of Marburton (an area with over 70 working men's clubs) is by no means the same as the national middle class culture, some of whose facets are reflected back by the wireless, the press, the very books in the public library. We are not concerned to choose or judge between the two cultures, merely to remark the difference. For it *is* a question of difference, and this report finds itself continually dipping into discussion or conflict where well-meaning people on both sides are fighting out battles between 'us' and 'them'.

Marburton has its prosperous middle class. Or, rather, it has two middle classes. The first is national, metropolitan in interest, mobile, privately educated. Such are the senior civil servants, doctors, executives, who stay a while and pass through the city; or who belong as natives here, but 'belong' elsewhere too. And then there is that other middle class, very local and rooted, of the self-made businessmen, works officials, schoolmasters clinging to their home town. Such a class is part of 'them' but in some situations can merge for a while with 'us'. This native, rather than national, middle class has been there from earliest days; drawing its money from the work of the men, but nonetheless close to them. There is a report by a hand-loom commissioner of 1839 that '. . . . the men of Marburton were constantly in their mills and taking their meals at the same hours as their work-people, but the clothiers of Gloucester were indulging in the habits and mixing with the gentle blood of the land'. It is just this native middle class we present here.

Marburton is one of the spread of cities that cover south Lancashire and Yorkshire, with wastes of moorland between them. Only a short journey, over the roads that curl through the moors, takes you into the opposing county. And on almost every side Marburton is hemmed in by other industrial centres, though yet with decent intervals of empty fields between. In only one direction have the open gaps been choked by creeping suburbia. We will not here describe the details of the city's streets and homes; such as matter will emerge as the survey gathers way. But the city's confidence in terms of work, of money, of pleasure, can be caught in a rapid glance. It is the confidence of the new industrial town after twenty years without recession. A correspondent who recently visited it felt that it was like nothing so much as the boom towns of the middle west, and touching on its satisfactions wrote, 'A sanctuary lamp in the parish church was placed there, by members of the local Home Guard, so a plaque blandly informs us, in memory of their own devoted service'. Had he consulted the latest guide book he would also have observed that Marburton, though on the Oxford Atlas some eighty miles north of Birmingham, officially considers that 'it may be said to be almost in the centre of England'.

Education in Marburton

Marburton then is prosperous, provincial, and confident in its material world. And as the word 'prosperous' covers over obscure pockets and cycles of hardship, so does the word 'provincial' merely catch the surface quality of a developed style of living within different social groups. Its material complacency, which is so easy to detect and illustrate, is also the more relaxed, if more normal, side of its essential citizenship. For Marburton has had other desires, and amongst them all we are now going to confine ourselves to education. This report illustrates how

7

different social groups—the working class, the local middle class—with 'cultural' strengths of their own, reach out for the central culture of our society as it is inherited and transmitted by universities, colleges and schools. We are concerned only with state education—and here a competitive situation arises.

A quick historical glance is useful, serving to fit Marburton within the common framework, and to introduce its four grammar schools. In 1838 the Non-Conformist manufacturers, whose entry to Oxford and Cambridge was still barred by the Anglican 'gentle blood of the land', founded Marburton College for the education of their sons and daughters. It offered a liberal training in the classics on traditional lines, supported by study in mathematics and the natural sciences. In 1894 the school was taken over by the city, and later divided into the two 'first-class' grammar schools—*Ash Grange High School for Girls* and *Marburton College for Boys*. Characteristically, their most distinguished pupil in the early part of the century was one of the great leaders of the Liberal party. Meanwhile, a small and shaky grammar school foundation from the seventeenth century still existed in a nearby village and, as the town grew and flourished, this school (*Abbeyford Grammar*) struggled into new life. A fourth grammar school, *Thorpe Manor*, was founded early in this century to handle the expanding numbers. These briefly are the origins of Marburton's grammar schools: founded, and often staffed, by the local middle class for the children of that class. Their ultimate model is the public schools and the eldest grammar foundations. To our own time they bring down the blended inheritance of the liberal subjects and the natural sciences; but now it is not for the children of the middle class alone, but increasingly for the new ranges of working class pupils. Such a line could be traced in many other cities.

But of course the working class had been seeking education for over a century. In 1841 the energetic and ambitious founded 'The Young Men's Improvement Society' which later gathered in hundreds of evening students and changed its name to 'The Marburton Mechanics' Institute'. It expanded, until in 1873 it was taken over by the local board, and developed into the Technical College of today, and the function of a secondary technical school was assumed by a new school of *Millcross*. Of course there were many other educational bodies formed by the working class

Introduction

—Co-operative Colleges, Labour Colleges, Forums and union centres, and such like—but the direct impetus from the working class did not create any *secondary* schools. The Technical College was an indirect result, and this is still evident today as the apprentices stream in from work; yet at the level of state education through the grammar schools, the middle class pioneers commanded the day. The working-class child today shares the final results of their energies. Four grammar schools then, stemming from the middle class; and today on the site of the old Mechanics' Institute stands a Working Men's Club.[1]

Before the passing of the Elementary Education Act of 1870 Marburton spent nothing publicly on education; in 1960 it supported almost 20,000 pupils. It offers 29 primary schools for all social classes, and around these is a fringe of seven small prep. schools. Since the war, nine secondary modern schools have been opened, and these are largely filled with working-class pupils.[2] For children who fail their eleven plus, there have been two private secondary schools with a strong commercial bias. Yet since the abolition of fees by the 1944 Act these two have lost ground, and one is now about to close down. The middle class parents who patronized them before, are either more successful now at getting their children through the selection examination, or they are well contented with the secondary modern schools, or they pay more and send their boys and girls to boarding school. Everyone working in this field knows that since 1944 there has been a shift in middle class education, but no one has altogether defined it.

Marburton seems not much different in its educational provision from other English cities, except that its wealth and its civic pride have helped it to be one degree more successful. We can

[1] Tylecote, M. *The Mechanics' Institutes of Lancashire & Yorkshire*. The Mechanics' Institute at Marburton was a genuine impulsion from working class life, and seemed to merit its description of 1849 as being 'essentially a People's College'. But the Mechanics' Institutes as a whole, as Mabel Tylecote shows, fell under the spell of their patrons, becoming centres for teaching those accommodating virtues which the nineteenth century employers wished to see flourishing amongst their work folk. At one Institute Sir Benjamin Hayward proposed as the right subject for the first 'popular' lecture: 'That security of property is indispensable to the welfare and advancement of society and that difference in fortunes and conditions of individuals must necessarily exist in every community.'

[2] There are organizational changes and new buildings every year—this report naturally reflects the physical details of a few years back.

measure this, in one sense, by the annual award of State Scholarships. If we calculate that the Ministry makes 1,850 such awards each year, then in 1960, by winning 15, Marburton gained three times the number expected for a place of its size. A similar prominence is reflected in the yearly Oxford and Cambridge lists.

We now want to focus attention on this upper area of the four main grammar schools: the road to college, university, and the middle class professions. Who are the children who travel this road? How does it affect them, and in particular how is the process felt by the working-class child and the family from which he comes?—for Marburton is very largely a working-class city.

TABLE I

SOCIAL CLASS OF OCCUPIED MEN

	Census 1951	
	Marburton	*Great Britain*
Higher Professional	3% ⎫	3% ⎫
Lower Professional	13% ⎬ 22%	15% ⎬ 26%
Clerical	6% ⎭	8% ⎭
Skilled Manual	50% ⎫	45% ⎫
Semi-Skilled Manual ..	16% ⎬ 78%	16% ⎬ 74%
Unskilled Manual	12% ⎭	13% ⎭
	100%	100%

Table I shows that at the 1951 census the city had rather more than the national average of manual workers. If we split the population up into manual workers and the rest, and call the former 'working class' and the latter 'middle class', then Marburton is 78% working class and 22% middle class. But if we now consult the records at Marburton College, Ash Grange, Abbeyford and Thorpe Manor, and examine the children who leave Marburton's grammar schools after passing their 'A' level, a different distribution emerges. This is shown in Table II.

Introduction

Taking the years 1949–52 as an example, we see that 36% of the children who passed had working-class fathers, and some 64% had middle class fathers. The balance between the two classes in the city is almost reversed in the grammar schools. This may have been common knowledge before the war, but since fees were abolished in 1944 there has been a general feeling that the

TABLE II

PUPILS PASSING H.S.C. OR G.C.E. 'A' LEVEL 1949-52 IN
MARBURTON: SOCIAL CLASS OF FATHERS

	Girls	Boys	Girls and Boys	
Higher Professional	17%	10%	12%	⎫
Lower Professional	32%	35%	35%	⎬ 64%
Clerical	20%	14%	17%	⎭
Skilled Manual	22%	34%	29%	⎫
Semi-Skilled Manual ..	5%	5%	5%	⎬ 36%
Unskilled Manual	4%	2%	2%	⎭
Total %	100%	100%	100%	
Number	84	145	229	

last major barrier frustrating the full education of gifted working-class children has fallen. And certainly very much indeed was altered by that Act. The number of working-class children going to grammar school has increased, and rightly so. But if we look at the vital upper reaches of these schools, and measure the number of children leaving with an 'A' level certificate, then it is clear that there has not been the proportional change at this point that might have been expected.[1]

---

[1] We would have liked to compare this exit from school with the social composition of the *entry*—but there were not sufficient records for this purpose.

TABLE III

120 GIRLS PASSING H.S.C. OR G.C.E. 'A' LEVEL
SOCIAL CLASS OF FATHERS

	1949–51		1952–54	
Higher Professional	14%	⎫	21%	⎫
Lower Professional	32%	⎬ 68%	39%	⎬ 74%
Clerical	22%	⎭	14%	⎭
Skilled Manual	21%	⎫	19%	⎫
Semi-Skilled Manual ..	6%	⎬ 32%	7%	⎬ 26%
Unskilled Manual ..	5%	⎭	0%	⎭
Total %	100%		100%	
Number	63		57	

For instance, Table III considers the social class of the 120 girls[1] who passed their 'A' level at Ash Grange between 1949 and 1954. Now if these results are split into halves, we are left with a group of girls who entered Ash Grange in the three years before the 1944 Act took effect, and a group who entered in the three years after the Act. They do not show any proportionate gain for working-class children. Indeed they point slightly the other way, (the middle class population increased a very little in these years). In 1949–51 68% of the girls were middle class, in 1952–54 this had *increased* to 74%. Such tiny figures are but straws in the wind, but they support the suggestions by other researchers that the wind has been blowing in unforeseen directions since 1944. There is some reason to believe that, in some sense, the middle classes have retained (and perhaps increased) their command of the sixth forms, and by that, of all the many avenues that open out from them.

These doubts about the social bases of grammar school education are well established elsewhere. In 1954 the Central Advisory Council for Education (England) showed that there was a large difference between the social composition of the

---

[1] The table is of girls only because there were no records of father's occupation for boys who took the examination after 1952. See our final comment on the need for records, the need to know these things (p. 197).

grammar schools on their samples, and the sixth forms within those schools. The swing was towards middle class dominance. In 1959 the same body presented the Crowther Report *15 to 18*. Here it was demonstrated that in the sampled population (men joining the forces for National Service) those young men with the very highest abilities—the ones we might expect to feed our university personnel, the senior ranks of management, the civil service, and so on—of these young men, 42% had left school by the age of 16. And of those in the second highest order of ability (which is well above average), no less than 87% had left by their sixteenth birthday. Whoever does stay on into our sixth forms, it is clearly not simply our most able children. Indeed the Crowther Committee go on to show in convincing statistical detail that this is largely a *class* wastage. Very many able working-class children either do not reach grammar school at all, or they leave without taking the full course. Using quite different approaches, the team led by Jean Floud, who published their findings in *Social Class and Educational Opportunity,* concluded a section of numerical analysis with 'It has now been established beyond doubt that there is a process of social as well as academic selection at work in the schools',[1] and their more particular findings are frequently referred to in our report.

This report is based on very small samples. They are not large enough for sophisticated numerical analysis. What we have done is try to go behind the numbers and feel a way into the various human situations they represent. But this intimacy with the living being carries certain risks. No one can present people speaking of education and social class in this way, without finding himself reflecting many kinds of personal controversy— and we have already mentioned the heavy charge on memory. But it would be sad if, for that reason, the attempt were not made; and we would ask the reader to try, as we have tried, to keep in play a certain sceptical habit of mind.

Had we been born 50 years ago, not only would this or any book have been an unlikely production from us, but the chances are that we would have spent our lives as weavers in the northern mills. State education has altered that for us, and for many more, and without intruding the personal overmuch, we would open

[1] Floud, J., Halsey, A. H. and Martin, F. M. *Social Class and Educational Opportunity,* p. 114.

by saying that the grammar schools have served us well, and that for us the writing of this is as the payment of a debt. If this has led to a too-generous assessment of the grammar school, or of Marburton and its social life, if it has pointed up failures of tone and distance, then the reader is invited to make his own correction. The invitation is, after all, not so much to observe with us the people of Marburton, as to observe us observing them.

2

TEN MIDDLE-CLASS CHILDREN

THE research problem posed by this preliminary scrutiny of grammar school records in Marburton may be considered in two ways. We may ask: why is it that so many middle-class children successfully complete the total grammar school course? Or we may enquire: why is it that relatively few working-class children do so? Our declared personal interest lies behind the answering of the second question; but before we follow the working-class child through school into a profession, it will be helpful to have a look at a group of middle-class boys and girls. We had neither time nor money for a full-scale survey here, but nevertheless thought it worthwhile to sketch in a setting for our main study, if only by visiting a handful of former middle-class children. There was time only to see ten. Their names were drawn at random[1] from the list of boys and girls who had passed their Advanced level at any Marburton grammar school between 1949 and 1952, and whose fathers were in social class 1 or 2. They are now men and women aged between 26 and 30. We also interviewed their parents, and the sketch that follows, while making no claims for typicality, does try to make up in detail what it lacks in range. It moves very freely around both the child and the family, to catch the texture and feel of life behind their success at school. We begin with the parents and their world.

Two of these families had been socially established by the parents. Both Mr. Chapman and Mr. Farrell were men of considerable presence and loquacity, who had countered the accident of birth with the spirit of self-help. Mr. Chapman is now a small tubby man with silver hair and the most direct blue eyes. His father had been a senior warehouseman in a local dyeworks, earning five shillings more a week than the other men in the gang. But the extra five shillings was not enough to help the

[1] The detailed procedure for drawing these names is set out in Appendix 2.

young and ambitious Mr. Chapman over his first educational hurdle. 'Oh yes, I sat the scholarship exam—and I passed it too! In fact I cake-walked it—but I wasn't allowed to go! I had too many brothers and sisters, and I had to get out and start earning a wage.' Before he could leave Mr. Chapman had to wait until he was 13, and the last 18 months of school were not wasted on him. He attended the evening institute where he came into the hands of a new teacher, the fierce and austere Mr. Lewis. Mr. Lewis gave severe but exciting periods in experimental science, which stirred new interests in his pupil. The master also lectured in science at the boys' grammar school, and when Mr. Chapman's thirteenth birthday arrived, he was invited to take the job of lab. assistant at the College. He was an able boy, and in Mr. Lewis he had found a sharp but proud patron who could direct his youth in ways that were beyond his own father. He was a kind of substitute middle-class parent. During the day Mr. Chapman worked in the College laboratory, and did various menial tasks about the school. After home-time he was permitted to sit in on the meetings of the school societies, to listen to talks and hear music. He began to play chess, and make fumbling friendships with boys of a much higher social station. 'I suffered from an inferiority complex I think, but one or two of the boys were very nice, and they took me under their wing. They saw that I didn't feel out of it. Mind you, I was conscious that a lot of the boys had a lot more money than I had. I used to go round and collect the dinner money—it was sixpence a day or something like that, and I'd see boys pull out a handful of silver, thirty shillings or more, and they'd say "How much is it, sixpence? Oh yes, here you are." And I'd think to myself, "Blimey, that's more than my old man gets for working a week!"' In the evenings he went along to night school, and tried to gain a more thorough grounding. Even during the day he kept his wits about him and picked out what knowledge he could from Mr. Lewis's daily lectures. 'I used to be setting out the apparatus and Mr. Lewis would give his lecture and even though the boys were three years older than me—some of them—I don't suppose it was all lost. When he'd finished, he'd ask them questions, and I'd think to myself what my answer would be, and quite often none of them knew what it was. They hadn't a clue some of them, I could have knocked spots off them. When he got really wild,

Mr. Lewis used to say to them, "Here you are, you've had the best education possible, and you haven't the faintest idea what I've been talking about, while Chapman here who's never been to grammar school.... !" Well, that did me no good at all. When I got outside I used to get some shocking looks, as much as to say 'bighead'—or whatever the expression was in those days.'

He was soon equipped for a better job with a chemical company, and after his new day's work still pursued his studies at the technical college, taking first his diploma and then his Higher National Certificate. He began to push his way up in the firm, at the same time improving his paper qualifications until he gained his F.R.I.C. Meanwhile he married the daughter of a small leather merchant who had fallen on leaner times.

Mr. Chapman told all this with spirit. He is now the overseas representative for his firm, and all his three children went to college or university. When they flagged, he knew how to drive them—though his parental energies circled mostly around the only son. 'When he was small I used to try and impress on Derek the need for work. I'd point to a man sweeping the road and say, "That's what happens to people who've got no ambition and don't work hard when it's necessary." ' Mrs. Chapman, a worn and quiet woman, seldom crossed her husband's flow of talk, but smiled support and looked longingly at her interrupted novel *'Hearts in Paris'*, laid politely on one side.

Mr. Farrell, the other parent who had forced his way up the social groups, was similarly self-assured and direct in manner. His father too was a charge-hand, who'd been offered and refused the chance to become a foreman. The young Mr. Farrell never sat an examination for a secondary school, and left school at thirteen for a nine-shillings-a-week job in the dyeing works. But he too went to night school for three years until he was old enough to win a scholarship to the Technical College—'But it was a poor way to learn. Many's the time I've fallen asleep at my work, you couldn't learn much after working all day. You were too tired.' The skills he picked up in his evenings were sufficient to open new pathways for him, and with no more formal qualifications he eventually became the firm's chief dyer. He married a girl from a mining village, and found more compelling demands than professional ambition. 'I told my lad,

Christopher, it's the easiest thing in the world to make money if only you put your mind completely to it—but I hoped *he* never would. I could have been a director, a very good friend of mine many years ago offered to take me into partnership in a firm in Belgium, but I put happiness first. My main aim in life has been to be happy and to make other people happy. I had a family with young children then, and it would have meant uprooting them and taking them to Belgium. So I decided I wouldn't go . . . . but Christopher says I haven't *enough* ambition. He's got plenty of ambition. He'll get to the top, he'll earn far more money than I ever did—but he won't be happy. He'll never be happy—*and he won't know he's unhappy*. But I think he's in for a lot of unhappiness.'

For all this Mr. Farrell had eagerly driven his son through school as long as he saw 'the use of it'. Now his energy for the boy is spent. His hair is going a distinguished executive grey and he is glad to guard his leisure time. On Sundays he plays the organ at Upperbank Methodist Church, and after opening a bottle he played Bach on his huge new radiogram.

Established middle-class families

Eight of our interviews were with more established middle-class[1] families. Mr. Firbank ran the family boiler-making business; Mr. Broomfield was a coal merchant. Mr. Denby was a works manager; Mr. Peters and Mr. Douglas were works chemists, and Mr. Ives a works engineer. Mr. Conway and Mr. Bancroft were headmasters of primary schools. Most of these families had been connected with local industries for several generations, and it was quite common for many of their members to be school teachers.

The detail of Mr. Peters' family catches this close weave of education, vocational training, and local industry. His grandfather attended Marburton Technical College in its earliest days, and his own father was one of the first members of Leeds University. He then returned to Marburton as head of the Dyeing Department at the Technical College, where Mr. Peters took his

[1] There are, plainly, many groups to be distinguished within the term 'middle class', just as there are within the term 'working class'. These are distinctions which we can't take up in this report. We use the general phrase 'Marburton middle class', both knowing what other truths it conceals, and hoping that it will not be confused with the Southern England 'image' of a quite different 'middle class'.

own diploma directly under his father's tuition. The family became either business men, or *science* teachers. One uncle was the first scholarship boy at Rastrick Grammar School, another took his degree in chemistry at the Technical College again. Both these became small business men. Mr. Peters' brother teaches science at one local grammar school, and his brother-in-law teaches mathematics at another. The rest of the family are in industry or small concerns of their own—often equipped with Technical College degrees or diplomas, or grammar school and university educations. All this lay behind the young Raymond Peters when he was first taken down the road to begin his schooling. A similar account could be given of most of these families. They had been linked with the new secondary schools and with further education at least since the 1902 Education Act. They were founder members; and their hold seems as firm as ever.

As families they display a wide experience and shrewd command of the possibilities of local education. On the whole they do not think in terms of whether their child's I.Q. is sufficient for a college or university education. This may be the way the teacher looks at things, but here in these households is a much more toughened and optimistic belief in the possibilities of industrious-ness, of self-help. They do not feel that their sons and daughters have to be brilliant intellectuals in order to carry off high edu-cational prizes. They believe that such things are well within the grasp of any energetic boy or girl providing that they go cannily and whole-heartedly to work. In Table IX[1] we try to chart visually the relative wealth of educational experience behind these ten children, and compare them (Table X) with those ten working-class children whose names immediately followed theirs in the Advanced level examination lists. The chart suggests merely, but it shows how the middle-class children began school with over six times as many educational 'units' behind them.

Relationship to the working class

The fathers earned between £1,000 and £3,000 a year, and none of these families lived in a working-class district. They were quite sensitive to social changes in the neighbourhood and would move if the district went 'down'. They favoured either the

N.B

---

[1] All tables quoted but not given in the text will be found in Appendix 2.

tudorbethan villa on the small private close, or else a blackened stone-built house surrounded by a wilderness of rhododendrons, laurels, and grimy trees, in that part of the town where the great nineteenth century woollen merchants once lived. Inside, their homes were often not so different from the homes of working class foremen. Most of the furnishings were old and conventional, handed on by their parents or bought in the inter-war years. A more recent purchase such as an angular new radiogram on black and brass legs, stood out oddly alongside the dark oak display cabinet sheltering its fragile collection of odd china tea things or a small silver golf trophy. A more firmly established family might have a somewhat Victorian air about its living room. Mrs. Firbank had a row of glittering brass candlesticks on her mantelshelf, and in place of the usual three-piece suite and fringed standard lamp, there was a grandfather clock, older chairs, and a polished mahogany table on which lay a closed copy of *Old Porcelain*. Yet though some rooms were richer than others, there was no sense of ostentation, no mere display of possessions. The overwhelming impression was one of 'homeliness'.

Living in such districts and having no employment of their own, the wives were seldom brought into contact with the local working class. This was so even when the woman herself had been a working man's daughter. Their surplus energies went into organizing the Flower Show, into the Townswomen's Guild, ladies golf and bridge. All these activities were beset with social tensions, from which the husband tended, rather belligerently, to withdraw.

In contrast to the rather refined manner of his wife, the husband might insist on his Yorkshire accent, converse long and loudly, pride himself on his 'independence' or his 'character', and call her 'luv'. He talked familiarly about the working men with whom he spent each day. Mr. Broomfield judged them to be unenterprising compared to himself: 'It's a question of using your imagination. A lot of these ordinary working people they're quite content to stand still, as long as they've got a fixed wage and a steady job. They don't want to look any further, that's all the end in view, so to speak. But you've got to use your imagination —when we were first looking around, people said to us, "Oh, don't bother, you're all right, you've got a good job, don't worry." But you have to think of the years to come, you have to think of the time when you'll be 30 or 40. I think what starts you off, you see people around you and you say to yourself, "Well, I don't want to be like him." You think you might be like them in a few years' time and that sets you wondering.' Mr. Farrell thought the working men were simply the unlucky ones in society, 'Well, they're the unfortunate people, the people who haven't had a chance. It happens that some people never get a chance in life, they might be very intelligent but they might never get a chance which would put them at the top.' But he then went on to insist that what distinguished the working class from the middle class was the fact that the middle class *worked*. 'The way some people talk you'd think you weren't a worker unless you'd got dirty hands. They don't realize that some professional people work far harder than they do. They work far harder than the average person. It annoys me when people talk in that way. All the directors, the mill owners' sons, everybody who's got on—they've got a bit of push. There aren't many *idle* rich now— they've all been killed off.'

It was true that these men did work hard, and true that they were not afraid of dirtying their hands. If Mr. Broomfield was short of labour he was ready to shoulder the sack and deliver his own coal. None minded the hardness of the work, so long as they had the authority. 'Well, put it this way, in whatever job I've been in for many years, I've always had somebody to say to "Do this!" ' (and he pointed with his finger in a commanding fashion) 'and if I had to change my job to where somebody started saying to me "Do that!" I shouldn't like it.'

Undoubtedly they knew much more than their wives about aspects of working-class life. They had daily and intimate contact with workmen around them, which indeed they preferred to the social world offered by their women-folk. For it would seem as if these middle-class families were surrounded by members of that other middle class—the doctors, the lawyers, the really prosperous merchants and directors, with whom they could never quite come to terms. Their wives sought to make links through their tea meetings and shows, but husbands were eager to keep clear of this. They had their own golf club, masonic lodge or even amateur dramatic company that they favoured, but it was with some scepticism. 'It's all silly really, if they join the golf club, or the rotarians or the masons, some people think they've

reached the top! Just imagine, if they join the golf club that's
the very top!'

Home life, their children and their work mattered. The more
elusive forms of social distinction they avoided. Habitually they
looked back and down to the working class, rather than up to
any classes beyond themselves. Their view of society was
competitive, and they spoke with a benevolent sense of that
superior 'push' or fortune which had distinguished them from
the working classes. Mr. Broomfield's daily behaviour illustrates
this in an interesting way. At home he has few friends, 'he likes
the district, but he hasn't any friends around here. I think Dr.
Smith put father off—he lives next door, *but he doesn't speak to
you because of that*', said his son. Nor is he interested in Mrs.
Broomfield's activities, 'No, he never joins in any of the things
with my mother. She's much more interested in clubs than he is;
she's a member of the townswomen's guild and the flower
society, but it doesn't appeal to him.' Instead, Mr. Broomfield
stays long hours at work during which he finds plenty of time
for tea and talk with his customers. His round is in one of the
poorest working-class parts of the town, which is being gradually
eroded by re-housing schemes. 'Oh yes, there are some very
nice people down there. I've known some of them 30 years.
I can just knock on the door and walk straight in, and have a
cup of tea. I get on very well with them down there. The place
doesn't look very nice, but there are some very respectable
families down there.'

In one case this friendly paternalism went to very valuable
limits. Mr. Conway, the primary school head, is a man fond and
capable of organizing. He is secretary of the ward Conservative
party, and his wife has been a city councillor. She inherited from
her father a sense of social responsibility, which her husband has
willingly shared. 'My father's was a life of public service. Before
they had National Assistance, he was on the Board—the Board of
Guardians it was called then. He had a weak heart, and my
brother used to say to him, "Why don't you get a taxi to take you
to the Board", but he wouldn't. He always rode on the tram, and
whatever was the difference in the fare, he would spend that and
buy a couple of ounces of tobacco or some packets of tea or
something, and take them along and give them to the people at
the Board. I can always remember the poor children there,

straining at you and touching you, just for a bit of affection. They were dying for some one to take an interest in them, so when I grew up I've always taken an interest in the children who haven't been so gifted. I don't see why the children who are most clever should have *all* the chances.' Mr. and Mrs. Conway, like Mr. Bancroft, have run a play centre and a youth club in the district for many years, and organized a host of local activities for the less fortunate. But now their eldest son has risen in the Bank and, feeling the need to 'entertain' on his behalf, they are preparing to move out to a more residential district.[1]

Seventeen of the original 20 parents were still alive, and of these 12 voted Conservative and five voted Liberal. In no case did wife and husband disagree, and in no case was there any support for the Labour party—though Mr. Douglas admitted passing through such a phase during his university days. It was impossible to collect full and systematic information about *their* parents' political loyalties, but from what we were able to gather it seemed that these must have been fairly evenly divided between the Conservative and the Liberal causes of their day, with a leaning towards the Liberal party. In discussing politics there was a marked retrospective bias: 'Once upon a time there used to be just the two parties, the Tories and the Whigs, and there were some very underhand dealings—a lot worse than now. That was what the Socialist party was started for, really to counter-act that—but now that's all finished with. The Tory party is coming down to meet the ordinary people and the Labour party is going more and more up towards them, so that you can hardly tell the difference.' They felt their political loyalties had been decided long ago and though they might comment lightly on such current issues as nationalization, there seemed no possibility that any event would make them change their minds again. This rigidity did not mean that they were not prepared to vote for

---

[1] More points of contact were possible with the local community through Sunday Church or Chapel—though on this we had little information. The families were almost all Non-Conformist, though this seemed, if not lightly held, then at least unasserted in conversation. They had once favoured the chapel schools in the same way that they now favoured the technical colleges, and still looked back admiringly to their *practicality*. 'My mother went to West Ing National School— that was where all the Non-Conformists went. It was in the days when there was a lot of controversy about whether you should go to church schools or not. You got a lot more teaching there, because you didn't have to learn all that doctrinaire Christianity, you got more arithmetic.'

another candidate as part of an electoral pact or similar tactic, nor did it mean that they aired their views eagerly and strongly. Mr. and Mrs. Conway were energetic though essentially *social* members of their local Conservative party, and Mr. Chapman who was right of Conservative ('whatever party's in power it's always a Socialist government; it's just that when the socialists are in we get *more* Socialism!') was the kind of man who always declared his mind on political subjects. But almost all of the others tended to avoid politics. Indeed had the interviews not been long, many of them might have gone down as 'non-political', for their first remarks were usually of that kind. Mrs. Broomfield, for instance, who has faithfully voted Conservative all her life, began by saying, 'We don't think much about politics at all, we're hardly what you'd call political', and then glided rapidly on to the subject of her Flower Society. There was a marked dislike of the political enthusiast ('I work with a politician—that's enough for me! He used to be the head of the whole lot, and I get fed up of listening to him talk'), and a considerable scepticism of the professional politicians even in one's own party. On the whole there was a tendency to contract out of what was felt to be a not altogether pleasant business. Not surprisingly this was most clearly announced by the Liberals; 'Put it this way, you can't say that anybody's suffered under the effects of a Liberal government, can you? You can say that now some people are suffering from the effects of a Socialist government, and there are still people suffering from the effect of bad Tory governments in the past, aren't there? But nobody can say that the Liberals have done any harm.'

These men and women would always take care to vote, but they did so only according to patterns already pre-determined. They used their vote today as they did ten or 20 years back, in accordance with that compromise or agreement they had reached in their earlier days: an agreement which seemed to have removed any marital discord, and to have harmonized social standing with family loyalty. They themselves felt that political loyalties were decided by two main pressures. First of all there was that loyalty to family opinion which experience only nourished and enlarged: 'I think it's more or less inbred. You might go to university, and you'll get more ideas and you'll see more and meet more people. But it won't *change* the first ideas. You'll still be the

same—it's just that your ideas will be more *full*.' And secondly
there was the sceptical view of social rising: 'I've seen it happen
so many times. You get a man on the shop floor who starts
off as a solid Socialist. Then you give him a bit of promotion and
make him a charge-hand, and then eventually you get him into
the office, and his views are changing all the time, and by the
time he's got into the office he's a staunch Conservative.'

They made distinctions between their political *views,* and their
political *behaviour.* Mr. Peters, who like the others was faithful
to his duty at the polls, made the remark which seemed to sum
up a common attitude: 'I follow my father, I think politics is a
very difficult subject. You have to know a lot about it before you
start blowing your mouth off. There are far too many people who
start shouting about things they don't know anything about.
I'm not very interested either.'

Their attitudes to politics and government, then, seemed to be
negative and sceptical. And their 'political' views were so
enmeshed in the details and emotional bonds of their domestic
and social life that current events seemed seldom likely to alter
them. But at the polling booths this generally meant a regular
Conservative vote: it always meant an anti-socialist one.

In many ways these homes may seem illiberal and narrow.
They do not, perhaps, have that breadth of cultural interest with
which to rouse an intelligent and sensitive child into total
adulthood. Mrs. Ives recorded a dominant note, 'Most of my
time is spent doing housework, and I play a lot of golf—and for
relaxation I play bridge. I haven't any time for any of these
intellectual pursuits.' She pointed to a cowboy film on the television. 'We just watch this for relaxation. We get very tired
during the day, and we want a bit of relaxation at night.' But at
the side of this 'relaxation' must be set the energies and 'push'
of the men who are determined to be amongst the masters in
their own societies. It was impressive to encounter in these
homely surroundings this record of determined industriousness,
this proven validity of the spirit of self-help. And though there
were to these interviews hard and ugly edges, we were nevertheless, in listening to Mr. Farrell play his Bach, or Mrs. Conway
tell of her father riding to the Board meeting on the tram, or to
the mother demanding less dogma and more arithmetic, moving
amongst the fragments of a fine non-conformist tradition.

In terms of the efficient *use* of educational facilities these families had much to give to their children. Their knowledge of this utility was so intricately woven into the very texture of their family life over the generations that they were well equipped to occupy and command any new fields that the state might make available. At the very least they would seem well placed to compel from state schools, colleges and universities an education which must give 'tone' to their daughters and a vocational training to their sons.

Sons and daughters

The ten sons and daughters from these families whom we interviewed in this small subsidiary enquiry, grew up in the older and more sombre middle-class districts. In their pre-school days they played in localities which were not marked by the galas, outings, walks and carnivals that formed a colourful part in the early memories of working-class children in the town. 'Oh no! There was nothing like that. Only V day and VJ day,' said Alice Douglas and she pulled a face. In place of the walks and carnivals, a girl like Shirley Fairbank might attend classes in Greek dancing, but this was unusual. Greek dancing classes and such like belonged to that other middle class which did not use the state schools. Shirley Fairbank found that all the girls at the dancing class went to private schools, and since in her opinion private schools were 'very snobby', she refused to make friends. This defensive hostility towards private schools was shared by most of the parents. For several of them hesitated about where to send children when schooling began; and there were often difficult family councils over this point: prep school or primary school? In these family decisions about the child's coming education the father's voice tended to count much more than the mother's—as it did right through to university. In seven instances this was certainly so; and in one only did the mother naturally take the lead. This was in direct contrast to our experience later with working-class families.

Why were these families so uneasy about private education? It seems that their own parents had less doubts and were much more ready to use these schools—particularly for their daughters. But now the question is argued differently. First of all there is the cost. This can and will be managed if the parents feel they are making a shrewd bargain, but the bargain is difficult to weigh up. Standards in state schools seem to have risen, and people are now much more aware if a school has the Ministry of Education's approval or not. There is a feeling that only the most expensive private schools offer better teaching than a good state school. What they do seem to offer together with or even instead of a good standard of teaching, is 'tone', 'polish', 'accent'. Mr. Farrell felt he would rather be assured of the excellence of the arithmetic, and the 'polish' could be attended to later. Again, and this seemed nearer the roots, most felt that the private schools belonged to the 'other' middle class, and that to use private schools with any seriousness meant contemplating a difficult long term commitment that would bring quite new and perplexing relationships. 'You see', said Mr. Denby, 'I wouldn't have sent him to a public school. I wouldn't have liked to be the *first* to do it. I wouldn't have liked to be trailing along all the time behind him. He'd always have that bit more polish and I should be made embarrassed, I'd be too embarrassed to go and see him.' There was no bridging the gulf; and then with an almost common voice the parents insisted on the primary school days as the time when children should mix freely together. 'I wanted them to have that experience, to rub shoulders with the ordinary people. I wanted them to meet people and get on with people.' With some bitterness and real puzzlement, Mr. Farrell wanted to know: 'What is it all for? They send them to private school, and they put a little fence round them to keep them away from the others, and they put them in a little corral so that they'll bleat like the other little ewe lambs. They're terrified in case they'll pick up a Yorkshire accent. And after that they'll send them to public school and they'll beggar themselves in doing it—and what is it all for?'

They could not quite see what it was all for, when there were reputable state schools to hand, tested by the weight of local opinion and kept up to standard by the Ministry's inspections. Moreover these families trusted in their command of all the ranges of state education for their children, and from the beginning thought of each school not merely as an instance but as part of a process. Mrs. Firbank when she sent her daughter to the primary school was already thinking of her ultimately going to Cambridge. 'Cambridge had always been in the family somehow. That's why I wanted to go—but I couldn't in those days, and that's why I wanted Shirley to go. I'm not sure how it was, but I had an uncle who discovered a star. He used to spend his spare time lying outside in ditches looking at the firmament, and he discovered this star. And they adopted it at Cambridge, or something like that—so Cambridge was in the family.' When they chose a primary school they chose with care. They chose one which not only promised well for a grammar school place, but pointed firmly in the direction of college or university.

This turned out to be quite a feasible forecast. We analysed the Advanced level pass lists at Ash Grange over an eight-year period to see which primary schools the children had first attended. There are some 30 primary schools in the Marburton area, but most of the Marburton girls who went to college or university came from only a very small handful of these schools —ones with a larger middle-class intake. There were some primary schools, and these were not small ones and not without excellent teachers, which never taught a child who finally passed Advanced level. We felt sure that these facts were not known in Marburton, even to teachers, in anything resembling this precise form. Nevertheless it would see that they were 'felt' amongst the Marburton middle class, if not elsewhere.[1]

Of these ten sons and daughters, nine were placed in what our calculations show to be Marburton's leading primary schools for long term results. Seven of the children did very well and were somewhere amongst the top six children in their class at school. We may assume that home gave them a vocabulary, a range and ease of speech and a positive attitude to schooling that stood them in good stead. And for these children links between family and school were frequently homely and intimate. There was one instance where the teacher came to tea and the little girl would be sat on her knee. There was another where the father invited the girls at a local teachers' training college to get extra practice by trying out their tests on his child at home. There was the strange and rather enchanting story of Patricia Bancroft, the headmaster's daughter, falling asleep in class. 'I must have felt tired at the end of one of Miss French's lessons. She told us all to lay our heads on the desk and rest a few minutes. Well, I put my head down and closed my eyes and actually fell right asleep. Next thing

[1] This point is taken up again in the section 'Early Leaving'. Appendix 1.

I knew I was in Daddy's office. Miss French had picked me up and carried me out and put me down there. She said to my father, "Pat's fallen asleep in class. I think she can rest better here.' That was the kind of thing, you see." ' All this meant that though the yard may have seemed large and noisy and rough, inside the school they knew what they were about, and trusted their relationships with the adults in the same way as they would have done at home.

Three of the children had real difficulty with their primary school work. Norman Conway, who later took a first at Leeds University was 'not successful' at this stage. Alice Douglas who ultimately went to training college, had considerable difficulty with primary school English. Her words came out in a peculiar order, and the teachers definitely forecast that she would not pass the selection examination. The parents arranged for private coaching, and she then passed very high up the list. Raymond Peters who finally took a first and a Ph.D. at London University had similarly severe difficulties with primary school arithmetic, and again the teachers warned the parents that he would not pass without special help.

Despite these weaknesses, all ten children not only passed, but passed well. Their brothers and sisters shared this success, for of 20 brothers and sisters old enough to take the selection examination, 19 passed. The twentieth was sent to a private secondary school, so that none of them attended a secondary modern or an all-age school at all. It would seem therefore that the parents' faith in their ability to use the state system successfully at this point was very well founded.

Grammar school

The authority offered the choice of four grammar schools and two technical commercial schools to those who passed the selection examination. All these parents seemed fairly well informed as to the relative merits of the different schools, and the varying prospects that they offered. Ash Grange and Marburton College undoubtedly had the most superior facilities, teaching and academic record, and eight of the children went to these two. The remaining pair were sent to grammar schools with which the family already had links. Table XI shows that though middle class children dominated the upper reaches of both 'second-class' (58%) and 'first-class' (64%) grammar schools, the children with professional class parents tended to command this section of the *best* schools to an ever more interesting extent. Thus 16% of the city population produced 33% of the passes at Thorpe Manor and Abbeyford—and 51% of them at Ash Grange and Marburton College. This does not of course put aside the point that in some respects these are possibly the best schools *because* of the social class composition of their intake.

All the grammar schools streamed their children in various ways. Five of these children were placed in 'A' classes and five in 'B' or 'C' classes. Not all the parents understood the significance of this, but they were all most prepared to see that their children would now work very hard and determined that this should be the gateway to a good job. When Patricia passed the selection examination, Mr. Bancroft called her into his room: 'I was called by myself into father's office, and he had the lists on his desk. "Look at that," he said, "You've come right at the top." I was at the very head of the list of all the children in the school who'd passed. "Now you can do anything you want," he said, "You can do anything!" I tell you this because it affected things later on. More was expected of me than I thought I could do later.' In their eagerness to assure themselves that their children were doing well, some were even prepared to join in the work themselves. Mr. Farrell recalled that 'At first I tried to push Chris along and I can remember the English master saying to him "and next time your father does your homework, tell him not to use such long words, will you?" Another time Chris was talking to Peter Chapman over the phone about the maths homework and Peter said, "Can't your father do it *either*?" After that I gave up helping. I still took an interest in it, but I stopped actually doing it.' Mr. and Mrs. Firbank more delicately concentrated on taking Shirley off on weekend trips to places of interest which might have some bearing on school work. But despite this marked degree of parental support, and even participation, some of the children were running into difficulties.

Helen Chapman had got herself into the wrong class. 'I was shy and quiet, and I'd made a bad mistake, a very bad mistake. After the first few lessons I thought I liked chemistry and that it was my kind of subject. And so I chose the science form, but

I soon discovered afterwards that I just couldn't do it. I couldn't do maths at all either and they both pulled me down. They were a very great trouble and I couldn't do them all the way up the school. It got so bad that the headmistress called me to her office and said that I was going to drop maths. So I went home and told my father that I couldn't do maths any more.' Mr. Chapman would never come to the school, for he was uncomfortable in the all-feminine atmosphere. Nevertheless he had a very real respect for a sound knowledge of arithmetic, and was not going to allow a decision of this sort to be made by the teachers. 'So he said, "Nonsense! You've got to do maths. Absolutely necessary. You go and tell the headmistress that you're doing it." ' And so I went back and told her. There was an awful scene. There was my form mistress and her (this was in her room) and she was saying thus and thus and thus about my not doing maths. And all I could say was, "My father says I've *got* to." ' In the end Helen continued with her maths, and in fact took a credit in it with her School Certificate.

Alice Douglas and Raymond Peters had both been placed in 'C' classes. On both it had an immediate detrimental effect which lasted for several years. The other children in the C classes were largely working-class children whose whole style of behaviour rubbed against the grammar school. At Alice's school the other 'C' Stream girls 'used to get their berets and tie them up at the back with a piece of ribbon to make them look like a halo! And they always wore them at a rakish angle or put them flat on top of their heads until they were told to stop it.' School records make it difficult to plot this drift of working class children into the C stream. But Tables XII and XIII which are based on eight entry years at Ash Grange, show that though a large proportion of the working-class entry usually *begins* in the C stream it has swollen considerably by the time that the fifth form leaving age is reached. Alice was content enough to join in all the fun and pranks that her lively class got up to, though she had a feeling of 'immaturity' at the side of the other girls. 'All they were interested in was growing up as quick as they could and getting out. Going out with boys and wearing make-up and high heeled shoes. They wanted to leave school. They always seemed much older than I did. I felt immature with them, I always felt as though I was one step behind. All the way up the school I was one step

behind. They were going out with boys much older than themselves, and having experiences that I'd never had. I knew they
could handle situations that I couldn't handle, and I always felt
much more immature than them.' When the fifth form was reached
all the other girls, except one, left. Mr. Douglas was troubled over
his daughter and wondered whether to transfer her to the Technical College. In the end he decided to keep her on into the sixth
form, and a quite new and satisfying phase of school began for her.

Raymond Peters was similarly affected by being placed in a
C class. He was intimidated by the masters who taught their
first form entrants aggressively, and he believed the weight fell
on a constant round of tests, examinations, and punishments.
Marks mattered very much, and the emphasis was 'on remembering and not reasoning.' A serious and industrious boy
he struggled hard with the daily round for five years, and then
quite suddenly, after always hovering half-way down the class,
he rose rapidly to the top. It was, he thought, a recovery of a
lost confidence. Again his C class had attracted most of the
working-class entry, and all except four members left at the end
of the fifth year. Mr. Peters wondered about letting Raymond
make a fresh start in local industry at fifteen, and a family conference was held. It was decided to keep him on into the sixth
form. Here he was attracted by a new master who worked his
pupils extremely hard, but taught them as individuals almost on
a tutorial system. His subject was biology which Raymond had
never tried before. Attracted by the man, he now concentrated
on biology in the sixth and soon met with considerable success.
The school could not quite escape its original assessment, and
suggested that Raymond should not try for a university but take
up, perhaps, hotel management. Father and son regarded the
suggestion as insulting, and pursued their way. The next year
Raymond won an Open Scholarship at London University, and
as mentioned before took a first class degree and did his Ph.D.
there. He is now a university lecturer.

Social life

Their friends were usually other boys and girls from similar
backgrounds who were in their own school class. They might
belong to a church or chapel, youth circle or tennis club, but as
often in this survey we found that these groupings tended to be

occupied exclusively, not only by children of the same social class but also of an identical educational background. (Thus one scout or guide troop would be favoured by middle-class grammar school children, another by working-class grammar school children, and a third by secondary modern school boys and girls.) They watched the drift towards the C stream and the failure to enrol for the sixth form course, and commented: 'I thought one or two of them were a bit dirty and their hair was tatty. It makes you wonder if it's worth them going to a school like Ash Grange if they are only going to leave.' The fifth form leaving, we can see, was a fact, but this 'tattiness' is more difficult to establish. Several of these middle class children referred to working-class children at school as being very 'scruffy' or dressed like 'tramps'. There may have been unusual cases of poorly dressed children at the school, but on the whole this was very difficult to accept as a general fact. We were inclined to feel that we were here recording on the borderline where the exceptional instance supported a social stereotype. Some of these middle-class children were almost obsessively sure they were clean and others were not. 'The domestic science teacher always used to say that Shirley was very good, except that she washed her hands too much. She'd never touch anything without washing her hands first, even if she just handled the flour she'd have to wash her hands before she went on to anything else.' It was extremely difficult to pin down this image of the working-class child, early leaving, and dirtiness—but it was often presented to us with some force. 'I don't think it's fair,' said Christopher Farrell, 'these snotty-nosed children should be given a chance—but not at a place like Marburton College. It's sheer waste.'

Alice Douglas began going out with a working-class boy at school, but here again the embarrassments proved too much. 'He was very working-class and a keen Socialist and very brainy. He was a year younger than me but he could understand the Chaucer I was doing. He spoke with a broad Yorkshire accent and he could understand it because the Chaucer was nearer to the way they spoke there.' But there was discomfort on both sides, and the relationship soon ended. 'Well, it was little things. I didn't think I was snobbish, but I found out then that I was. His clothes were very old, and he wouldn't come in and meet my parents. He thought that they'd be too middle-class.'

Two of the boys seemed to have had a much friendlier relationship with working-class children at grammar school, and this had an important effect on their school and social life. For three years at Abbeyford Grammar School, Norman Conway was a quiet and conscientious pupil who took second or third place in his class. But in his fourth year he began to make a new kind of friend and to spend his evenings with working-class boys in the park. 'I began to break out. I'll give you an example of what I mean. I used to start playing pontoon in the park, and if we got a chance at school we'd go round the back. We'd play pontoon and smoke there. It was all very silly, we only did it because we were immature and we thought it was great and big to do things like that. I was still quite good academically, but I was more *against* the school in those days.' This adolescent eruption made it seem for a while as if he were completely identified with boys of a lower social grouping. In the evenings he began courting a miner's daughter who had not been to grammar school, and at school itself adopted an instinctively antipathetic attitude. 'Silly little things showed it—like smoking so much. Or for instance one master was very go ahead, and he organized a mock election between the three parties. There was a conservative candidate and his agent, and a labour one and his, and so on. Well, the kind of thing we did—see, silly lads!—we had to put up a communist and his agent. And that was me, that's the way I was.' Norman stayed on into the sixth form ('There was no question of leaving. I would never have been allowed to'), and his courtship of the miner's daughter slackened and ended. When he left school for university this phase of his social relationships was left behind for good.

George Denby seemed to have had a much milder form of this experience. At first his social life outside school centred around the local tennis club, but when this closed down he was attracted by new friendships in the classroom and pursued these by joining a youth club dominated by working-class grammar schoolboys. For several years he held a half-and-half position at school. Like his newer friends, and unlike his older ones, he refused to join the school scouts or the school corps. But he was reluctant to go further than this, and took great pains to define his position. 'I wasn't against the school. It was a dislike of anything connected with joining in. It was a dislike of those who were pro-school. You might describe it as anti-pro school.' When the youth club too closed down, those friendships weakened and he began attending the parish church youth group. This was a well-defined centre for children from more prosperous background. His wife who comes from a middle-class home also attended and she said, 'The congregation was very middle class. I should say you got few manual workers. I don't think they go to church. I don't think that the middle classes are more religious. It's more of a social occasion. The manual workers go to the pubs instead.' He too passed on to university, and shook off this phase of dissatisfaction.[1]

Six of these sons and daughters went to university and three went to training college. Christopher Farrell was also thinking of moving on to university without any very definite ideas of where he was going, when his father abruptly forced the issue. '*Why* do you want to go? You're not very good at any subjects, and I don't think you're really interested in them. Wouldn't it be better to get out into industry and get your teeth into something?' The son agreed, and left school to take a two-year commission in the army. He then began very successfully to make his way as an overseas salesman for English textiles.

Of the nine who went on to college or university, six did so supported by the successful co-operation of school and parents. The school advised Mr. Denby to let his son try for the law, and family, school and student persevered together whilst he took his Advanced level three times before he got a sufficiently good one to take him to university. He is now a practising solicitor. Patricia Bancroft, helped by staff and urged on by an eager father, gained a university place, and then feeling that she was being forced beyond her capabilities, turned it down herself in favour of the less arduous course at a training college. Mr. Chapman asked the school to help him choose the best training college for his daughter—a request for both excellence of training and distinction of 'tone'. Helen was sent on a three-year course to the Froebel Institute. Mr. Douglas' family believed, through personal connections, that the National Training College of Domestic Science was both professionally good and socially superior. The school co-operated, and Alice took a place there.

---

[1] For another comment on the working-class friendships of these two boys, see the diagram on p. 105.

Norman Conway went to Leeds, and Dorothy Ives to London. Shirley Firbank finally went to Cambridge, though the headmistress on grounds of age had first of all suggested that she shouldn't take the scholarship papers. Mr. and Mrs. Firbank immediately saw the Education Officer formally, and communicated with a member of the Education Committee informally; the difficulty was straightened out and all impediments removed.

We have already quoted the case of Dr. Peters where the school thought university too ambitious and advised hotel management. There was a similar difficulty over Allan Broomfield. The school informed the parents that he had no prospect of getting to university. The parents disagreed. Allan was withdrawn at eighteen and sent to the technical college. There he won a scholarship to Edinburgh, and read his degree in brewing.

Men and women

All completed their college and university courses successfully, except for Dorothy Ives. Severe eye trouble compelled her to abandon university after one year. This brought difficulties, but her parents were able to help both her and her husband establish themselves in a small business. The other four girls became school teachers, and all but one are now married. The boys spread out into education, the law, management, brewing. Most of them seem to have inherited their parents' drive and ambition. Miss Firbank, though still very young, is Senior Geography Mistress at a large girls' grammar school. She works her pupils extremely hard and her father refers to her as the 'slave driver'. She is very keen on teaching girls who might follow the same course as herself and ultimately go to her college at Cambridge. Christopher Farrell considers himself to be moving rapidly up in his own field. 'I'm quite satisfied with what the old school's done for me. Look at me now. Going to South Africa next month. I must be one of the youngest overseas reps in the business. I'm only 26 and it usually takes you till you're 32 to get my position.' Norman Conway applies himself with immense energy to promotion in the grammar school. 'I reckon I can do A level chem. in four terms. Four terms flat out, mind. We have to go really fast. We have tests twice a week, but we get the results. For instance, last year I got an open at Pembroke, Cambridge, and an exhibition at Trinity Hall, Cambridge, and then I got half-a-dozen places. I've got 14 places in the last two years and then these opens. I do pretty well; my results are all right. The way we teach, we teach for results. I want the passes, the schols, and all those things. Tests all the time, and scrub the teaching methods, forget about the educational side. Yes, it *is* like that; not altogether of course, but there are two ways, aren't there? There's the one way I teach and there's another way. Well, let me give you an instance: if a boy asks a question it might raise some interesting matters. Now, the other way you'd waste the whole period and follow up those matters and that's all right. But that's not our way. We've got no time for any questions or anything that leads off the syllabus. You've got to get through it. I like teaching our A stream boys but you should see our C stream! They're shocking, absolutely shocking. I don't like teaching them at all, and I don't know what it can be like in the secondary modern schools. I'm not made out for missionary teaching. What I want now is a head of department in a really good school, and then I'd do what our head of department has done. I'd put on the pressure, really hard. Really work those children, tests, tests, tests, and get the results. Get them the results they should have, and that would establish me, wouldn't it? It would give me a reputation. People would know that I could do the job. I might slacken off when I got established—perhaps after ten years or so, I might start looking around and thinking more about the educational side. But you've got to establish yourself first, haven't you? Right?'

Three of the sons as well as four of the daughters are now married. Christopher Farrell wants to be free to travel and make his way in his profession without the encumbrance of a fixed home, at least for a few years. Raymond Peters toys with 'the wild idea of going off to New Guinea and collecting plants. And at the moment, frankly, I'd rather do that than get married. I couldn't do both.' In six of the seven marriages the spouse had also had a grammar school education. In the other instance, Dorothy Ives married a working-class boy who failed the selection examination. She met him through her church as he began to prepare himself for the ministry. Four of the partners came from middle-class homes of the type we have been illustrating here, and three of them have come from originally working-class homes. Norman Conway married a girl from such a background who had been sent to grammar school and training college. Alice Douglas' husband has an identical history. Where there is a working-class spouse, the new family seems to have attached itself more to the middle-class parents than the working-class parents. With these latter there is a marked degree of discomfort. Norman Conway said:'We don't get on well with Anne's side of the family. You see they want things different.' His wife explained: 'What my mother would really like is for me to live in the next street and for Norman to take a job in Preston. In Preston, you see, it's all the family and all that, and everybody whom you know. They want to get me back there—but I don't want to go there for anything.' 'Anne's right,' added her husband, 'her parents are very nice, but they're so naïve, you see. When we see them they start giving us advice! Advice, I ask you! Their experience, what is it? It's quite different from ours, it's got nothing to do with it. They know nothing about the things that affect us, but they want to give us advice.' For Dorothy Ives things are less easy. 'We see his parents as little as possible. About twice a year. He lives in a very dirty house, and she doesn't look after it, and when he was living there he always had to cook his own meals. She just sat by smoking a cigarette. Perhaps at the bottom of her, she's got a warm heart, but she's a very loud-mouthed coarse woman. We once called unexpectedly, but never again.'

Marriage, then, has confirmed the social class of the new family, rather than pulled it down or up in any way. There is no case in which they have significantly married 'up', and in this respect the social gap just above their parents seems not to have disappeared for them. But under certain circumstances of proved educational merit, new blood has been introduced from markedly lower social groupings. Again this follows the pattern of the parents. Marriage means the setting up of a new home, and except once this was in another part of the country from Marburton— Hampstead, Kew, Stafford, Lincoln, Norwich. The new couples make four or five visits home each year. They live in flats or perhaps are buying a new house on a small private estate. It is a first home and they are proud of it, but they expect to move around a little yet and own other and better property. When we came to see them, they were not embarrassed or much perplexed. They knew what social surveys were, and very much enjoyed exploring their own lives in this way. They shook hands at greeting and parting, and spoke easily in unforced and 'educated' north country tones. Their local accent was still there, but it was very mild. Inside the home was usually sparsely but quite expensively furnished. They had not bought everything immediately on hire purchase terms, but had preferred to choose and buy one piece at a time. They were enjoying the excitements of first colour schemes. Alice Douglas had had one wall of her living room strikingly papered with a contemporary orange and black pattern. She had now bought a deep blue carpet and hadn't quite made up her mind whether it matched or clashed. In a corner there was usually a small half-filled book case. Most of its contents were old books from school and college days, filled out with a handful of Penguins—four or five of the green-backed thrillers, one or two fatter Penguin Classics. A television set would take up one corner, and it would be on each evening. They had inherited no furnishings from their parents, and given this start it was difficult to see how the two kinds could blend. Perhaps the most remarkable difference from their parents' rooms was the colour, the bareness, the complete lack of small ornaments and knick-knacks. There were few mirrors and no flying ducks on the walls: only a small print of a Dufy or Van Gogh.

The women had quiet religious convictions, and occasionally attended church or chapel. They insisted firmly on white weddings and the baptism of children. The men did not seem to feel the reality of this part of their being. In politics, both were not very much different from their parents, except that they were not so diligent in using their vote. Seven were Conservative, two were Liberal, and there was one Socialist. The Socialist, on his own account, was of a very temporary kind, registering a personal protest against local bad housing conditions and the inadequacies of his own income. He hadn't in fact used his vote at the last election and these views came as a surprise to his wife. 'Well, I didn't know that before. I didn't know you'd have voted Socialist! I've been brought up a Liberal myself, my parents were Liberal and I never had much time to think it out, but I'd have voted Liberal like they do—or if it had been a Conservative candidate I should have voted Conservative. As a matter of fact I didn't vote at the last election. It was my evening in, or something, and I couldn't be bothered to go out.'

Marriage also brings children, and with them a new cycle of social and educational problems. The Conways have a small girl, but are disturbed that the neighbourhood might affect her. 'All the people round here have been moved out of the slums near London. They've got nice houses, they've got lots of money. Some of them earn as good wages as I do. But the old ways still linger, don't they? Let me give you an instance: on Sunday afternoon all the kids round here are out in the street kicking a ball round and playing football. Now I'd never dream of letting my child go out in the street playing football on a Sunday afternoon. Not for religious reasons, understand. Not for the religious reason of playing out on a Sunday at all, but just because it isn't the proper thing in the kind of society that we live in—and thinking of other people.'

What kind of school should these new children be sent to? Like their parents these couples too are puzzled about choosing the state or the private school. They have been gaining a keener sense of what public schools have to give socially and are a degree more interested than their parents. Those original parents knew very little of the public schools and had not had much personal contact with men and women who had attended them. But in the years after school the sons and daughters began to realise the effect of this alternative form of education. Helen Chapman met public school girls at college and was both surprised at, and hostile to, their assurance, their loud and confident accents. George Denby attended a legal course at Guildford when he was twenty-two and had his first full encounter with public school-boys. He too commented hostilely in an identical way. Christopher Farrell first moved amongst them when he was commissioned in the army. He admired their bearing and leadership, and liked to talk to them about their schools. He approved warmly of their training in sport. 'It was a different kind of education altogether. They're just as intelligent as I am, but I don't suppose they've got G.C.E. in more than two subjects. They concentrated much more on sport. I share rooms with three public school boys now, and they had a well known cricketer for their coach, and he used to belt them with a cricket bat when they did anything wrong.

That's the sort of thing we should have had more of at Marburton College. My old man doesn't believe in public schools. He'd probably say that I'm snobby about this, but he doesn't know. As far as I can see, it's no good coming to London unless you've been to public school.' He himself talks much about his 'old school'. 'Don't let anybody tell you that tradition doesn't matter. It does matter, to be able to play cricket and wear the old school tie,' he looked down at his chest, 'I'm not wearing it today, but I was yesterday.' It was a strange and novel experience for them to mix with young men and women from the public schools. When it did come it came late, and was for most of them casual and passing. But it set old thoughts gnawing, and new hopes stirring.

Conclusion (ᴠⱼᴍᴘ ‖

The sons and daughters in this small 'middle-class' group turn out to be men and women who in very many basic respects are close to their parents. They have inherited their parents' spirit of self-help, their drive, and many of their social sympathies and antipathies. In politics they are similar but much less conscientious. At church or chapel the line of interest descends through the women. But grammar school and college have given them wider interests in some fields. The odd Van Gogh and the few Penguin classics in the book-case may not mean much, but they do seem to point, if slightly, to something. Whether or not education has enlarged and sensitized their personalities in new ways, they have certainly found in it an efficient training for a particular job, and on the whole they now pursue their professions with considerable vigour. Like their parents, they have a realistic sense of their social position. They seem also to share the same dual attitude to social groups below them. On the one hand they are much more closely in touch with the working class than they are with the upper middle class (if only because of the shared schooling) and yet they seem much harsher than their parents in commenting on it. Whether this is comparative youth or whether it has to do with their high degree of geographical mobility, their lack of close and regular contact with the society of a particular place, is hard to tell. In the other direction, they have a more alert sense of the existence and benefits of the private system of education. The family conferences are beginning again.

They are likely to have the money, if they wish to use it in this way—but so had their parents. What they have not yet got is that range of informal, intimate contact with public school men, women, teachers and pupils, which would give them the information and the confidence to seriously consider contracting out of state education. And then, to weigh the balance down, they share their own parents' confidence that *their* children—even unborn —will receive the grammar and college education that they themselves enjoyed. The inheritance had descended to them.

We began this chapter with a problem. How was it that the upper reaches of the Marburton grammar schools were—quite against the run of the population—dominated by middle class children? These accounts have suggested an answer. We have seen that in a host of small but telling ways the middle-class families had an educational inheritance with which to endow their children. State education had been worked into the very grain of these families since its first major stages in Marburton. In half of these instances there was a shrewd and trusting understanding between school and family, supporting the child. But when things went 'wrong', the family was able to interfere and maintain the child even against the schools' opinion—whether it was preparation for the eleven plus, grammar school streaming, early specialization, staying on into the sixth form, choosing a university, deciding on a career. In a variety of social and educational dilemmas which might have damaged another child, the family was able to prevail. It could support him through periods of dissatisfaction, apparent unintelligence, patent idleness. These fathers and mothers were not able to bequeath to their children any vast amount of capital, but they were able to hand on an increasing skill in commanding the state system such that their sons and daughters ultimately received a high standard of education, and one which helped them move smoothly into satisfied and energetic citizens. It is worth pausing to wonder what could have happened to these children if, though of equal potential, they had come from a lower social class. How many would have passed the eleven plus? How many would have sunk into the C stream? How many would have left before the sixth form? How many would have left the sixth without a university place?

Now clearly it is a good thing that so many children from these

families receive such a high standard of education, and an
excellent thing that able children have not been allowed to fall
by the wayside, as well they might. We have sketched an answer
to the first problem. But this problem only opens the way to
another and larger one. How is it that—against the run of the
population—there are so *few* working-class children in the upper
reaches of Marburton's grammar schools?

3

WORKING-CLASS FAMILIES

'Of parenthood and reverence towards ancestors. . . . .'

HAVING very lightly sketched in the middle-class world, and the histories of ten middle-class children at school, we next considered the working-class children who remained at grammar school until they were 18. As Table II had shown, only a minority of those who passed their final grammar school examination were working-class despite the city's predominantly working-class population. We wondered who these children could be, and whether from a study of their time at school we could see what made, and what did not make for success at grammar school. Further, we wanted to know what kind of men and women they became, and where they would be found in our society today.

We therefore examined the pass-lists of the Higher School Certificate and G.C.E. Advanced level at all the Marburton grammar schools We selected the pass-lists for the years 1949 to 1952, since the men and women on them would now be between 25 and 30. This was important because we wanted to talk to adults, many of whom would now be married and parents themselves. We expected that they would have moved along in their chosen professions, and taken their general bearings in life: the turbulence of adolescence and the possible vagaries of college days would be behind them. From these former pass-lists we then drew the names of all children whose fathers were working-class. To define this we used the Registrar-General's classification of occupations. The sample[1] drawn like this provided us with 49 boys, but only half that number of girls. This was our first problem, and a discovery of interest. We increased our number of

---

[1] The detailed procedure for drawing the sample, and our use of the Registrar-General's classification, is described in Appendix 2.

girls by extending the years for them only, back to 1946 and forward to 1954. Some girls whom we saw were as young as 23 and some as old as 32. With boys and girls together, we now had a sample of 88 former working-class children.

But before we interviewed these people, we took up a suggestion from previous research. It had been well-recognized that the answer to many of the questions we were raising would partly be found through a study of family life, and not of children in isolation. In *Early Leaving*[1] the Central Advisory Council for Education urged more than once the need to throw light on the known statistics by documenting the home life of working-class children at grammar school: 'We considered the possibility of making a direct study of the home itself, but we decided that this was beyond our means. We believe, as we shall emphasize later, that there is a great need for such a survey. This is the only reliable way of finding out the many details of home background that need to be known before any precise judgment can be made.' In our study we therefore interviewed the parents as well, and separately from the children. This chapter is a consideration of those interviews, and part of our aim here has been to catch those 'many details of home background.' In our sample there were two sets of sisters, so the following account is based on 86 working-class families.

The home

Although Marburton has its share of poor and squalid housing, we did not visit any such homes. The poorest homes we entered were old weavers' cottages with their many small windows and stone 'flagged' roofs, built on the hillsides around the town. These were once working-class hamlets grouped around the isolated mills, but now often lost amid the acres of middle-class suburbia. Almost always they had been bought by a thrifty family in difficult times between the wars. The lavatories were outside, standing at the end of small paved yards across which the washing hung. And looking on to the yard would be the often crowded living room/kitchen in which the family spent all its time. Housing of very similar quality was found in irregular

[1] Early Leaving, Central Advisory Council for Education (England), p. 4. See also the plea by Floud, J., Halsey, A. H., and Martin, F. M.: *Social Class & Educational Opportunity*, p. 127.

stone terraces nearer the town centre. Here the roofs were slate and the facing stone. Inside there was a front room used only for such formal occasions as Sunday, Christmas, a wedding, christening, funeral or special visitor. It is a subtle test of welcome to see if you are guided into the front room or brought into the kitchen. There were very small square gardens at the front, usually supporting a few evergreens. A low stone wall—just the right height for children to walk along—hemmed it in from the street. A line of iron stubs marked where the railings—lost for scrap in the second world war—had once been. Gates too had gone at the same time, and had seldom been replaced. Many of these homes stood back to back and also had outside W.C.'s. The hilly streets produced the most awkward house plans, with the backs much lower than the fronts, and with dark and dank passage-ways tunnelled beneath them. Nevertheless these were the homes of prosperous working-class families. They looked structurally sound, were usually in good repair and were more likely than not to be owned by the family. The building stone was often excellent, but they gave the impression of being not so much planned as improvised. People and their needs took a command over buildings, yards, and streets in a way never seen in other parts of the city. When we called on Mrs. Beckworth we had to leave the car 20 yards from her door because a line of washing was strung across the street. Coming out, two hours later, we discovered that further lines of flapping washing sheets had appeared both behind and in front of the car. Cars were simply not recognized in that street, and there was a prevailing attitude of no compromise. As one of the neighbours explained when called to the door, 'Oh, it's always like that. Some of the cars don't bother at all. They dirty your sheets and make a right mess of it all—and them coal men, they're the worst. They break your line. It's always happening, but people won't have it! They don't like it—but it's always happening.'

Sixteen of the families lived on council estates. These tended to have the lowest incomes on our sample, but the quality of their housing was good. Though the estates were dreary and unimaginative in the extreme, the houses had three bedrooms, a bathroom/toilet, and were surrounded by more substantial gardens. The council had provided good-sized living rooms but smallish kitchens. All was well when the family used both rooms freely, but there were cases in which the old customs prevailed and most of the 'living' was actually done in the kitchen. This produced a curious kind of 'overcrowding' more severe than in the less well-equipped weavers' cottages.[1]

Some families lived in distinctly better homes. These were tudorbethan bungalows along crescents and avenues populated by minor clerks and school-teachers. Others were larger semi-detached houses perhaps on unmade roads. They had red tiled roofs and broad bay windows. There was usually space for a garage, though only a few had one. The housing officer typed these districts as 'nice residential areas' for us, and few inter-viewers working on a subjective basis would have termed them 'working class'. The one feature that all these houses had in common was an insistence on leaded lights. We seldom saw a clear window, and never in the lounge or front room.

Most of the homes, though not all, were slightly better than their neighbours. Frequently they looked better cared for. The paintwork, subdued browns, greens and maroon, was in smarter condition. The garden was trim, with staked flowers and small rose bushes, orange labels still strung to them. All this indicated care and pride; but the extra features such as the door bell that lit up at night or the fresh and fancy name-plate marked a new prosperity in the home.

Inside the homes the relative prosperity of recent years had again left its mark. After the long lean years during the education of their children, they found themselves relatively prosperous before retirement and old age changed the prospect again. In material terms this did not mean such a lot. It meant a new electric cooker instead of the old gas stove. It might even mean an old second-hand car. But after the comparative privations of a lifetime, purchases such as tnese were charged with intense satisfactions. Mrs. Morley put it this way. 'After all you've got to admit that we are better off. "We've never had it so good"— you laugh if you're a Socialist, but at one time we'd never have dreamed of even possessing a car, but we've got one now. We've spent our money on Barbara for so long and now she's finished

[1] For an account of a similar situation, see the story in Mogey, J. M., *Family and Neighbourhood* of uprooted working-class families in new housing, building their own 'front room' with movable partitions placed across a 'through' lounge. Mogey tells how these must be dismantled and hidden whenever any official appears on the scene, such as the weekly rent-collector.

her education we've spent it on ourselves.' Not all the homes were like this. For one or two widows whom we saw this account would have to be altered. But even they could draw upon the extra support of their educated sons and daughters in ways presumably not so readily available to other working-class widows.

Inside, there was a new buoyancy which was changing rooms that must have looked very much the same for the past twenty years. In the 'front room' was the chunky three-piece suite bought in their early married days and still in good condition. A dark patterned carpet picked up its sober colours, and in a corner stood a glass display cabinet. The cabinet housed a few crinkly china cups, very bright with gold edging, shining metal teapot, and small silvery or gilt trinkets from Blackpool or Morecambe. Either here or on the piano would stand wedding photographs of the children, and sometimes a degree portrait. It was always worth noticing whether the educated son of the house went to his wedding in plain dark suit or whether he hired tails and a grey topper.

In the kitchen/living room the fire was usually burning and the fireplace itself was an indication of the family's prosperity. The poorer homes had huge black-leaded fireplaces with oven and shelf set in and the maker's name stamped heavily across the top. The grate itself was placed rather high; these were the kind of fireplaces on which the big blackened kettle had once boiled, and heavy flat-irons been heated. Better houses had replaced this with a much smaller version but one of the clearer gradings of relative prosperity is the difference between the home with the metal fireplace and the home with the small tiled one. Kitchens were clean but untidy. Or to put it another way, the tops of tables, shelves, window-ledges and sideboards were never clear or simply adorned with symmetrically arranged trinkets. They overflowed with old letters, packets of eggs, pins, buttons, birthday cards, collars and ties, newspapers, broken ornaments. The clocks might run ten or 15 minutes fast. Over the door hung the husband's overalls and there was sometimes a string of small washing across the fireplace. Signs of washing and ironing were usually much in evidence no matter what day we called. Television sets were almost universal, and much depended upon where they had been placed. If they had gone into

48

the front room then the special function of that place was much altered. The TV drew it into the living space of the household.

All these features held in the general run of houses, but were toned down in the bungalow or semi-detached homes. Dirty or squalid homes were so rare as to be remarkable. At the outside no more than four or five could be classified in this way. But they did exist. In one home the room was cluttered and dirty. Beneath the small sofa the baby's pot stood unemptied. On the table stood a mixture of jam jars, opened packets of biscuits, half-emptied pint mugs of tea thick with leaves, and all the remains of the last three meals. The floor was scattered with scraps of papers, a children's ball, small toys, more biscuits, a tube of Smarties. In the middle of it sat the baby sucking a dirty dummy and sharing its biscuits, bite for bite, with two collie dogs. This was not an instance of poverty.

The presence of the child, whom we were later to interview, had left its mark faintly. Besides the photographs, there was sometimes a small National Gallery print bought for the parents, or a line of abandoned school books. Other signs were there but harder to catch and classify. They lay in the parents' vocabulary, or in stray incidents such as Mrs. Morley calling in the cat, ' "Come in, Sam!" Samson Agonistes he's called. That's a bit of *her* coming out.'

Most of these homes suggested that we were dealing on the whole with the prosperous upper layers of the working class. Altogether 57 homes were owned, 24 were rented—on five we had no information. The quality of housing varied—a third had outside toilets and the rest inside. Again the figures are deceptive —all this meant was careful couples had bought sound but old property with their savings. It had nothing to do with poor families living in condemned districts. Indeed in very many cases we were looking at homes that many observers would have subjectively termed 'lower middle class'. And of course their owners might think this, too.

The average length of these interviews was just over two hours. Most parents had difficulty in grasping what we had come to see them about, though they had all received a preparatory leaflet. This was only too natural since we ourselves were 'selecting' one child only from the family for attention. The parents' normal conversation flitted from child to child, and not all of them judged 'success' by the measure we had applied—total grammar school education. ('My younger daughter didn't pass at all and she's the brainiest of the lot. She could buy and sell the other two.') Sometimes they were more eager to talk about their fuller relationship with a son or daughter who had received very much less schooling. But once the interview got under way they glowed with pride, rummaged old photographs from drawers, and even school reports and a child's treasured work—talking so freely that it was hard to get the questions in. This happened even as they protested taciturnity. 'I'm not one of them that talks, am I now? You know when you go in a railway carriage and you see that man that says nowt all the time. Aye, well I'm him!' As the past was unfolded they chuckled or got angry, telling stories in direct speech, and backing the incidents with gestures. Several such as Mr. Lucas moved from side to side, like Launcelot Gobbo, as they acted both parts—their girl and the head teacher, themselves and sceptical work-mate. Towards the upper social levels there was more consciousness of 'being interviewed', but even here it was slight.

Many husbands were well-shaven, red-faced men, rather small in stature. They had hairy arms, stubby nails and greying hair. Often their wives, though slightly younger, had been grey for some years. Many of the men sat through the interview in pullover and a blue-striped flannel shirt, held at the top with a gilt stud. Working boots and shoes were replaced by slippers, and collar and tie lay on one side as they took their ease. The wives nearly always seemed much larger. They were mostly fat and bulky, with thick arms and legs. Their hair was frequently frizzy from home perms, but it was very rarely tinted or dyed at all. A flowery dress with a flowery pinafore was common. Again the more prosperous families were distinguished by the wife's superior hair-do, and interest in face powder.

Similarly in speech the women took more care over their accent and grammar. Few of the men troubled at all, and 'tha' and 'thee' might replace 'you' as the interview relaxed and suspicion disappeared. Both husband and wife had larger vocabularies than they could pronounce, and larger too than they would easily find in their daily paper. The syllable length would be unusual in words like 'preparatory', 'compromise', and similarly they would wobble over facts or dates that they knew well enough. One man, for example, spoke of 'the battle of Waterloo right back in eighteen fif . . . .' and then faded it out in case 1815 wasn't correct.

There was never the break for 'drinks' that came in the middle class interviews, but there were some pressing invitations to stay for a meal and many suggestions to 'bring your wife with you next time'. It was very many times presumed that there would be a 'next time'. The half-understood 'interview' was forgotten, and it was taken for granted that this was the beginnings of a normal social relationship.

This is the context in which our information was obtained, and words like 'interview' which seem so firm and precise in print do not properly represent what happens. With many working-class families the 'interview' became seemingly absorbed in the work-a-day rhythms of home life, and to some extent flowed over into a different kind of personal relationship. These details do not quite hold true of those 'upper' working-class families which had, or sought, some strong association with middle-class life.

Who are they ?

Who belong to this minority of working-class parents whose children successfully complete the grammar school course? A visit round the homes has shown that by and large they come from the most prosperous, house-owning, reaches of the working class. Table I had indicated that although all sections of the working class were under-represented, the children of semi-skilled and unskilled fathers were strikingly less in evidence than the children of skilled workers. If we divide Marburton's working class population into three such groups and compare it with our sample, we can see that 64% of the working class is skilled, whereas 78% of such children as appear on our lists have skilled fathers. On the other hand 36% of the working class population is either unskilled or semi-skilled, but only 22% of children from such homes qualify for this sample. (Table XIV) This heavy under-representation of unskilled or semi-skilled workers was noted, at the point of entry, by Jean Floud and her team in the Hertfordshire survey 'An analysis of the social composition of the entry to grammar schools in 1943 shows that although the

proportion from the unskilled group showed some improvement, it never surpassed their peak proportion of the total entry—5 per cent—which had been reached as early as 1922–30.'[1]

Something like this was reflected in our sample. Despite Marburton's continued prosperity and despite the removal of school fees, children from the relatively poorer homes do not usually complete the full course, even if they manage to gain admission. Though grammar school success seems to be as distinctly related to the prosperity of the home as it has been in previous enquiries, this in itself does not explain the blockage. Most Marburton parents could afford to send and maintain their children at grammar school. By and large the differences are differences of relative prosperity, not relative poverty. Are there then subtler ways in which economic pressures work? Is it for example partly a question of family size? The relationship between intelligence and family size has been remarked elsewhere. For whatever reason, children from small families score better on intelligence tests than children from large families, and this holds in all social classes. It is not therefore surprising to discover that only children bulk large in the grammar schools. This is mirrored in the present sample: 29 are only children, 32 have only one brother or sister. Well over half of the children come from very small families then, and though it is difficult to compare these figures, the suggestion is that a remarkably high number of the working-class children at grammar school are only children. Again the figures turn out to be slightly deceptive when set beside the particular conditions of the families we met. For example, some of the children with siblings have really been brought up and educated *as if* they were only children—perhaps 10. These were families in which the gap between child and child was so large that each had virtually an 'only' childhood; or where the brother or sister had died young, and further ones, difficult to measure, in which the sibling had been rejected and largely brought up by a distant 'auntie'.

Yet despite this, there were 9 who had more than two siblings, and this is sizeable enough to make us pause. Especially when we consider the number where all three children went to the grammar school. It is clear that the successful working-class children come mostly from the more prosperous upper levels of the working

[1] Floud, J., Halsey, A. H. and Martin, F. M., op. cit. p. 22.

class and that, further, they come from small families within this group. But neither of these explanations is exhaustive, even at its own level. The same would be true if we analysed these successes in relation to the material quality of their primary schools, or any similar factor. Such an analysis is conducted with great delicacy and acumen in *Social Class and Educational Opportunity,* but the relationship revealed is more one of 'support' than 'cause'. That is to say, good primary schools in themselves do not so much cause more working-class children to attend grammar school, as support and reinforce children who are already moving in that direction.

Are there then other ways in which we can distinguish these homes from other working-class homes? Obviously there are several, and one of the first questions that pushes itself upon the attention is that stirred by the sight of one or two of these homes, with the new car standing outside the front door, and the £60 knitting machine humming away in the lounge. Are *these* working-class homes at all?

The sunken middle class

Like most workers in this field we have abided by the Registrar Generals' classification and use it as some kind of rough and ready, but recognized, measure. These were all manual workers' homes; yet manifestly this did not always fit either with the bountiful display of material possessions, or, more importantly, with their whole style of living. Were we to some extent dealing with new or temporary accretions to the working class? Were we looking, not so much at upper working-class homes, as sunken middle-class families? This was one of the first suggestions we tried out. We analysed these families from various angles, looking for meaningful ways of describing them. Table IV lays out the basis of our discussion.

Six of the fathers had once owned their own small business, and they had turned to their present manual work when that collapsed. A further 25 couples had a middle-class father on the husband's side, the wife's side, or both. Mr. Waite's family, for example, had owned a small factory, but his own father, though a jovial and respected citizen had given little thought to the possibility of bad times coming. 'He was too generous. He was a Liberal councillor and a big man in the church—whenever they had a

TABLE IV

86 WORKING-CLASS FAMILIES

'Sunken Middle Class'

formerly owned small business	6	—
at least one middle-class grandparent	25	—
with middle-class aunts and uncles	3	—
TOTAL	34	34

'Foremen'

total foremen	28	—
foremen not included above in 'sunken middle class'	—	14

Education

total families where a parent had secondary education	20	—
total not included in previous groups	—	6
total families where a parent had further education	14	—
total not included in previous groups	—	1
total families where a parent was unable to take up an award to a secondary school	16	—
total not included in previous groups	—	7
total families where an aunt or uncle attended secondary school	31	—
total not included in previous groups	—	3

Local Organizations

total families with a parent holding local office ..	18	—
total not included in above groups	—	4

Others

total families not included in any above groups ..	17	17
TOTAL	—	86

collection he was the one who 'guaranteed' it. But he was silly. Sometimes he'd meet a couple of my sisters down in Marburton, he'd put them in a taxi and send them home. He was *too* generous, and when the slump came he hadn't the capital to meet it. The factory banked, and he had a nervous breakdown. My brother who's a director in Liverpool took the family in.' In the circumstances Mr. Waite couldn't be sent, like his older brothers and sisters, to the grammar school and he had to take up a manual job. Lacking education he has followed this all his life. Now his only son has been encouraged through grammar school to university and a position in the civil service. After the long years during which they have regarded themselves as the 'poor relations', the family now has a new 'face'. At university their son, Richard, was offered both the presidency of the union and the presidency of his university Conservative association. Through state education the family has regained contact with its lost position in the middle classes.

This note of being the 'poor relations' came again and again. ('We're the only ones that live in a *council* house!') Families which had come down in the world or failed in business seemed more ready to re-invest their energies in the education of their children than in building up a new concern. 'We're the poor relations', said Mrs. Wimpenny, 'and it's educating the boys that's kept us poor.' Aunts and uncles who advised on the schooling of the children were often solicitors, businessmen, teachers. Sometimes they were very rich, but the poor relations always seemed to remain 'poor'.

> 'Of course,' said Mrs. Barker, 'she's very rich now. Her husband left her 30 or 40 thousand, but she's not my type. I'm not saying anything wrong against her—she's my sister—but . . . . well, people have different kinds of life and she's in a different station in life. Everything has to be hectic with her. Her husband was a member of this masonic lodge and that masonic lodge, in Liverpool and Derby, and all over. And they were always going off to places. When he was sixty they were planning to retire and live in a hotel by the Thames which had got lovely sweeping green gardens going down—whether the back or the front, I can't remember—but I remember about these gardens. They were the kind that always had to be moving around.'

But though the poor relations found themselves in a different station in life, they took pains to preserve their former distinguishing ways. They did not, for example, have the same interest in close neighbourliness as the working-class housewives in their street. 'People round here are always popping in and out of each other's houses, but I didn't like to do that. My mother had never done it, and I wasn't brought up to it. . . . One day the woman next door knocked at the door and opened it to show me something. And I must have looked so queer at her. I opened

E.

my eyes very wide and it must have been the look on my face because she never did it again. When they talk about me they say. "Oh, she wants to keep herself to herself does yond!"' '

Together with this lack of free 'neighbourliness' went many other distinctive traits which told with increasing force when the child went to grammar school. These will be illustrated later, but here we have to record that right at the beginning of this 'working class' survey we find ourselves dealing with a large number of homes that reveal themselves to be submerged wings of middle-class families thrusting their way upwards through free education. The actual proportion comes to over one third of our sample. It suggests that one of the consequences of throwing open grammar school education has been that middle-class families who have collapsed through ill-health, bankruptcy, foolishness or any of the stray chances of life, have been able to educate their children out of their fallen condition and reclaim the social position of their parents and grandparents. All those who spoke naturally of themselves as 'middle-class' did in fact belong in this section.

The foremen

After the 'sunken middle class' the next largest section was made up of families in which the husband was either a foreman or senior chargehand. Such families accounted for a further 14 of the sample; 14 in the former section were also foremen, but they have not been counted here. 'The foremen' in the sense that we are now going to use that term belonged to a distinctively different group from the submerged middle class. They are thoroughly working class in that when we explored their parents and grandparents' working lives, little else was revealed save generations of manual workers. 'The foremen' are a kind of working-class aristocracy, and it is curious to note how in many families the position had been handed on from father to sons: 'Aye, he's a foreman, and his father was a foreman in the same trade. All his family were foremen—his brother was the foreman up at Aggridge, and his younger brother too was the foreman down at the mill in the bottom.' In very many instances, the intelligence and long hard work which had earned the foreman his position was everywhere evident. Mr. Rawnsley, for example, had begun work as a common weaver, but after meeting him it was no surprise to learn that he now had fifty-four men working under him. With others the rise to foreman level seemed almost capricious—or so family legend would have it. 'My father worked in the quarry, on the face there. That was a bad job, you know. No work in the winter months, six or seven weeks you might have and no work. As soon as the frost came the whole job was stopped. They'd cover the face up in case the frost and water got at the stone and make it break when they didn't want it to break. So there was no work at that and he had a go at navvying, digging the roads. And one day they were on the roads digging the ditch along, and he was the only chap that had a watch. So they made him the man that blew the whistle—and after that he was in charge.'

But though the foreman is an aristocrat, he is like that other aristocrat, the policeman, separate and isolated from the rest of the working class. In *Man the Social Animal*,[1] Professor Gluckman remarks, 'The problem of the strain caused by the conflicting loyalties which centre on the bottom-most official in any hierarchy is thrown up in every society, and it is the general problem which interests the social anthropologist. We find it in the case of foremen in factories. They belong to the working class, they depend for social life on their fellow workers, but as foremen they are officers of the management. There is some evidence to show that, like the village headman, they may have a higher rate of illness, though so far it has proved difficult to work this out.'

Several wives bore witness to this strain upon their husbands. Mrs. Black illustrated it like this: 'Sometimes at nights he gets worried about it. I can tell he's thinking about it all the time, about things at work. You see these young ones aren't the same. Only the other day there were two young lads standing about, and father went up to them, and in the Post Office where they work there are some boxes. Now they used to paint underneath the lids of these to keep them nice and bright, and father said, "Oi, you two—you're not doing anything. Get some paint and paint under there!" And they said, "What us? Not likely, we're not painters!" Well, father can't understand that, and he worries about it when he comes home.'

Many foremen brought their worries home like this and

[1] Gluckman, M. *'Man the Social Animal'* reprinted in *The Listener*, 22 October, 1959.

troubled their wives with the doubts and dissatisfaction that they could take to neither their managers nor their men. From their men they took pains to distinguish themselves, and it is remarked elsewhere how the foremen tend to be Conservative in politics where their workmen tend to be Socialist, and how the same man will veer politically as he tastes promotion from the ranks. In many other small ways they dissociated themselves too. There were the important distinctions of dress at work, which were pursued after hours into a host of tiny habits. They might drink, for instance, in different bars. In many honest and earnest ways the foremen were much bent upon 'improving' themselves, and for their children grammar school education seemed to offer the long-awaited invitation. For themselves promotion beyond foreman seemed difficult and elusive, and not always to be secured by the most lengthy and devoted service to the firm. This brought the inscribed clock which stood so frequently on the mantelpiece, but the entry into management itself was quite another matter. Just as the sunken middle class aspired to reclaim their lost ranking, so the foremen sought to satisfy their frustrated longings, by pushing their children through the grammar schools into the senior ranks of local society.

Education—the frustrated and the excited

Over the whole sample there were 20 families in which one of the parents had actually had a grammar school education themselves. There were twice as many instances in which this was the mother rather than the father.[1] In these homes the child had been born into an atmosphere of educational excitement and ambition; ambition which had been thwarted in the parents and now pressed intensely on the growing boy or girl. Of course many of these fell into the 'sunken middle class' grouping, but there were others where a working-class family had broken through into the grammar schools in a previous generation. The curious, almost accidental, way in which grammar school had connected up with the local mesh of working-class life is illustrated by Mrs. Dibb, 'Just at that time when I was nine or ten, we had a new headmaster and with him being new I suppose he was more up on things that were new in education. He encouraged four or

[1] 31 Homes had had an aunt or uncle attending grammar school.

five of us to go in for the scholarship exam., as it was called then, and I passed. Now in Moortop at that time there was what was called the Moortop Trust. And that provided a scholarship for a girl to go to grammar school every two years. Now if I couldn't go, there was another girl who was second on the list, and she was an only child and she would get the scholarship. It was strange how it happened. It was Co-op voting day and my father went out and there he met the father of the other girl. The other one said, "I hear thy lass has won t'scholarship to go t'grammar school—but I reckon she'll noan be going, so our Sarah will be able to go." Now that was the first my father had heard of it. I don't think until that moment that it had ever crossed his mind that I might go to grammar school. But anyway, that got his back up and he said, "What makes thee think our Helen is noan going?" and the other said, "Why I don't think tha'll be able to afford it with a big family like tha's got." So my father said, "Well, that's where tha's mistaken—because she's going!" Mrs. Dibb had to leave grammar school because of a family misfortune, just at the point when her hopes were turning to university. 'I confided in my mother just before she died that I would dearly have liked to have gone to university at Oxford, and she said, "Well, you never know, you might see your ambition realized in one of your children—let's hope it's a boy." ' A son was born to young Mrs. Dibb who ultimately found his way through grammar school to Cambridge.

But by and large those with grammar school experience themselves were also of the submerged middle class, cherishing the tone and polish for their children. 'It was in the family', continued Mrs. Dibb, 'My mother came from a good family, although grandfather had lost all his money, but she always tried to speak nicely and so did I. I was trying to get out of the rut, I wanted to go on and make the most of my chances. My youngest brother used to speak as broad as ever he could just to annoy me —and it did irritate me. When I used to have friends in— oh I was so ashamed.'

Yet for most of the parents grammar school in their generation was a thing for other people. In 16 of the families at least one parent had passed the scholarship exam., but had not been able to take up the place. In most cases acceptance was so much out of the question that the matter had never been seriously discussed.

Mr. Turnbull speaking of the 'otherness' of grammar school education caught it like this: 'There were only two passed in our year, one was me and the other one he was a genius! I can remember the teacher now, he stood this boy up on a desk and he said, "That boy's a genius. We've never had another boy from this school who's won a free place at the grammar school. Absolutely free!" Oh, he was out of this world was that lad. He died when he was 23. His hair turned white, he was too brainy to live. Too clever altogether!' And Mrs. Wallace trying to explain how grammar schools had seemed to belong exclusively to the middle class, the teachers themselves, and the odd eccentric on the fringe said: 'Now there was only one family round here ever went in those days—that was Josiah Firth's. We used to call him the 'whipper-in'; he was the school board man. All his daughters went, but I don't think they were a right lot cleverer than we were. But it was like this, my father used to say, Josiah Firth was no good at the weaving and he couldn't get into weaving —so he became the 'whipper-in'. And you see Josiah Firth was this sort—he read a lot and looked into things, so that he saw more into things than most people round here.'

Table XV shows how those working-class families in which a parent had passed their scholarship examination without being able to take it up, were almost as successful in getting their children to grammar school as the families in which one parent had actually been themselves. Both are seen to differ markedly from the families where neither parent had either of these experiences. In this latter kind of household very few parents could remember sitting any such examination, and it was clear that for many of them school had always seemed irrelevant to the central business of living. Their attendance appears to have been erratic and frequently troublesome to the 'whipper-in'. Mrs. Robinson recalled, 'I used to go along to the school and the teacher used to say, aye it was the head teacher too! "Esther, tha's quite a clever lass, and tha does thy work well, but I wish tha'd come to school more often than once a week." ' As young boys and girls they are eager to be out into the world; too eager in their more mature view. Though the official school leaving age for them was 14, most had passed 'the Labour Exam.' (a sign of ability) which allowed them to end schooling at 13, and many of the older ones had begun 'half-timing' as early as

11 or 12. Under these former regulations, early leaving was paradoxically associated by working-class people with ability, and longer schooling with dullness.[1] 'You see in them days schooling was different. It wasn't like our Mary's had. You learnt to read and you learned to write and to do figures up and take them away, and that was that! You never thought about anything else except work. Work was a wonderful thing. It was a wonderful thing to be a workman and earning a wage, and that's all you thought of. It was as if your brain was closed in. So I was right glad when I left school. I thought that was the finish of that, and I was right glad to get a job. Like I said your mind gets closed in, but you're satisfied and you're happy. Now it isn't everything, but you don't know. Nay, you don't know these things at the time. It's only experience that teaches you, and your experience is written in bigger letters than what's been told you by the school teacher. Aye, it's in bigger letters. It stands out clear like this' (and he made a gesture with his hands). 'You see what it means, but you didn't see at the time. It's only afterwards.' And afterwards many of them had tried to get something of their education that they had not received as children. All that sizeable minority which had been associated with one of the political parties, the Co-operative, the trade union, the working men's club, friendly society or such organizations is dealt with later. These had all experienced some form of further education, though the sheer variety and oddness of courses baffled measurement. But there were others still, a small minority who had played no part in any organization but who yet had seriously attended further education classes of some kind. For example, until the last war, Mr. Ellis had followed a workers' educational class and, with even more interest, courses in further education organised by the local Quakers. These ran a week's school every summer in the Dales, and for many years this had been his annual holiday and refreshment after his unskilled labour in the mills. 'Oh, we had literature there. We had *Shirley* and *Silas Marner*—sort of the psychology of it all. *Silas Marner* had to do with mill workers back in the last century. And we've had poetry—that one about *Daffodils* and Gray's *Elegy*. And once we had a good course on Honey Bees. We had microscopes and looked

[1] As John Sharp says (*Educating One Nation*) 'it is shameful to record' that part-timing was not abolished until 1921.

through them and saw where the wax came from—we all got really interested in that one. We had theology once, and once we had music—that famous singer that there was such a lot of fuss about when she died—Kathleen Ferrier—she came and sang to us. And we had old Egyptian things too.'

Others such as Mr. and Mrs. Abbott had never attended any formal course of further education, and yet they too clearly had a lifetime of 'self education' behind them. Their particular speciality was reading travel books and collecting large Geographia maps to set alongside them. Though they themselves had never been further than Blackpool, their collection was as curious and as impressive as their geographical knowledge. 'Here, look at this one. You can follow the travels in that book just as if you were there. That's Alaska, look! Can you see? And there's the Yukon, and over there are the Aleutian Isles. This here archipelago goes right across to Russia, that's what it does. We've met people that's travelled along there. Here, what's that one underneath? Oh yes, map of the Holy Land. Where all them scrolls were found. You can see the very places on this map—look, look! We get this map out of the Holy Land on a Sunday night and settle down to it. Others can have their TV. We don't want that row!'

One or two of the self-educated shared this hostility to television. 'What's television? Just like radio—been prostituted! Poor stuff. Radio was better in 1931 than it is now. Television, we don't want that. Give me a book. Them chaps can't put that picture that you can see when you read them books. on to them screens, can they? No chap can. It's here' (tapping his head). 'Another thing. It's their opinion, is television, not your opinion. When you read a book, it's your opinion, but what you get on that there television is their opinion, what they're telling you.'

Thus there were a very large number of homes already educationally excited or thwarted even before the birth of the child, and instance after instance of men in cramped mechanical jobs, or women bringing up families on small wages who kept before their children some wider vision of social possibilities. Those most articulate and energetic in stating this were the ones who had held active and responsible office in one of a host of working class organizations. This group of parents, overlapping to a large extent with some of the previous categories, deserves special consideration.

Leadership—the articulate and the energetic

In 18 of the families one of the parents had held responsible office in some kind of local organization. The immense variety of organizational life at neighbourhood level was bewildering. Mrs. Williamson is women's secretary of the Conservative party branch, Mr. Bleasdale is a Labour councillor. Mr. Mountain is president of his union branch, Mr. Turnbull is a scoutmaster, Mrs. Batley is social secretary at the chapel, Mrs. Dibb sits on the Old Folks Committee and the Unmarried Mother's Committee, Mr. Holroyd presided over the supporters section of a first division football club, Marburton City A.F.C., Mr. Rawnsley is national president of a friendly society, Mr. Wallace sits on the Co-operative Committee, Mrs. Rushworth is prominent at the Churchill Tea Circle. . . . . and there were a host of other positions connected with brass bands, choirs, allotment societies, working men's clubs, and so on.

One parent had held distinct office at the local church or chapel in 11 of the families. Sometimes this was combined with district prominence in one of the three major political parties. Church or chapel attendance did not associate itself with a particular one of the three political parties. It was rather the mark of the widowed or the socially active. Mr. Mountain, who in younger days had sought election as Labour member to the city council, now concerned himself increasingly with his union branch and his Baptist Church. The widowed Mrs Barker works hard for both church and her ward Liberal party. Mr. Priestley whose health compelled him to abandon the secretaryship of the local Conservatives, now gave his energies to the parish church.

Very few of the parents spoke easily and naturally about religious matters. Their faith was quiet and inarticulate and conversation busied itself with the direct, practical details of work at church. There was a sense of difference, but not much open feeling about the 'church-chapel' division. The two groups promoted different circles of friendships and acquaintances, and members of the other body tended to be strangers rather than rivals or enemies. Crude re-housing schemes had sometimes placed church or chapel members out of contact with their natural centre, and they had tried attendance at one another's. If this had disappointed it was not so much for reasons of faith, as that the manner of it had been alien. 'I don't like the church services. They don't *sing* there like they did at the chapel. I went to this one and I started off *singing* away at the same strength as usual, and I felt out of it. I had to soft pedal it, and after a few verses I gave up altogether.'

But church offered something that was to matter a lot in the education of their children. It offered them direct contact with people in other social circles whose experience and advice they could use. School problems could be put before an educated chapel acquaintance, and here they might even meet and talk on more intimate terms with the teachers themselves.

There were parents whose sole outside activity was organizing a cricket team, a band, a tea-circle or a gardening group. But the proliferation of these activities was immense, and they came most to notice when a father or mother pulled many such posts together around a political office. Support for the Liberal party in the sample was substantial though office holders were rare; on the other hand, quite a few parents had taken posts with a Conservative group. The father might combine this with being sidesman at the local church, whilst his wife ran a women's section and organized the tea-circle. Yet it was unusual for active Conservative support to be connected with more of the subsidiary local activities than this. This may be because the very active Conservatives largely came from the 'sunken middle class' and 'foreman' groups. They were consciously divorcing themselves from many of the characteristic working-class bodies, and tended to talk in general and 'international' rather than 'neighbourhood' terms. They were indeed highly sceptical of the political intelligence of the workmen around them, and felt the local Labour vote to be either thoughtlessly automatic or narrowly selfish. 'I think,' said Mrs. Coates, 'that the lower intellect people are mostly inclined towards Labour, aren't they? I think it's because they're the sort of people that won't do things for themselves. They want everything doing for them instead of working hard and saving up a bit of money and buying a house. They'd rather live in somebody else's. They'd rather live on a council estate.' And Mrs. Turnbull, thinking along similar lines, said: 'You get these women down at the launderette, and you ask them what are they going to vote. And they say "Labour," and you say, "Why do you vote that?" and they say, "Eeh, I don't know—because our Lawrence votes Labour." '

But more parents were active members of the Labour party. They came from the skilled workers rather than the 'foreman' group, though there were exceptions. It was curious to note how men who had held highly responsible offices for many years, speaking from the platform at National Conference level, did not yet become foremen in their own workshop. It again suggested the general divergence between the two groups of working-class leaders.

Mr. Rawnsley is a cross between the two types. As a boy at home he experienced the benefits of Friendly Society membership. 'When I was very young there used to be men come to see my mother and about a week after they'd come, we'd have a new pair of shoes or trousers, so I decided that that's what I'd go in for when I was older.' He joined the Friendly Society and rose to be National Secretary, at the same time became a lay preacher and foreman at work. These positions gave him many friendships and contacts among local professional and business people. He was nominated president of the local Liberal club. Nevertheless he was uncomfortable about the attitudes of his more prosperous acquaintances, and the many small irritations and differences came to a head. 'I was in the Liberal club one night, and at the time there was a big agitation for 50s. a week for the weavers. And there was a chap in the club who spent that much every night on cigars and whisky. He was on about this agitation and saying, "What do they want with bloody 50s.? What will they do with it? They'll all be millionaires," and I said to him, "Now correct yourself, Peter, you wouldn't speak like that if you hadn't had too much to drink. You spend that much every night on smoking and drinking." And he said, "I'd say it whether I was drunk or sober!" And I thought to myself, "Am I barking up the wrong tree?" Later they came to me to put up as Liberal candidate for the ward, but I said "no". After that I changed my politics and I've voted Labour ever since. But I sometimes wonder if my life's been wasted. I went in the Friendly and Trades Club, and there were a couple of fellows there worse for drink. And I thought, "Well, what's the use? Have I been working all my life for such fellows as this?" And the other day

I met a chap on the road—he's a good union man—and as we were talking, three men came staggering out of the Wool Pack Inn, and he said to me, "I think we're wasting our time, you know." You sometimes wonder if you are; and then you think that perhaps for every four fellows that are like that, there might be two somewhere that have improved themselves a bit.' Many of Mr. Rawnsley's hopes have centred on education, and his only surviving child went to grammar school and training college. She became a teacher and a member of the young Conservatives.

A more characteristic example of the working-class Labour leader is Mr. Bleasdale. In him a host of local groupings draw together. He is a Labour councillor, president of his union branch, director of the local co-op, secretary of the allotment association, and a member of the district youth committee. His father was an active Socialist and his mother a suffragette. He had been born into a politically articulate unskilled workers family.

'When I was a young lad and came home from school, my father would say, "Take these bills round for me," and he'd give me a wad of political bills, notices of political meetings and such like. And at the school when I used to fall out with the other lads—as all lads do—they'd shout names at me. They'd shout this and they'd shout that, but it always ended the same way—"Yah, yer mother's a suffragette!" Ha, yes all those days are behind us. My mother now— you'll hardly credit this—she used to read a lot. She used to read the *Clarion* and the Labour Leader and all that—but she couldn't write! You wouldn't credit that, would you? I'd pick up a lot from home. Oh, there'd be lots to read from there—not the kind of books that you get at schooling like, but books that you wouldn't have heard of, books that would have been put out of print a long time ago. Robert Blatchford's *Merry England*, William Morris' books, and books that made your flesh creep—about the jungle and the Pacific. Ha, yes there were lots of them!' His father apprenticed him to a trade and he was soon holding office in local organizations. 'It's up to us to go out and take these jobs, to show that we can run the place as efficiently, better, more decently than the others have done. It's up to us to take our chances, to take Council places, to take this committee and that committee. It's up to us to let our children go to university like our Stanley did.'

'When our Stanley was a lad, I'll tell you what—I wanted him to go into politics. Aye, more than anything I wanted our Stanley to be

Prime Minister, to be Labour's first Prime Minister. You see, working-class organizations are all right so far—but they've got to have a man who can put the case and knows how to make a point. Look at the miners! A hundred years struggling, and then in 1921 they'd got to make their case—and they had to go and get Tawney. They've always had to go and get people from the universities and higher classes to help them through. Gaitskell you see, and William Morris, Ramsey Macdonald (he were a bit of a duffer was Ramsey—but he was one of them too!) Attlee—another one. That's what I thought our Stanley could do. He could come back and take on the responsibilities. You see, it's very saddening when these lads that's come from working-class life grow up and don't remember it. They ought to do something for it. They've got brains, they know how to make the points. They know all the details. That's what we haven't got—the *details*. But it never seems to happen.'

Mr. Bleasdale too is sometimes disillusioned about the working class. 'I've always been interested in people. All people round here, whether they vote Tory or Labour. You're interested in them, you can't help it. And you get more interested as you grow older. I suppose you get dafter, but the hard thing is to make people interested in themselves. That you can't do. They want to talk about the football club draw, the Liberal club draw, Real Madrid on television. . . . . If you could make people interested in themselves, you could *do* something.' His only child went through grammar school to Cambridge. He is now a time and motion officer, who wavers between Liberalism and the right wing of the Labour party.

Politics

It will be seen that political statements are particularly revealing as to the values, desires and frustrations behind the successful working-class child. The relationship is often quite tangible; whether the situation is one in which the parent is pushing the child away from the sourness of working-class life, as Mr. Coates is, or whether they are moved by the rather different vision of Mr. Bleasdale. We have therefore thought it rewarding to pause at this point and present the political nature and opinions of our sample as telling shadows playing behind the children's lives. The political views of the children are considered later.

Of the 128 parents whom we could directly ask, a clear half

were Labour voters. But the proportion of Conservative voters was high (34%) as was that of the Liberals (16%).[1] The high proportion of Conservative voters is not perhaps surprising after the analysis we have just conducted. Very many of the 'foreman', 'sunken middle class', or 'grammar school' groupings were Conservative, and more easily found their values and aspirations reflected in that party. But Labour and Liberals also drew substantial support from these sections, and the dividing lines did not run so clearly as all that. Indeed, the more we scrutinized voting behaviour the more firm outlines melted before us. At first, for example, it seemed as if the Conservative voters tended also to be the ones who owned their own house. (Table XVI). 'Sunken middle class'—house ownership—Conservative vote,' did indeed cohere together as an intelligible unit, but there was a sufficient degree of political behaviour decided by random or non-political or less self-centred factors as to muddy over all the outlines.

We have seen that the Conservative working-class voter was frequently in the upper working-class grouping, but this was not exclusively so, for the Conservative vote went right down to some of the poorest homes on the sample. This was not so with the rather special case of the Liberal vote which floated amongst the skilled workers with no real anchoring at all amongst the unskilled or semi-skilled. What then was there about Conservative politics which associated itself with educational aspirations, and which was not tightly related to wealth in the home?

To begin with, many of the Conservative voters felt isolated. For reasons it would take more than this enquiry to fully define, they were out of touch with the neighbours, the yard, the street. They had this powerful sense of being surrounded by vast numbers of orthodox Labour voters. ('If a donkey stood for Socialist candidate here, he'd get in!') and had to draw their sustenance directly from the Royal Family, the figure of Churchill, their daily paper. Whereas the Labour supporter could *assume* that the man on the next bench or the woman at the bottom of the yard had similar sympathies, the Conservative had to presume hostility and move with caution. In these isolated circumstances, it is not surprising that their assertion of selfhood was

[1] Owing to local electoral pacts the Liberal figures are possibly deceptive, and may be too high.

sometimes touched by a certain shrillness. Mr. Abbott is a pensioner who lives in an extremely small house. He is one of the few poor people in the sample. Behind him he has a long and toughened hostility to local opinion, and much of the above runs through his conversation. Here he is talking freely about politics—

'Take the slump. That's when I fell out with Labour. Come out on strike, they said! All of you, out on strike! That's what Labour said! And you can't do that. It stands to sense you can't beat governments. Governments top the lot! All the world isn't going to stand still while you go out on strike. Of course it's not, and it shouldn't, I say. Since then I've been with the ruling party.

'Take family allowances. Good theory is that. But no good in practice. The days are gone when they wanted family allowances. Everybody's in work—what do they want with family allowances? Labour party, all lies and fiddles!

'Take National Health. There's that chap Nye Bevan, he started this national health service. Free teeth. Free glasses. What happens? All the foreigners come over in their ships and pinch the lot. All the people from round here, they rushed down for new teeth, new glasses, the lot. Some people hang back, and wait to go when the rush is over. By the time they go for theirs, what's happened? You've got to pay. The whole shop's been skint out. Of course it has. Ridiculous!

'Take Africa. All these blacks. Seen it coming for a long time, I have. Now I was reading in my *Daily Express* today, and it's just what I thought. It's all the fault of the propagandists. These Labour people, going out there, sending propaganda out. Rubbishy stuff. Daft, silly, daft, when you listen to it! Crackpots, they go out and tell all these black people what they ought to have and things they ought not to have, and it's not right. Like it says in my *Daily Express* 'only a veneer of civilization'. They're different from us. These natives, they pinch anything—can't trust a thing. They've got different mentalities. But all these propagandists come out, these Labour party agitators—why they pour it into themselves so much that they believe it. Crackpots!'

The extreme patriotism, the 'international' outlook, the sense of the Socialist crowd, is echoed by Mr. Hammond: 'I'm a Churchill man. I think that England would still be a great nation, even if she never had Australia, Canada, and all those other places. It's that that's in us. We're a great race. I always vote,

I'm like this—if there were twenty men at the corner and they were all Labour supporters, I should tell them to go and vote. We've fought for that vote and we should use it.' And few Labour supporters showed a keener sense of hard times past than Mrs. Ash: 'The working class always voted Labour, of course. That was the only thing they could do to help themselves. Anybody who'd lived through the war and the slump would vote Labour. Things were shocking in those days. You've no idea the things the employers used to do. If you were two minutes late, they used to send you back from work; and the employers —that used to be the Conservatives—used to treat you like a worm. Something to be trod on. You'd no rights—everybody voted Labour then to try and improve things. But I think voting Labour now would be going back to the days when things weren't as good. I mean looking round you can see that things have never been as good, can't you? I think that any of the working people that are intelligent, any with a bit of education, or that's managed to save their money and haven't wasted— they'll vote for who's doing them most good. They'll vote Conservative. Mind you, if things got worse I might vote for the other side again. But things are all right.'

For Mr. Bottomly politics largely centred around the Royal Family, and the way in which his desire for closeness was obstructed. 'Now take this here Prince Charles. I think it's a real tragedy that lad hasn't been sent to a proper school. Just an ordinary school in a decent area, a local day school. If he mixed with the ordinary lads, he'd know summat, and they'd know summat. I don't know what they're frightened of. Are they frightened of the Royal Family knowing how we live? I remember Princess Elizabeth as she was then, coming to Marburton. The way they decorated it up! The way they dolled the mills up! And the way we had to go to work in special overalls that day! We weren't allowed to dirty them, we daren't do a spot of work in case we got a bit of dirt on us (mine's a filthy job, you can't work two minutes without being black all over). But no, you'd got to be bright and clean for when she saw us. Now that's all wrong. Wrong altogether! I've tried to fathom this out, but I can't study it out no way. Don't they like the way Marburton looks? Do they think she won't like it if she sees it? Nay, it's altogether wrong.'

The Conservative voter had an immense respect for men trained at the major public schools, and a large belief in the claims of businessmen to be able to run the country. All this went with a turning away from the immediate life around him, and a reaching for figures and images which seemed more richly charged with life. These speaking voices, taken alongside the educational history of their children, suggest with what a quickening interest they prompted their children through school and university. Grammar school seemed such a *practical* disengagement from the sheer mass and density of working-class life around.

But it would be misleading to associate this tone and colour exclusively with the Conservative voter. We have seen there how unhelpful the customary social stereotype was, and conventional expectation was often similarly defeated by the Labour voter. The militant worker crying Revolution! was not present on our sample, and a large wing of the Labour voters could not easily be distinguished in terms of political opinion from the Conservatives.

Nevertheless for reasons outside our compass their loyalties were given to the other side. Mr. Mitton might represent this 'Conservative' voice which has yet a lifetime of steady Labour voting behind it. 'These Public Schools, Eton and Harrow, they're very interesting, aren't they? They must be very good. Like Macmillan's been to one of them, hasn't he? Now he came to be Prime Minister at a right rum time, and nobody thought much of him for a start, did they? But he's coming off all right. yes! And one of the reasons why that is, is you've got to have these people from these Public Schools, because they can see all the job at once. Like me, now if I had a little bit of a job to do in the house—fix some cupboards up—I'd have to sit down and think it all over. I think this would go there, and that go there, and yond piece would go at the back. Now I can only seem to do little things like that, but somebody like Macmillan he can look at the country, the whole country! And see how *all* the job's got to be done. Right from the beginning to the end! Now I could never do that. And I don't think folk around here could either. It's because they've had this best education; they're very good are these chaps, you know. I say England wouldn't be England—and it's the best country in the world—without these Public Schools.'

F

Against this had to be set the quite different reading of forma-
tive experience which welled up in the conversation of most
Labour voters. Here too educational action and aspiration are
never far absent from political statement. First of all there was
the defence against the unthinking voting charge. 'What any
working man is doing voting for the Tories I don't know, I'm
sure! The only thing they'll get from the Tories will be the
crumbs from the table. I've been a Socialist all my life. It's the
natural thing for a man in my position.' And then there were the
bitter memories, swamping all cognizance of the current events.
Mr. Pollard pulled up incident after incident from his past
employment.

'There was once I heard of another bloody job. It meant walking to
work, but I didn't mind that because it was more bloody money.
So I went to the office and said, "I've got another job, and I'll be
handing in my notice." And they said, "Nay, lad, tha' can't do that.
Sir Thomas is up at London today, he isn't in the office." So I were
bloody stuck. I hung around works and I asked about Sir Thomas,
and they said that he was coming back from London that night.
Now in them days it were all Sir every other bloody word, and cap
in hand. I waited until the train came in, and I went up to Sir
Thomas' bloody house. Sir Thomas Wheelwright it was, and I
knocked on the door and I were shown in. And inside there were
a right big bloody bloke with a right white beard. This were Sir
Thomas. He says, "What does yer want?" and I said, "I've come to
hand my notice in". "You don't hand your notice in here," he says,
"you must wait until next week. I can't receive it." I said, "I'm sorry,
I've got another job and want to leave. I want to hand my notice
in!" And at that he began to curse and bloody swear. "You bloody
young thing," he says, "coming and picking our brains, taking our
ways to other firms. Don't you ever show your bloody face in our
firm again." '
'And as I said, I'd got another job, and this bloody job were at
28/8d. a bloody week. And that weren't much. Tha' could get 23s.
on the bloody dole, see? But if you went on the bloody dole, they
treated like you like bloody cattle. I was *glad* to work for 28/8d.
a week. Now I worked bloody hard for this chap. Well, one day
the boss comes along and he says, "I've got a schoolboy here. He'd
like to be a starting hand. Show him the job." These bloody lads,
sithee, came along from school and worked part-time for nowt.
It were only way they could get a job when they left. He worked

with me, did that lad for about six weeks. One day as the bloody boss was walking along the shop, the young lad went up to him and says, "Well, I'd like a job now, please," and the boss says, "We've no bloody jobs, no bloody jobs at all," and walks away. (He didn't want to pay him, oh no, he were getting the job done for nowt.) And then all of a sudden the boss swung round, came right across the shop floor and he says, "Ah! perhaps we have a job, perhaps we have. Carry on there. I'll give thee 5/- a week." Well, five bob were no bloody money, were it? But five bob were better than nowt. That afternoon the boss came along with another school lad and said, "Now show this one." And I showed that lad till he knew how to do the job just like the first one. And then the boss came in one morning and said, "Now Pollard that will do." "That will do?" I says, "What does ter mean?" "Tha knows what I mean," he said, "I say that will do. Tha'd better start looking for another job." "Looking for another job, what does ter mean?" "I mean what I bloody say," he said, "tha go look for another job. Tha's bloody finished here!" I were sacked. He'd got these two bloody school lads, five bob each a week, and me 28/8d. He were saving 18/8d. week. That's the way they bloody were in those days. We were in a right bloody mess. I goes down to the employment exchange, and by God, didn't they treat you rough in them days. You'd think them buggers were giving you the money . . . .'

It would be hard to under-estimate this past frustration as a major force pushing working-class children on, over difficulties that might have defeated others. The voice was heard so often protesting against insufficiency, indignity, and the perpetual toils of the master-man relationship. Current political events played a very minor part in these loyalties. Yesterday's headlined news was obliterated by today's, and last week's lost altogether. At a time when many of them felt that the major political parties were now so similar as not always to be distinguished, it was the clear battle-calls of the past that dominated their conversation. 'Do you remember that Mrs. Pankhurst?' said Mr. Cowan, 'well, she hadn't much money and when she travelled all up and down the country making speeches, they had to rely on people putting them up. The Labour movement supported them and when she came to Marburton she stopped at our house. Her that chained herself to the railings too. We had to sleep on the floor, while she slept in the bed. Next day we'd follow them when they were giving speeches. Sometimes the ordinary working men used to throw sods at them! They wouldn't have it! They used to sod 'em did the people. And then we'd walk miles among the canal bank into town where the I.L.P. ran a Sunday School for us. That was where I learned the principles of Socialism. The Socialists stand for the brotherhood of man. That school was down St. Peter's Street. Socialists stand for the betterment of everybody all round. They were fiery speakers then. They were real good 'uns!'

Around this sense of Socialism clustered so many attempts at self-education; the debating forums above the Co-op, the classes in literature and economics at the working men's clubs, the yellowed sixpenny books still to be found around. It still had everything to do with educational aspirations that manhood in a prosperous society had not satisfied. It connected naturally with hopes for the children. 'I once read a Jack London story. I've always remembered this one—*Mutiny on the Elsinore*. In it there's something like this. The deck hands are all round, and there's Jack the cabin boy, and he's going to be something like the midshipman in the end. And they say to him, "Now you won't forget when you're in the high places." That's it, "in the high places". That's what I thought about our lad. I always thought "Now our lad's going to be in the high places, and we want him to remember." '

Thus the voices of the parents playing freely around 'politics', dredging up from the past critical memories, projecting into the future hopes nourished in long and often very lean years, suggested again and again the charged pressures from the home. The common aspirations went with loyalties to all three political parties. There was a difference, but it was hard to define. Perhaps it can be indicated by saying that in the Conservative home grammar school offered an educational *release* from the cramping conditions of working-class life; in the Socialist home it seemed to promise the long-awaited consummation.

Of the 17 families that are not covered, save in the pages on 'political' comment, something more needs to be said. Some of them might be associated with the desire for 'improvement' or the frustration of patent ability. A visit to Mrs. Wallace found her deep in Thomas Hardy ('it's not fairy tales, love') and one to Mr. Kingsley urged him to display the host of unsightly but highly intelligent mechanical inventions which had both saved hundreds of pounds for his employer and made life easier for his crippled wife. 'Come round the mill with me,' he said, and led the way up ladders, through long work-rooms, over the flat roof, pointing all the time at small inventions and improvements he'd made in his 30 years as an unskilled workman there. In particular he paused by the long row of huge wicker baskets ('skeps') in which the woollen pieces were piled. 'Now look at these here skeps. They used to be pulled along by a metal hook—like that one that's hanging on the wall there. Fellows did that in the mill for years and years, for donkey's years! And of course when you pull them skeps along the floor they get battered and battered, and they soon get worn out. Come Bonfire night and the Boss would chuck out about a hundred of them skeps to the children, for them to have a big fire down on the canal bank. I thought and I thought and I thought about this, and I invented these—see? These little trolleys, sithee. Tha takes one of these up to the skep, and it's as easy as lifting a baby: tha pulls it along the floor and the skep's still all right at the end of the job! When the kids come along to collect for the bonfire now, they only get six skeps. So that were 94 skeps I'm saving the Boss each year. I made him these trolleys in my spare time, out of my own pocket; and he said "That's a real good idea—you've saved a lot of work and trouble there." He gave me £2 for it. . . .' There were half a dozen families like the Kingsleys where the husband was unusually energetic, and yet had nothing 'formal' to show for it—no promotion, no money, no local prominence—nothing, except his son or daughter's education.

In six or seven families the parents seemed uninterested in education, and of very few gifts themselves—though this comment, based on only a few hour's conversation, is offered very tentatively. From such homes the child had moved through school almost totally by his native wit, drive, accommodation. Finally, there were just one or two homes in which the family had been actively hostile to schooling; but most such families had clearly had their own way long before their children could qualify for this sample. No doubt this is not a total statement of hostility to grammar school education. In a number of families there had been a suspicious and resentful partner as well as an eager and pushing one. But such hostility and resistance can be hard to document after the accomplished fact: few people bet against a winning horse.

Conclusion

In this chapter we have considered the homes from which the successful working-class child came. We have looked at them in several different ways, and it may be useful to summarize. First of all these were mostly families with fewer children than usual. On average there were rather less than two children to a home, whereas a national sample[1] yields three or four children for similar working-class homes. This is only a crude calculation, for there are many subtleties involved, but it is enough to show that in Marburton only small families could fully use state education. This is no new discovery, though it has perhaps been covered over in the buoyant years since 1944. Leybourne-White[2] presented a similar thesis in 1940 and we might in fact expect to find a majority of small families at any point in education where economic handicaps are severe. For example (we have no proof) this might hold true for families sending a child for the first time to public school.

Secondly, very many of these families came from districts where the social classes were mixed, and where there was an important minority of middle-class children attending the local primary school. In many tiny ways, picked out in this and the next chapter, the successful working-class child was carried along because of contact with the local middle class, or because he shared the same facilities, knowledge and teaching. The sketch map of Marburton opposite shows this very clearly. Five out of the 29 primary schools are underlined. These are ones with a large middle-class intake. It is noticeable how the successful working-class children cluster around these schools. The many streets of totally working-class housing in the Railway Street district near the old city centre provide us with no children. The vast pre-war housing estate at Carthorpe with a probable population of over 7,000 gives us only three; whereas the tiny estate (a few hundred people merely) set amongst the wooded hillsides of Beech Green, and surrounded by crescents of middle-class bungalows, supplies four children.

Most children therefore came from small families and went to

[1] 'National' figures are calculated from *15 to 18* vol 2. p. 125 and p 128.
[2] Leybourne-White, G., *Education and the Birth-rate*. This relates too to the distribution of measured intelligence, and the many subtle emotional influences on the life of children in small families. For a comprehensive review of the papers on this subject see *Current Sociology*, vol. vii No. 3. p. 218.

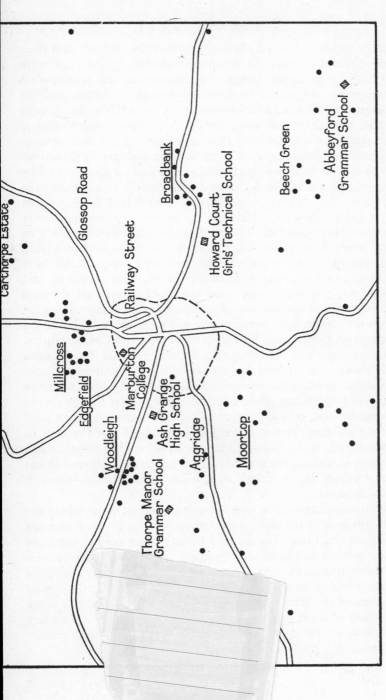

Sketch-map of Marburton—showing the most 'successful' primary schools (underlined) and the homes of working-class pupils on our sample.

schools in which the influence of middle-class children and their parents was distinctly felt. When we considered the homes more intimately, we again noted the importance of middle-class connections and access to knowledge trapped within middle-class groups. We tried to communicate some of this in the concept of the 'sunken middle-class family'. As 'measurement' this is very sketchy, though it has a light numerical edging. It is more an emphasis, an 'ideal type'. Yet its very firm reality is shown by comparing the two kinship charts, (reproduced on pp. 79–80). The Rippons are a traditional working-class family, coming into the city from the Victorian countryside. Their first four children either did not pass the selection examination, or, passing it, were unable to take up a place. The handicap of a large family on top of many other deprivations was too much. But fortunately for Neil, the youngest child, he both passed his eleven plus, and did so at a time when his sisters, Violet and Mary, were working, and money was coming a little more easily. He passed on through grammar school and university to become a scientist working on advanced problems of aeronautics, whilst his brother became a journeyman painter, and his sisters worked in factories and shops. Compare this with the Priestley family. Here is the 'sunken middle-class': a prosperous family which lost three separate businesses through the slump and ill-health. Here too is a large family—four children; but allied to native gifts, the Priestleys have ambitions, contacts, knowledge, that enable them to send all four children, not only to grammar school but through to university as well. (Though here the children had considerable difficulty in making the academic grade). The new generation has re-established the Priestleys as a middle-class family—through state education.

We documented other types of working-class home where the pressures behind the child were unusually strong: the foreman's child; the child from the isolated Conservative family; the child whose parents had been to grammar school themselves, or who had been unable to take up a place they had won; the child whose father or mother were leaders in local groups; the son or daughter of the active Socialist. A certain number did not come under any of these headings, and here we could only offer a few comments on the qualities of a parent, or the wit and accommodation of a child—and little more.

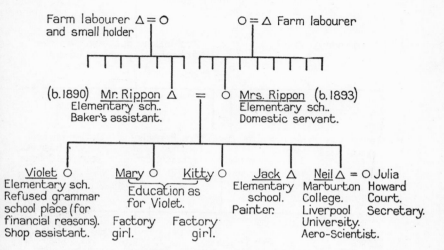

BACKGROUND CHART I. First child to go to grammar school in this family. The chart begins with two families of Berkshire farm labourers in mid-Victorian times, whose children received the earliest form of state education. Mr. and Mrs. Rippon left the country to find work. Mr. Rippon became a baker's assistant in the towns—where Mrs. Rippon followed him as a domestic servant. The search for work brought the married couple to Marburton after the 1914–18 war. Here they raised a large family—though not as large as their parents. Four of their five children passed for grammar school, but it was only when the older ones had begun work that Neil Rippon, the youngest, could be permitted to go. His brothers and sisters remain in manual jobs in Marburton whilst he becomes a scientist specialising in aeronautics, and living in London.

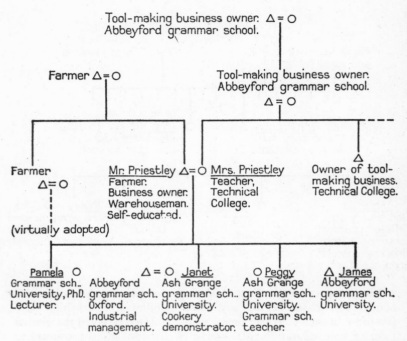

BACKGROUND CHART 2. (Sunken Middle-Class Children). The chart begins with a local business family connected since the nineteenth century with the small foundation grammar school of Abbeyford. The business declined so far that Mrs. Priestley and her brother could only be sent to the Technical College, where Mrs. Priestley later taught. She herself married into a local farming family, but Mr. Priestley left the farm through ill health and later lost another business in the slump of the 1930s. Mr. Priestley's brother helped them by taking the eldest daughter Pamela to live on the farm: he later sent her to grammar school and university. The remaining daughters went to Ash Grange, whilst the son took up again the family's old connection with Abbeyford. One daughter remains temporarily in Marburton as a grammar school teacher. The other married a working-class boy who had been to Abbeyford grammar school and later won a scholarship to Oxford.

Working-Class Families

Such is the world from which the children come. The homes seem more remarkable by the wealth rather than by the paucity of background which they offer to children beginning school. And if we accept this wide span, then many kinds of experience, desire, longing, knowledge and ambition are converging here to focal centres, as money turns more generously and the state's schools open themselves to all pupils on liberal terms

4

88 WORKING-CLASS CHILDREN

In the last chapter we presented the home background against which the children were born. Our suggestion was that whereas the middle-class parent was quietly and justifiably confident about handing on an educational inheritance to his children, the parent of the successful working-class child was more often nervous and anxious to break through and snatch grammar school education for his children. Of course this is only a rough attempt to catch a central thread; the full picture was more elusive than that. But at its centre was the working-class home in which frustration, drive, ambition, was such as to impel evenly the modestly-gifted child through all the difficulties of primary and grammar school into the 'middle-class' invitations of college, university, and the professional career.

Before we begin the illustration of school and college days, it is useful to indicate again a crucial difference between the middle and the working-class home. Such pointers as could be gleaned from the slender middle-class sample drew attention to the father as the dominant parent in matters of education. But behind the schooldays that we are now to examine, it is clear that the centres of power usually lay with the mother. In two thirds of the families there was either an equality of interest, or else the child could not or would not attest the major influence of one parent. In the 29 families where the child made distinctions about his parents' influence 23 claimed that the mother was the important and pressing parent, and six claimed this for the father. This could not altogether be accounted for by the mother's education or her superior station before marriage, though both these mattered. Its roots seemed to push much deeper into the basic rhythms and expectations of working-class life, belonging to that whole pattern of social living in which the mother rather than the father was the organic centre.

But this does not mean that husbands were not prominent: often they were—but usually supported by their wife. Many of the working men were resentful of their lot, and eager for hard bread-and-butter reasons that education should come to their children. 'To put it bluntly,' said Mr. Beresford, 'I didn't want him to finish up in the same street as I'm in—whistled up at half-past six in the morning, working on short time. I had seven solid months off work just before we got married, and I knew that if he got educated, he wouldn't be in the same position as me. That's the top and bottom of it.' Others spoke of strongly 'cultural' expectations, of pictures and Shakespeare becoming meaningful to their children; but perhaps the commonest feeling was that education promised a kind of classless adulthood in which you could mix freely and talk with every kind of man and woman. This was illustrated in a host of homely ways from talking without embarrassment to the Queen down to the confident handling of patronizing shop assistants.

It was no wonder then that out of this mesh of hopes and anxieties the moment of birth itself should look so especially rich in promise; almost oracular even. 'When our Richard was born, he had a funny head,' said Mrs. Beckworth, 'he had the funniest shaped head that you can imagine. It stuck out here, like that! And I said, "Oh Dr. Sykes, look at his head. I've never seen one like that." And Dr. Sykes said, "I have. It's a long time since I've seen one like that. Don't you worry Mrs. Beckworth, those are brains. Those are brains pushing out, and as long as you take care of him until that head's firm, you mark my words, something will come of this." '

As the child began to talk and play, there was sometimes distinct parental effort for a more than common correctness of speech, for a purer English than the parents themselves had hold of. With this might go rules on play with 'rougher' children, a whole series of *extra* precautions, demands, and trainings, in which love has a tang of harshness and restriction for the growing child. 'His auntie came over, and she said to him, "Let's have you talking, give me your pandy," and I said, "I'm not having any of that! If they are going to speak, they are going to speak properly, right from the beginning. We're not going to have any of that sort of talk here!" '

Primary school

Nevertheless, when the moment came for schooling to begin, many of the parents were less sure of their choice and guidance. This was the point of entry to unfamiliar worlds. Those families with blood relatives in the professional classes, or with middle-class links through church or club, sometimes took advice about the choice of primary school. There were eight instances in which the nearer school had been shunned and a farther one preferred, as a result of canny recommendations. Like most cities, Marburton is divided into loose zones with a primary school in each. The working-class population tends to accept the zone together with its school. This after all unites with convenience and the many ties of 'neighbourhood'. When the middle-class population resides close together it too tends to take over a distinct school, and is satisfied. But the whole system, as elsewhere, is reasonable and elastic and a certain degree of free movement to schools out of the native zone is tolerated. Now there are many critical areas in the city where very good and less successful primary schools lie close together, or where several less successful schools command a whole sector. Middle-class parents are much more aware of the relativity of procedures of selection and rejection, much more aware that these things are not decided by acts of God or infallible scientific procedures. They know that all kinds of advantages may flow in from choosing the best school for results, rather than accepting the school which is simply nearest. Consequently they use the system's elasticity, and by doing so reinforce differences in standard, tone and expectation.

Few working-class parents fully realized this. Apart from those with middle-class connections, they accepted the local school in a natural 'neighbourhood' spirit. When they seemed equidistant from two schools, their reasons for preferring one rather than the other were warm and child-centred, but extraordinarily short-term. Mrs. Black chose in this way for her little girl: 'Yes, there *were* two schools in Broadbank but we didn't know much about them. Well, there were some children passing on the road, and I said, "Which school do you go to?" and they told me the Church School. So I told our Doreen, "Those children go to the Church School. Would you like to go to that school?" And she said, "Yes," So I went along there, and after that she went to school with the children.' The consequence of this kind of situation is that certain Marburton primary schools provided no members for our samples. If the children attending these schools passed their eleven plus, then they did not stay at grammar school to pass Advanced level. The fortunes of able children from two such schools, children of parents who chose 'wrongly' at this stage, are examined later in Appendix I.

At school the children quickly showed promise, and began taking very high positions in class. Those who appeared on our samples were the able ones who had taken easily and quickly to primary school. Not surprisingly, there were no stories of children being pulled through by extra coaching outside school, if their gifts had not immediately begun to develop. Parents were not in touch with this kind of thing, even if they could afford it; nor was as full a knowledge disseminated about the selection examination at that time, as there is today. It is worth suggesting that for the working-class child *early* success in the primary school was a pre-requisite to any further achievement.

Early success meant firstly a quick and eager mastery of reading. A facility with figures counted next: but to begin with, it was from the ones whose literacy came young that the successful children emerged. Many parents reported their child's relative quickness with the printed page, their almost hypnotic concern to unravel written language. 'One summer's evening talking to our neighbour,' said Mrs. Robinson, 'we looked out, and there was our Arthur sat on the wall at the bottom of the garden. It was a windy night, and there were bits and scraps of paper being blown along. A bit came rolling on just past our Arthur's feet, and didn't he off and pick it up, and sit on the roadside and start to read it! There you are! Read owt, read any scrap of paper that came his way. "That lad'll be Prime Minister one of these days," said my neighbour.' This rapid literacy became a proud badge of difference and more than one ambitious parent with a little money to spare and intoxicated by her child's success, was persuaded by some doorstep salesman to buy expensive encyclopaedias on credit. Many of the volumes still stand unused, others were sold at half price years ago.

Meanwhile, at school the children discovered themselves sorted out into 'top groups', special classes, and similar bodies marked by the teachers as good prospects for selection. At least

50 spoke of receiving special or extra attention. The numbers were clearly much larger, for many whom we elsewhere discovered to have been members of highly coached groups had forgotten, or come to feel that this was the 'normal'. Before the 1944 Act took effect most schools were all-age establishments taking their children through from the infant department to school-leaving age. Their official title of 'all-age schools' seems never to have taken root outside the education offices, and their older names—the 'Board School', the 'Council School'— were the ones still in common speech. In all but the smallest schools there were systems of pre-selection enabling the teachers to give particular attention to the needs of those likely to go to grammar school. Some, for instance, were moved up into the 'scholarship' class two or even three years in advance. For most this meant that hard work, many tests and a thorough grounding in those skills of arithmetic and language to be examined by the 'eleven plus', began at seven or eight years of age. A certain 'apartness' from less successful children was experienced even before the examination was taken. But the gulf, though there, was not a wide one. Future dustmen and future physicist sat side by side, though they received a rather different kind of teaching. Most of the children were schooled under this older system.

But after the 1944 Act the senior parts of the council schools were cut away and formed into secondary modern schools. The junior sections, covering the years up to eleven, became our primary schools. Both secondary modern and primary schools tended to gather larger numbers of children within a shorter age span, and the result was that whereas in the old council schools one class for the seven-year-olds or the thirteen-year-olds had sufficed, there must now be two or even three classes for each year. Children were divided up into school classes according to ability; the ablest class in each year being the 'A' stream, and the less fortunate the 'B' or 'C' stream. The division into streams generally took place at seven, and there was not very much movement up or down. This account does not always hold true, but it may be that in the present system where a firmer pre-selection is often accomplished at seven, there is a greater rigidity, a less accommodating way of handling children who develop at different rates and under different pressures. It may be; for there is little certain evidence either way, and one must be wary of over-emphasizing the elasticity of the former mode. We had not sufficient informants schooled under the present system of official selection at eleven, and unofficial pre-selection by 'streaming' at seven, to anchor down any firm remarks on the change. But amongst its possible effects could be an increase in the need for very early success by the working-class child, and a heightening of their nascent sense of separateness. For that majority of working-class children who fail the selection examination would find themselves in different classes, not different desks, from the children likely to pass.

The schools' teaching then seemed centred on the grammar school examination, though not perhaps as attentively and efficiently as it may be today. The atmosphere could be sharply competitive, and at the top of the class one girl said, 'We didn't have friends, we only had rivals.' Given all this, there was still a certain breadth of childish friendship. They found themselves working and playing as members of a wide social group, a more inclusive body than they have belonged to since. Orchards were raided in company with future navvies, plumbers and civil servants; skipping rhymes were picked up from girls who were going to spend their working lives as weavers or bus conductresses, and their first car rides were enjoyed when they were given lifts home by the professional father of a new school friend.

And to some extent they were aware of this at the time. Aware certainly of more tattered and rougher children than themselves, aware too of boys and girls from prosperous homes whose wider experience yielded fuller vocabularies, and an imposing range of reference. Some felt the need to 'cover' themselves against this competition and Malcolm Astin recalled, 'Every year we had to write essays about where we'd been for our holidays, and our family could never go anywhere. But I used to write essays about having gone for a week's holiday to Rhyl. The others were talking about where they'd been, so I'd write my essays too. I knew it was 'expected'.'

Other touches of the middle-class world were felt as they reached the age for joining the junior sections of clubs and troops. In some districts the boys brigades, the cub packs and similar bodies were full of working-class children and part of the whole neighbourhood complex. Children who joined these strengthened those local ties that had to be reconsidered when they reached grammar school. But in other districts a scout troop might be a fairly exclusive middle-class body, perhaps associated with a church drawing on few manual workers. Some socially perceptive and ambitious parents, anxious to thrust their children out of the working-class world, actively urged them to join this kind of group. Others were hostile. James Wood wanted to join the cubs, but his parents 'wouldn't let me. They said it was a Fascist organization,' and it wasn't until he got to grammar school that he had his way. Other boys, like Richard Beckworth, were hostile themselves. 'Let me say that the sort of kid I was wouldn't join the Scouts. There's a social difference. Now even when I was seven or eight all of us scruffy, low, working-class kids would be playing around St. John's Church, and the brownies and cubs would meet in the church hall there. Up we'd go into the yard and climb up to the windows, and we'd push our faces right up— a right scruffy lot we were—and stare at all these brownies and cubs inside with all bright clean uniforms. They seemed so pretty, so clean. I always hated them.' A few years later he too is to find himself on the 'inside' and wearing 'bright clean uniform', but his hostilities were undiminished.

As the eleven plus drew nearer, one or two children were hurriedly moved across a vital boundary line, on to the side where there was more substantial grammar school provision. These were cases where the family had middle-class relatives or friends. 'I never thought anything about this exam.,' said Mrs. Waite, 'until Mrs. Beardsell came down to talk to me. She was Peter Beardsell's mam, and he was our boy's age. She came down and she talked and she talked until in the end we took him away from that school and sent him to Broadbank.' But few parents were aware of these important discrepancies, and though many were looking forward hopefully to their child's success, many others did not properly understand the significance of the exam.—and amongst those who did was a small group which feared rather than welcomed success. 'It's funny,' said Mrs. Trafford, 'but when it came to that exam., to go to grammar school, I didn't think I properly realized what it was. I might have said "good luck" when he set off, but I didn't seem to be bothered about it. That's funny, isn't it?' A few children had failed to tell their parents at all of the exam's imminence, and the first they heard was when the results came out.

Almost everyone was eager to point out that knowledge and concern about the eleven plus had now increased out of all proportion to what it had been in those days. Perhaps this explains why we came across so few of those pitiful cases in which the child had been offered substantial presents if it passed. Those forces other than active ability and good teaching which made for success at this point have already been explored, but perhaps their potency at a crucial moment is caught by this boy. 'Well there was nothing in particular. My mother didn't offer us prizes or money or anything like that. There was never any money about. But she was always hovering in the background, very emotional about things. For instance, when I took my eleven plus, she was there getting all worked up wanting me to do well. She was always very reticent, but you were aware of things like that. There was an almost psychic atmosphere about it, and that helped us to do well. And once you've passed your eleven plus, you've made the decision, haven't you? It was the natural thing to go on to university, in some ways going to university was the easiest way out for me.'

At that time the local system was to announce the eleven plus results in three separate lists. The first list with the top passes might precede the second by two weeks, and a third list followed later. Custom usually had it that the results were read out at school; and there were painfully tense periods between the lists, and hard moments in class when your name was not called. It is outside the province of this enquiry to document how it felt to be rejected, and we can only offer up memories of relief and joy, by the successful.

For with the results of the exam. came warm scenes, full of pride, excitement and promise, remembered still with remarkable precision. 'I was cooking down in the cellar (I do all my cooking down there for fear of accidents) and he came in and stood at the top of the cellar head, waving an envelope, and I said to him, "What's that, love? Has the post been or something?" and he shouts, "I've passed my exam. mam, I've got my exam., I'm going to grammar school." ' Other children responded to their own fears and their parents' anxieties in curious ways. Lillian Ellis said how she 'ran home and went into the house, and do you know what I did? I said my name hadn't come on the lists, and I waited until her face fell, until it really dropped. Then—it was a cruel thing to do—then I told her I'd passed. What do you think of that?' And in some homes they were met with a more worldly-wise reception. 'When I passed,' said Kathleen Holdsworth, 'I came home and told them it was a load off my mind. They said I needn't be so cocky—it was a load *on* theirs.' But for almost all it was a moment to be eagerly recalled ('When I passed. . . .') and a moment that seemed to bring overnight the most perplexing weight of worries.

To begin with there was the grammar school to be chosen. For the girls this was fairly easy since there was not so much grammar school provision anyway. But for the boys there was in the city both a first grade and a second grade grammar school, and for many it was the choice between these two that was so difficult. Children on the first list had the priority of choice, and the informed naturally tended to choose Marburton College. Most of the children on the second and third lists had their difficulties automatically resolved by the filling up of places at the more popular schools. They then took what vacancies were left, and these were often at the technical secondary school at Mill Cross. This whole procedure has since been somewhat changed in Marburton, but of course similar kinds of gradings still operate in most places.

Its interest here lies firstly in the dilemma of working-class parents in discovering the best school, and secondly in their tendency to choose one distinctly below the level of their child's potentialities. Knowledge as to the best and the second best only circulated freely in those families with some history of grammar school education or with middle-class connections. Many of the other parents had obviously been quite concerned, but both ignorant and embarrassed at their own ignorance. Those with church, union or political connections held a distinct advantage when it came to seeking advice. Others tried the neighbours, workmates, even a friendly bus driver. Some went to the school, but in that atmosphere felt antagonistic or defensive.

'That's right, I saw the headmaster, and I said: "We've got this form with all these schools down, and we don't know anything about any of them." "Well," said the headmaster, "What's his father's job?" "He's a lorry driver." "Well, then you'd better be sending him to Mill Cross." "Mill Cross? Why, is that the best school?" "No, it's not, but it's the best school for you." "How do you mean, it's the

best school for me? Where would you send your lad?" "Oh, I'd
send *my* lad to Marburton College. . . ." So what do you think of that
story? Fair cheek, isn't it?'
'Oh yes, I went up to see the teacher, Mr. Crowe, and asked him
which school he thought was best, and he said straight away,
"Marburton College of course. Don't you know that?" And I said,
✗"Yes I do," but I didn't.'

A few visited the City Education Offices for the first time and
retired defeated and unenlightened by the clerical staff. They had
an instinctively personal vision of the situation, and assumed the
accessibility of the Education Officer and the possibility of a man-
to-man chat with him. Mr. Pollard was more persistent.

'One dinnertime down at the foundry when the whistle blew, I came
out through the gates and round the corner to see the Education
Officer, Mr. Pike. "Can I have an appointment?" I said. "Oh no,"
they said, "you can't." "Can't? I want an *appointment*, I don't want
to see him now." "No, Mr. Pike can't see you. Mr. Pike's too busy."
I had all the lot. . . . Well, I wouldn't have that. I banged on the
counter, but I got nothing, no. They wouldn't make anything.
I went back to the foundry and I said, "Oi", to Councillor Boggis.
He was a stonemason and he'd been put on the Council like. I told
him the story, and didn't he play pop! He got on the telephone and
he said "Who's there?" And they told him. "I don't want thee,"
he says, "I want Mr. Pike." So he got Mr. Pike in the end. "Sithee,"
he says, "tha's a public officer like everybody else, and tha can make
appointments like everybody else. . . ." '

The result of this ignorance, embarrassment and bewilderment
was that in many cases a vital decision was taken for quite trivial
reasons. A school was chosen because it was near enough for the
child to come home at dinner time, or because it meant one bus
journey instead of two, or because its situation seemed to offer
a greater abundance of 'fresh air'. Faced with a lack of knowledge,
there was at this and many future points a strong tendency to
choose that which was nearer, less divorced from the world of
home. There were, of course, those homes (very few) in which the
surface hesitation had nothing to do with lack of information,
but mirrored the more reluctant depths. The most extreme case
of such hesitation was one in which not only the responsibility
for choosing the grammar school was left to the child (for this
frequently happened), but the basic decision itself was abrogated.

'My mother got all the papers signed and put them in an envelope for me, and she gave it to me and said that if I wanted to go I could post it, and if I didn't then I could leave it.'

Of those who chose the school for themselves, most were following a group of friends whom they were reluctant to lose. At the centre of this group could sometimes be found a middle-class child whose parents had made an informed decision, and unwittingly chosen for his friends as well. Others were attracted by a particular uniform, or merely the name of the school. This was a kind of reason sometimes confused with their reading of comics. 'Do you remember those comics that we used to read? *The Wizard* and things? Well, there were stories in there about these public schools—Red Circle. Big 1914 stuff, all colonial kinds and that type. Now that's all I knew about colleges, and somehow I mixed that up with the name Marburton College.' More than one parent supported this by saying that all their knowledge of 'grammar' schools derived directly from Billy Bunter's Greyfriars, and they fully expected something rather close to that establishment. Their inaccuracy of judgment had led to a downward current of choice in certain instances. Children enrolled at a secondary school a degree below their apparent abilities. And the downward tendency was strengthened by some of the fathers' distinct preference for a clearly understood technical training rather than the more nebulous grammar school course. Similarly a few mothers—even at this point—feared the possibly longer grammar school course might lead children away from them in either place or spirit. Both these numbers were small. The other doubters had presumably drawn their children out of grammar school before eighteen.

What of the children, their classmates, left behind? Sixteen spoke of themselves as being isolated, almost friendless anyway, and perhaps the accounts of background and pre-selection help us understand this. They lost nothing in friendships at eleven plus, for they possessed little. Eighteen reported that, since all their friends had passed the exam., they had no links at all with such children. A further body began with this statement, and then as memory brought back lost relationships of some intimacy, they pointed out how it began to *seem as if* all their friends had passed, after the links were snapped. But there were many times in which close friends had failed the exam., and one in which a

92

twin had done so. Here the relationship became immediately tense. The child left behind was quickly defensive, and undeserved charges of 'snobbishness' might break the friendship. Relationships that lasted best through this critical period were the ones rooted in a very local society, such as an outlying village, or the ones bound by a common organization such as the boys' brigade or a Sunday school. And this opens a theme to be developed throughout the grammar school days.

Notwithstanding the above, most felt that the ones who failed 'didn't care', 'weren't bothered', 'hardly noticed', and there was a distinct harshness in their description of them. They were 'the illiterates', the 'dim ones', 'the future teds.' Only in one or two cases were the validity or the efficiency of the selection techniques questioned. By and large they believed that a correct and distinct line had been drawn between two kinds of children, the 'intelligent ones' and these others. There was no doubt at all but that they strongly affirmed the rightness of selection at eleven plus. And it was interesting to note a periodic tendency on their part to over-estimate rather heavily the number of children in their school class who had gone to grammar school. Marburton had at this time grammar school provision for rather less than 20% of the population, but many here thought it had been twice or even three times as much. Some spoke of 75% or 90% of their class passing. It was as if the majority who had failed had gradually shrunk in their memories, and success with the selection exam. taken its place as the 'normal'.

Here, then, was the ending of the more inclusive primary school days; an ending full of excitement, fear, loss, sudden charges of 'snobbishness', and new looks from the neighbours. For many it marked a sharp and immediate ending of all neighbourhood ties outside the home, though not for most. For those who were to find grammar school an unhappy experience it was their farewell to their 'real' school. Ten years after leaving Scarcroft Council School, Brenda Sadler took her degree. 'I sat down and wrote to the teacher at the school there thanking her. I wrote and thanked her for starting me off on the right foot.' She did not trouble to inform the grammar school.

Grammar school

The first weeks at grammar school were strange. For the children who already had contacts, they were exhilarating, the exciting prelude to promised satisfactions. Whole new areas of inviting study presented themselves—Algebra, Physics, Latin, French. 'I took to Marburton College like a duck to water,' said Ronald Turnbull. For children who had broken most friendships and connections with the old neighbourhood, here were fresh children, fresh clubs and societies, the school scouts and the school corps to join. The invitation was irresistible, and many were glad to accept it in full and become from the earliest days loyal and eager members of the school. Their wholeheartedness was naturally reflected in their first pieces of work, and finding themselves soon well placed in class, they were conscious of latent power thrusting through, of their ability to command new and more testing situations. We have shown that most of the parents came from the very upper reaches of the working-class, and once their child reached grammar school, these parents were whole-heartedly behind the enterprise. In very many small ways they influenced their children to accept, to belong. Both grammar school and home supported the child in orthodox and receptive attitudes. But under particular strains and pressures, this home support could, and did, break down; and this happens more and more often as either the school disturbs the parents (directly in an interview, indirectly through weight of homework and so on), or the parents find no way of obtaining vital knowledge, or coming to terms with the middle-class ethos of the grammar school. The parents may have been 'sunken middle-class', but many of these discover how different this can be in knowledge and evaluation from that range of middle-class life endorsed by the grammar school.

For the majority of the children, unlike Ronald Turnbull, the entry to grammar school was uncertain and confused.[1] They had suddenly lost in some measure that mesh of securities, expectations, recognitions, that we have called 'neighbourhood'. 'I had this feeling of not *belonging* anywhere,' said Patricia Joy. They found themselves surrounded by more middle-class children than they had ever met before. These children spoke better, seemed more confident, some already knew bits of

[1] The 88 children spent 636 years at grammar school. 165 years (26%) were in war-time. Of the 196 sixth form years, two were in war-time, We do not believe that this has much altered the situations we describe.

94

French and Latin, their fathers had told them what 'Physics' was about, a few even knew the teachers. *They*, evidently, seemed to belong. This insecurity was heightened by confusions over getting the right books, the right sports equipment, the right uniform. 'I didn't like it,' said Rita Watson, 'my uniform seemed too big all round—long sleeves—I suppose my mother had to do it like that so it would last longer, but I felt awful. All the other girls' uniforms seemed all right. *I* was wrong.' On top of this came the new subjects, the new vocabulary (not 'kept in' but 'detention', not 'playtime' but 'break'—and was it 'yard' or 'playground' or 'cloisters'?) the masters' gowns, the prefects, the whole body of customs, small rights and wrongs, that any well-developed grammar school holds. Some of the schools made a practice of teaching the new children aggressively for the first weeks, to 'break them in', and, presumably, to nip behaviour problems in the bud. The effect on children already bewildered was to knock them off balance rather than 'break them in' and to create, rather than cure behaviour problems. This was obvious in our study of the middle-class child where a highly gifted boy could be so robbed of confidence in the first term, as to *seem* dull for several years afterwards. For some of the working-class children, confused by a genuine loss of part of their social life ('neighbourhood'), perplexed by the strangeness and sheer difference of grammar school, conscious of new *social* barriers thickening the normal barriers between pupil and teacher, and unable to turn to parents for explanation and understanding—for these children the beginnings could seem almost hallucinatory 'I had that feeling like when you were in the forces,' said one boy, 'after you got your jabs and you got inoculation fever, you felt away from it all. You felt in a bit of a haze, everything was a bit bleared. Well, that's how school felt at first. I felt just as I did later when I'd got inoculation fever.'

It would be gross exaggeration to offer this last statement as the 'typical'—the spectrum spread between the first and last quotations in this section, but there was an impetus towards *this* end. For many the 'haze' always seemed to hang about grammar school. And not grammar school only, the world outside had suddenly changed. If they forgot to speak to someone in the street, or failed to notice a passing neighbour, there were sharp accusations of 'snobbishness'. Even neighbours who had never been spoken to much before were illogically insistent that they were now being scorned. Sometimes they had grounds for their charges ('I must have condescended to them. I thought how unlucky they were not to have been to grammar school'), and perhaps small children compensated for their insignificance at school by their surface confidence at home. But many were very scrupulous about these matters, they soon learned what a remarkable tact was required from them. Still it all meant a loosening, or a straining of neighbourhood ties, and it was hard to know where the next challenge might come from. It might come from a neighbour: 'An old woman who lives nearby was always asking me what standard I was in, and I didn't know what "standard" meant. We didn't have "standards" at Ash Grange and I could never understand what she said. So I was always embarrassed with her. It was always *me* that was embarrassed. I felt as if *I'd* done something wrong.' Or it might come on the bus, 'If you were on the bus and you were in uniform it didn't matter how many Briggshill children there were on the bus, *you* had to stand up. The conductor would say, "What do they teach you at Thorpe Manor?" Little things like that meant a lot to a child.' Or more simply and more manageably it might come from other children; 'When I got to Ash Grange and wore the uniform, the other children used to shout about that. I didn't mind so much. I felt superior. But I had a violin as well, and I used to dread carrying that violin case. I used to plot my way from the yard at home to the teachers, but that violin case seemed to stand out—that brought more bashings than anything else.'[1]

Classroom

Eighty of the children were in grammar school years in which there was some form of streaming, of dividing into 'A', 'B' and 'C' classes. (Table XVII) This division has usually taken place by the end of the first year, and sometimes was complete after eight weeks. It looks as if it decided a lot about the future for these children, if not others. Sixty-six were in 'A' classes, and only two came from 'C' classes. For them there was not much movement between streams after the first decision. We only recorded five such instances. Almost all those children who were graded 'B'

[1] What Dr. J. C. Daniels calls 'the self-fulfilling prophecy' in the streaming system is, of course, extraordinarily difficult to disentangle. R. R. Dale writes suggestively on this aspect ('Prediction and the Crystallization of Differences').

or 'C' at this early stage did not last for the sixth form course. (On our very small middle-class sample, half the children had come out of 'B' or 'C' classes). And of their experience we can give little in this section. This whole point must be developed later, but at this stage we must either credit the grading system with very remarkable accuracy, or wonder whether working-class children, lacking a particular kind of parental knowledge and support, and rubbing against the school in all kinds of ways, did not over-accept the gradings given them. Once declared 'C' children, did they not begin to learn, play, act, think and feel as 'C' children; precisely that?[1]

From now on then we are, to a large extent, talking of children in 'A' classes. And to begin with we must report what thorough workers they seemed to be. As they felt it, the atmosphere was sharply competitive. The note sounded before the eleven plus selection vibrated still. 'There were four or five girls at the top of me. Anne was my friend, but the others were just competitors. To be truthful, I half hated some of them.' But now it had a deeper ring; when so many other things seemed unsure, work was basic, clear, markable. Success here was a peculiarly potent security, and even those children who refused to identify themselves with the school, largely identified themselves with the *work*. Its compulsions could have touches of 'guilt' and 'obligation' about it. One boy summarized it with 'I always had the feeling that I ought to do well in exams because I *owed* it to somebody being at grammar school.' And another who had rejected 'school' all along said, 'No, I didn't like that school at all, but I was keen on the *work*. I was very keen. But school was just the place where I went to learn things, that's all it was, no more.' In the years that we covered those children who stood out in everyone's minds as the really phenomenal workers, the ones catching at every mark and grinding their way to quite brilliant 'O' level results, were working-class children in just these situations.

Meanwhile some of the social difficulties were resolving themselves and some of the 'haze' beginning to clear. Speech and accent had been an early difficulty. Some spoke of their sudden self-consciousness over accent, of their discovering that they actually had an accent. Boys were troubled at having to read

[1] Young M. & Willmott, P. *Family & Kinship in East London* includes a small study touching on similar ground, see pp. 144–154.

aloud in class, girls feared to ask questions. 'That bothered me quite a lot. I thought that if I mispronounced words or said them wrongly the other girls would pick me up and correct me and tease me. . . . Oh yes, they did. Oh yes, they certainly did. These things did happen.' But, as confidence gathered, some of these troubles were deliberately overcome. Parents with middle-class ambitions were as conscious over this particular difficulty as their children, and a small number (especially girls) were soon taking elocution lessons. Others spoke of themselves as good 'mimics' who quickly learned to speak as others and the teachers spoke. This group, 'the mimics', were perhaps the largest body, and they certainly knew what they were about. 'Fairly early on I decided what changes I was going to make in my accent and I made them. That's perhaps why there was that drifting apart that I told you of from all the other children.' So shifts in accent too play their part in loosening 'neighbourhood' ties, and it was as if the process continually gathered momentum and the breach grew wider. But accent, even if changed, was still a burden and created other difficulties. That it offended the neighbours and old friends goes almost without saying ('stuck up', 'speaks la-di-dah'), but this time it cut into the home and family life. Again the need was above all for 'tact', and there were children who became bilingual, speaking B.B.C. English at school but roughening up when they got home. But the situation was not as automatic as this, and the tact was not always forthcoming. Some kept the new accent at home as well as at school, and though this was approved by parents paying for elocution lessons, it thrust a touch of discord into other working-class homes.

Yet, as social difficulties altered and most children began to melt into the school, to become *of* the school, other problems arose. As early as the second year important decisions were being made by teachers or by the children as to the range of subjects they would study. There were decisions about going into a 'science' or a 'language' class, about dropping or keeping geography, or Latin or chemistry, or physics or German. Many of these decisions had of course to be taken, and we have shown how for the middle-class child and parent with some sense of *consequences* a reasonable arrangement was often possible. But few working-class children knew what in the long term, they were deciding when a subject was dropped; and no working-class parent ever raised objections at the time on such grounds. So the decisions, if the child's, were taken for childish reasons. 'I chose the Latin stream because I couldn't manage the bunsen burner and I'd got told off.' Or else they were taken in the familiar 'haze'. Clifford Tate recalled, 'The others seemed ready to take decisions and look after themselves. They'd go and talk to the teachers. They knew what they were doing. Whereas I very seldom knew what I was doing. I daren't ask and I didn't seem to know what was going on. There were a lot of decisions you had to make at 11 or 12. You had to decide between Latin and German, and you had to choose between history and geography, and as it turned out the subjects I dropped would have been a lot more use to me.' The extent or seriousness of this dilemma was hard to measure, for of course it is a common indulgence to blame present weakness on past decisions; but without being able to offer anything near precision, two areas did locate themselves. Firstly children who had ambitions to be doctors discovered very late in the day that they had made things extremely difficult for themselves by wrong specialization from the age of 12, and with most, their ambition was defeated by discovering themselves at 16 or 17 so far along the wrong path. Secondly, some who later wanted to go to university, and some who obtained sufficient marks to get a scholarship there, were startled to find (often casually when they were 17) that they lacked basic 'O' level qualifications for entry. Or similarly, that they had severely restricted their choice of university. For example, this might arise by a child preferring German to Latin when young, or being streamed into a German ('B') class rather than a Latin ('A') class. When the sixth form was reached and a scholarship won, the discovery is made that only at one English university is it possible to read an Arts degree without a Latin qualification.[1]

[1] Since Oxford and Cambridge have now altered their Latin requirements, part of the difficulty has been removed, or rather its surface nature has changed. For of course they have (rightly) laid down other entry qualifications and the suggestion here is that, *whatever* qualifications are required, the working-class child, *in the situation we report,* is going to find himself frequently without them. This is something to put alongside the Crowther Report's cry that such a vast number of our most gifted children fail to take the sixth form course or go on to university. If they *did* take it, then many would find themselves still without the bases for university entrance, for decisions nearer the roots might well have put them into 'B' or 'C' classes at 11, 12 or 13, where in place of Latin, physics or a second foreign language, they would find themselves engaged with 'O' level Art or Domestic Science.

At the point of university entrance there were two particular effects. The first was a blocking of the way from the sixth form to Oxford and Cambridge, and the second was the diversion into training college of girls whose 'A' level result would have promised a successful university course.

Something then of these final consequences seems to have been pre-determined at a very early age, and with it also had gone an essential decision about the *pace* of schoolwork. Practise varied between schools, but most of the children in 'A' classes found themselves on a faster course. The basic idea was to do the first five years' work in four, so as to give the children who stayed on more time in which to pursue specialized studies. The need then (as the school saw it) was to save a year, to push on younger children with good qualifications to the universities. There was no doubt that this thickened the competitive, the highly mark-conscious atmosphere, some sign that—here and there—it produced nervous troubles with distinct physical symptoms, and perhaps most clearly of all it emphasized the importance of homework. But, considered later, the year's saving seemed to have offered hardly any lasting advantage.

Homework

The schools usually had a graded system of homework.[1] In the first year something up to an hour a night might be expected, by the end of the fifth form it would have risen to near two hours. There were children who kept to these times, and there were children who did it in less. But for most the prescribed time was merely nominal and a considerable under-estimation of the hours they spent. This was not because the schools were demanding an excessive weight of private study, though there were instances where a too-fast timetable spilled heavily over into evening work. It had more to do with the children's own need for success, for marks—a need we did not encounter at this intensity with middle-class children.

Few working-class homes had easy provision for home study. Some children went into the front room, others retired to a bed-room, but many did their homework in the living-room/kitchen at the very centre of family activity. This immediately produced

---

[1] There is much excellent documentation of the effect of homework on social and family life in Stevens, F., *The Living Tradition*.

difficulties. Should the wireless be on or off? Could the younger children play noisily? Could the father stretch his legs and tell the day's tales? To ask for silence here was to offend the life of the family, was to go against it in its natural moments of coming
× together, of relaxation. So many learned the early habit of working with the wireless on and the family talking, of building a cone of silence around themselves. To a certain extent this worked well, but it meant that the boy or girl had to continue at his tasks after the others had gone to bed, or he had to learn to snatch those moments of emptiness in the house immediately before tea or breakfast or during the week-end. And the family was not always untroubled at this, for the private concentration could produce an abstraction, a forgetfulness, an off-handedness that also gave offence. Those who retired to front rooms and bedrooms met with other difficulties, especially in winter, when they could hardly ask—in their peculiarly dependant and 'obliged' position—for two rooms to be heated. 'Sometimes he used to go up into the bedroom and do it. Aye, he'd have the eiderdown wrapped all round him to keep him warm, wouldn't he? And many's the time he'd be up early on a morning—before breakfast —working away at his problems and things. They gave him such a lot.' But it wasn't simply a case of their being given 'such a lot'. Other children, no more able, managed it within the time; yet we were given here 20 accounts in which homework loomed monstrously large.

'There's been times, isn't that right?' said Mr. Beresford to his wife, 'when he's started after his tea and he's gone on and his mother's gone to bed and I've gone to bed, and then I've got up again at half-past one and there's still been a light under his door. I've gone in and taken the books off him, and there's been tears in his eyes because he wanted to go on. But I said, "They're not giving you so much homework at Thorpe Manor. Either you're spending too much time on it, or you're not taking it in at school." ' Some parents made gestures of help, but there was little they could do, the studies were beyond their training. Some accepted it as inevitable and came to terms with it in other ways. Mrs. Hudson insisted on her son going straight to bed for two hours when he came home from school. 'Yes, straight to bed at half-past four and then he'd come down and have tea and go into that front room and work right through. And I didn't mind when he came to bed at one o'clock or two o'clock, because I knew he'd had two good hours' sleep.' There were arguments; arguments in which the children tried to explain the urgency to them of their work. Mrs. Lynch recalled, 'He'd stopped up till midnight studying, and I said to him, "Surely you know enough to pass by now, Clifford?" And he said, "I don't just want to *pass*, I want to do *really well*." ' And these arguments flared into the open when one of the parents (often the father) was reluctant about the whole grammar school undertaking. 'Our Alfred would be doing his homework in the front room, and his father wasn't a bit understanding. He'd make it in his way to go through that room as many times as he possibly could—to disturb him. First he'd go for his coat, and then for his cap, and then for his collar and tie. Eeh, we'd have some rows in this place on a Saturday evening when Alfred was doing his homework! His father would start off talking about Rugby League and stuff like that, and I'd tell him to shut up.' These long homework hours, even more than 'accent', cut into the vital centres of family life, dislocated the whole household's living. It could generate hostility, misunderstanding, irritation, jealousy; and many mothers had to make a special effort to take it under their protection, to create a new rhythm around it.

But of course much was evidently lost, and looking back not everyone felt the price well paid. Neil Rippon was spilling over with opinions:

'Christ, no, I didn't like Marburton College. Too fast, they just got me there and they crammed my nut from the moment I arrived. That school doesn't turn out human beings, it turns out people to read and write, that's all. Look at the facts they rammed into me. School Cert. in four years. All these facts, Christ, just think of them! All that geography I did period after period, and now I hardly know where America is, and I've been to the place! Yes, I worked quite hard. I'd be about fifth or sixth in class. You do a day's work at school, you go home and you've got two and a half hours' homework because you've got to keep up to schedule, kid, and then you do another two and a half hours. You don't play out any more, and you don't see anybody except on a Friday night. Christ, what a way to grow up! You go back to school next morning, and perhaps some kid hasn't done his homework, perhaps he's been out! What, you'd think he was a bloody communist the way they carry on. Christ, kid, they don't believe in leisure. Leisure means laziness for them. It means sitting around and loafing with your feet up, that's what leisure means. No time for all those other things like reading serious books (not that I read any serious books, not after having all that crap about Shakespeare and Dickens rammed down my throat. I wouldn't read a word of it now.) But leisure, that's what you need in growing up and, Christ, you don't have any leisure.'

The loss of social life outside school—'you don't play out any more'—a loss which some regretted, and some regarded as a natural and quite normal stage of growth. (A few insisted that *nobody* played out after the age of about 13, *that* belonged to earlier childhood.) But not all children were prepared to give everything to school like this, and by the third year most had taken their stand, for or against.

School versus neighbourhood

There was some evidence to suggest that the third year had been an important kind of pause, a point after which it was clear whether you were for the school or not. We were not asking for particular statements about this in the interviews, for it was only as the survey developed that the conflict began to claim more of our attention than we had foreseen. But, without prompting, 48 children spoke clearly of themselves as being identified with the school ('I was very much an establishment man. I was all establishment man!') whereas 15 were just as clear that they had declared *against* the school, and 25 held some intermediate position. As pointed out above, being *against* school did not necessarily mean being against school *work*. For all kinds of children interest here was intense, and success of supreme importance.

We pay a great deal of attention to the children who refused to accept the school. This is because we believe that they often represent the very large numbers of gifted working-class children who abandon grammar school at 16, and do not progress (as well ✗ they might) on to university and the professional life. Certainly the children we spoke to remembered large numbers of dissident pupils up to the fifth form, but few of these remained at school after this, and only a minority fall on our sample. The rebels left.

Who are the ones who *did* remain, and who especially are in this inner group of 15, who stand out uncompromisingly against the grammar school ethos? Five of the 15 come from 'sunken middle class' homes; eight have fathers doing unskilled or semi-skilled work; 11 live in rented homes. Lightly sketched in like this we see that they come from all ranges of our sample, with perhaps a slight emphasis away from the very top reaches of the working-class. A more illuminating way to look at them is in terms of their friendships. We chart these in the diagram below:

Two of these 15 were very isolated children at grammar school. Another two belong to groups that do not concern us here. But the other eleven are joined together by a very tight mesh of friendship. Ten of these 11 were at one school, the city's largest; Marburton College. Leslie Barron, who joins many of these children up, was at Marburton College an unusually long time, and his friendships, based on neighbourhood rather than age, crossed several school years. So we can summarize by saying that though large numbers of working-class children may have been hostile to the grammar schools, most of these left before the sixth form course began. Only at Marburton College, which was large for a self-supporting group to form and maintain itself *within* but *against* the school, did many stay on into the sixth. This self-supporting nucleus had friendships both with working-class children who left at 15 or 16, and dissident middle-class children who, in minor ways, helped to drag the group over the gap between the fifth and sixth forms. But this is to glance forward.

The essential choice which these 88 children faced in the early grammar school years was one between school and neighbourhood. Some children had begun with few neighbourhood links, and for them this was no crisis. But the others who found themselves firmly, or sporadically, against the school, were boys and girls who were still involved in neighbourhood life, and who preserved their other style of living. It was more than a matter of joining a youth club rather than the school scout troop; it had to do with deep differences in response, feeling, judgment—which recoiled against common images of 'dominance' or 'leadership': school uniform, teachers' gowns, prefects, the Honours Board, the First Eleven, the Scout Troop, the School Corps, Speech Day, Morning Assembly, Expected Public Decorum. The children who drew back from this spent their evenings in youth clubs, or

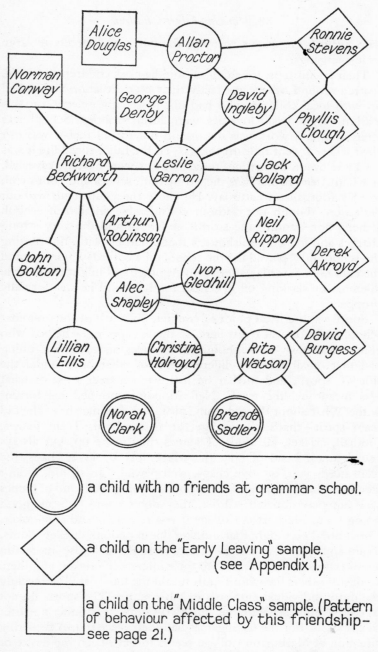

○ a child with no friends at grammar school.

◇ a child on the "Early Leaving" sample.
(see Appendix 1.)

▢ a child on the "Middle Class" sample. (Pattern of behaviour affected by this friendship—see page 21.)

Working-class children against the school—the mesh of friendship.

with cycling groups or roaming the parks and streets in large inclusive gangs.

Their friendships, touching on middle-class children at school, centred around others in exactly their own situation and linked up with local children who had not passed the selection examination. Their basic loyalties were local loyalties. School was interesting and work was important, but for all that it was *only* 'Just where I went to learn things.' To the fuller social life it was hardly relevant. Sometimes these loyalties were nakedly revealed, as when Alec Shapley was picked by both school and youth club to play football on Saturday. He chose the youth club without hesitation, though not without considerable friction at school. Others, not wanting the storms at school and the very strong charges and indeed punishments that could go with 'not putting the school first' played for the school on a Saturday morning and the club on a Saturday afternoon. Another still might resolve the dilemma by slacking off in school football until he was formally dropped.

Sport was a critical point of conflict. So much of the grammar school tradition was overt here, so much expected. The boy who clung tenaciously to neighbourhood modes of feeling and doing had first of all a rather different idea of what came under the title of 'sport', and further he had a much freer sense of what was meant by 'the team'. Neil Rippon continued his torrent with, 'What about the old team spirit, eh? Ask me about the old team spirit—that's all you get at that school. Team games, football, cricket, all kinds of games they make up, but always team games. Load of crap the whole lot! By jove, chaps, the team needs you, by jove chaps, well played. Christ, kid, I can't stand that kind of thing. Load of bull, all of it. The kind of games you can play yourself, Christ, they don't count. It's no good going on to Marburton College if you're a dab hand at snooker, Christ no! Too tough, that snooker doesn't count, cricket counts. Team spirit, by jove chaps!' There were those whose interest in snooker was more intense than their interest in cricket, and there were still others for whom sport meant the lonely skills of cycling the more individual emphasis of table tennis. The sports do not of course quite separate out into two camps, it is rather a matter of emphasis. For the team games had their place too. A recurring situation at Marburton College seems to have been the desire of working-class boys to play rugby league football (the northern professional game) instead of soccer. When this reached the state of groups of boys organizing themselves into something like unofficial school or house teams at this unofficial game, then the school might put out feelers for compromise, and suggest the difficulties of catering for *rugby union* as well as soccer—difficulties, say, over fixtures of the better kind. The whole point, of course, of the rugby playing was lost in this, for the school failed to see that whereas rugby league was very close at heart to northern working-class life, and whereas soccer could occupy a kind of neutral and classless position, rugby union was almost as remote as lacrosse, and not what was wanted at all.

But it was not only a question of what came under 'sport', it was a question too of how a team game should be played. Here again the same freer feeling was evident. For some there was a root disinclination against highly organized sport, and for those who were ready to play there was not the feeling that they had to play wholeheartedly all the time. The twin ideas that the team should be bound tightly together in uniform and spirit, and that every member should give of his uttermost that the school might win, were ideas that these children had to learn at school. And some refused to learn them. At football they never quite had the complete rig-out: if the school didn't provide the socks, then their socks were odd, if it did not provide shorts, then theirs were the wrong colour. Small incidents arose out of their refusal to call the master 'Sir' at football on Saturday morning as they would unhesitatingly have done in class on Friday afternoon. At half-time they had no conscience about avoiding the lemons in favour of a quick smoke, and about their whole play was a friendliness that was not quite the same thing as 'sportsmanship'. It carried with it a freshness, almost an ironical touch, a readiness to take rests, to applaud the opposing team, to enjoy the game but to be not much troubled whether the school had won or lost. And since this often went with quite excellent abilities at ball play, sparks flew between master and boy.

But difficulties over the right style of playing football were as nothing to the disagreements over cricket and its rituals. Richard Beckworth tried to reconcile playing for the school at cricket with playing for a local club, and this is how he spoke of 'official' school cricket. 'Simon Carpenter was captain, and he was dead keen that we all walk on the field in a straight line behind him, like professionals. Well, I'd never do that, nor would my pal Hopkins. And then the master, Rylands, he always insisted that we had whites, white shirt, white shorts, white shoes, white socks, all dressed *properly*. Well, George Hopkins would come along wearing green corduroy pants and one of those tee-shirts with cowboys across the front, and I'd wear my shirt outside my trousers. No. . . . I don't seem to have that certain something that makes cricketers and prefects and officers. I don't know what it is.' The way school sport threw up the different behaviour patterns, tested the different loyalties, could be developed much further, but sufficient is indicated here to show the kind of thing it was.

Meanwhile, similar difficulties were arising within school. There was the school uniform. To illustrate the divergence over sport we drew largely on the experience of boys. But school uniform had an equality of effect, and met with an equality of rejection from boys and girls. Lillian Ellis said, 'Another thing, I didn't like school uniform. I'd keep my beret in my pocket and only put it on when we were walking into school, and I'd get out of that uniform as soon as I could. When I got home I'd change into a print frock to go out in the park. I wouldn't go out in that uniform. I wouldn't wear it at weekends or holidays or anything like that.' The uniform had nevertheless to be worn, and though the rejection could be heightened by financial difficulties ('It was a bit tight, it was a case of washing the school blouse one night and wearing it the next morning. They were the only clothes I really had.') this clearly had nothing basically to do with it. The children who objected so strongly to school uniform were not the poorest children by any means. It seemed as if the objection was aimed at all those aspects of 'school' that did not have to do with 'work', but had to do with the school as an alternative community, as a particular code of living together and growing up. And the dislike of school uniform spread out into a dislike of all uniforms—scouts, guides, O.T.C., A.T.C. It also had something to do with the working-class children's pace of growth. Working-class girls were often quite early turning towards boy friends, dress and make-up; the life of the evenings was becoming a central part of their living. To them uniform which required the dress styles of the young to be worn up to the age of 18 could be very irksome; and indeed it *was* embarrassing to walk the streets when they felt like young women but looked like young girls. Boys felt they belonged to the world of men when their uniform kept them in the world of boys; and their parents supported them. Mrs. Proctor said of the headmaster, 'He used to send me notes about how our Allan shouldn't go to Speech Day in his trilby hat when he was still a schoolboy. Why, there was nowt wrong with it. He looked daft with a little cap perched on his head.'

Almost any official side of the school was rejected by their children. They would not join the school corps, they would not join the school scouts. Nor would they even buy the school magazine. 'All the way down the school I'd refused to buy the school magazine. I wasn't interested in buying it and I wasn't even interested in looking at it. I wasn't the only one, no. There were quite a bunch of us and the masters would come and bark at you and tell you how ashamed they were and how you were letting the side down, but I wouldn't buy it. And even when other kids bought it I wouldn't go and look at their copy.' It was odd to hear these consistent incidents in which children—often quite shy children—had taken a painful stand against the school over something which must have looked quite trivial to the teachers. Again it was not a case of the lack of money, though this might reinforce a stand, and it was not that the children could themselves explain why they were having nothing to do with this or that aspect of the grammar school. All they could say was, 'I won't ,' and stick.

On the other hand, it was by no means clear that the school understood either, and often there was the sense of two strange worlds finding themselves side by side, yet with neither fully aware of the other's sheer difference. Head teachers saw that some boys and girls retained neighbourhood links through youth clubs and similar bodies. Most tried to dissuade their pupils from membership. Speeches were made in assembly suggesting that youth clubs really belonged to secondary modern school children and should be left to them. For grammar school children there was the school community with its societies, and homework. 'I joined the civic youth club,' said Peter Waring, 'and the organizers used to ask for the head master's signature from anybody who joined. But Mr. Lewis wouldn't have it. His attitude was, "If you haven't got enough homework to fill in your time, we'll give you some more." It didn't make any difference, I joined all the same.' But it is reasonable to suggest that it could make a difference sometimes, that it did play its part in further stratifying children's society by breaking down the last links between grammar school children and the rest.

Other head teachers were bolder and struck right into the question of 'friendships'. 'There was the time we had the drive to get all boys to try and get friendships centred on the school,' said Harry Dufton, 'He used to think that this would draw all the circles into the school. But my father thought differently. He thought that I should have friends outside the school.' And this was precisely it. These children *did* have friends outside school. 'You have two kinds of friends. I had the friends that were at school, and then you had the friends that you had at home—all the ones that lived in that maze of alleys and streets around Barker Street.' Though for all this, relationships with non-grammar school friends could still be tense, and the easiest relations were only with those in a like position. If the parents came up to the school, the master might put the question to them directly. 'He was saying to me, "So-and-So is very good, why doesn't Alan make friends with him? Why doesn't he make friends with boys who would be a better influence?" '

And daily from the teachers came a host of warnings, injunctions, suggestions, that spoke of the gulf existing. Working-class children felt themselves being separated from their kind. The choice between school and neighbourhood was faced daily in small concrete incidents. For the teachers these incidents were merely part of the pattern of manners, part of that training in 'tone' which distinguished the grammar school from the general community. They were honourably conceived and held, but for the child something much more central to his living was being locally but continually strained. 'She said you weren't allowed to eat ice-cream or sweets in the street. All sorts of silly things like that that you'd have done *naturally*.' (Fish and chips seemed to have given as much trouble as football.)

'And Mrs. Mackintosh was very snobbish in some of the things she said. They used to have gardeners at Ash Grange to look after the garden and she told us that we had not to speak to them. The way she said it, it sounded as though they weren't the kind of people we should speak to . . . She wouldn't let us speak to the caretaker either, but the way she said it, it sounded as though *they* weren't the type of people we should talk to either. . . .'

We recorded a lot of evidence about the school's insensitivity and the child's hypersensitivity; the school's determination to hand on the grammar school modes, to spread its standards as the best and the only standards, and the child's awkward, clumsy and stubborn desire to preserve the other ways, to remain 'natural'. This gaucherie soon moved into rudeness, tactlessness and the impolite. And the children who clung to 'neighbourhood' seemed to attract to themselves the full weight of the school's punishments. Again it was all part of the 'haze'. 'I got showers of detentions, showers of them, and 'Saturday mornings' as well. Canings, tests, detentions, crying at night over my arithmetic homework—that's all I can remember of those years. I don't know why I got so much punishment. I was quite a mild child, and I was interested in my way, too. I just don't know how it was.' At Marburton College one of the punishments was to bring the offending children back on Saturday morning for extra school. 'Yes, you got three detentions and that made it so that you came in on a Saturday morning. But somehow 'Saturday mornings' were better than weekday school. The whole school was quieter, more relaxed, less intimidating altogether. Somehow it was better than going to school in mid-week.' A similar note could be recorded about the quietness and freedom of the art room, the laboratory after school, or a meeting of the music group. 'I liked relaxing, stretching out on the desks with my feet up on the seat—all the things that you couldn't do in lessons. And some brainy sixth formers would sit in the master's desk and put these gram records on.'

So it was not then such a simple case of being anti-school. School had its attractions, and for these, its very deep satisfactions, but it was only a part of life and often an alien part of that. 'No,' said Alec Shapley, 'we weren't anti-school. School didn't enter into it. School was like work, you went to school in the daytime and in the evenings you went out to enjoy yourself.' Those who tried to keep all their evenings to themselves seldom lasted into the sixth form, though some did. Others were caught in the tensions between the evening life and the need to do well, to establish themselves securely in terms of marks—as a counterpoise to the ambiguities, the discords, the losses of living. By the third year the lines were clear: on the one hand were the working-class children who had thrown their total self into the school; on the other hand were those children (largely in B and C streams now) who clung to neighbourhood, and whose attitude, clumsiness and inarticulate divergencies attracted that rebuke and punishment which merely stiffened the will to resist. Most of these children were moving towards the escape from grammar school at the end of the fifth form. From their ranks only the very small minority survived.

The majority of our sample had preferred school to neighbourhood and become hard working, accommodating members of the school community. They survived into the sixth form, where they began to assume responsibility to lead and command themselves; and they are best illustrated at that point. We turn now to the parents' vision and to the winnowing of the G.C.E.

Parents and the school

As the earlier discussion on the parents suggested, grammar school for their children was a new extension of living for themselves too. This does not hold true in every case, but in almost every interview with the fathers and mothers we recorded some flicker of excitement at knowledge for themselves as well their children. For some whose abilities had been particularly frustrated or under-developed, the grammar school was as rich an experience as for their sons and daughters. And though with some this was a mere spurt of life lasting a year or two only, with many it burned throughout school and college days and has not since lost its hold. Here is one voice playing over the whole experience. Mr. Lucas is a bus driver who left school at 14; a man in whom large areas of curiosity, delight and intelligence had lain dormant until his daughter passed the scholarship exam. To hear him speak now is to hear him use words like 'culture' and 'civilization', if not with full confidence at least with a very real sense of what their meanings reside in.

'Now when your child is coming along and going to grammar school, you begin to get excited, you begin to be interested, and you want to know more things. That's how it was with us. It was a wonderful thing for us our children learning all these new things. Now when I was at school we learned history and geography and it was all battles and such like. But for our Mary history and geography aren't all like that, they're bigger things. It's as if she can see ten times, a hundred times, as much as we were taught. She doesn't talk about *battles*. Now we went out on a coach trip up in the Yorkshire Dales and she goes poking in the fields and she hoicks out of a field this here thing. Come and have a look out in our garden. Dost tha' see it? Now that's a fossilized fern is that, and you know I'd have kicked a dozen of them things over and I wouldn't have known what it was. Aye. she explained all this and how it happened thousands and thousands of years before all these battles were thought on!

'Na then, I've been 35 years with the Bus Company and you get to be having privileges after all that time—like free travel. Now we never used that, but when the childer got to school we started having this free travel. Coach trips all over the place. We went to Sherwood Forest—now that's a funny place—have you ever noticed what it's like yourself when you go through it? . . . No, you haven't. I didn't think you would have done. Next time you go through Sherwood Forest, just you stop that car of yours and get out and get a hand full of soil and have a look at it, and you'll find it's all pebbles and sand as if it was on the beach. And that's just what it was —a beach! Our Mary told us all about that. She explained it all to us, and it was wonderful. One time I saw rocks, they were just rocks and stones, and I'd kick them over and never think about them. But now I look at them, and I wonder whether that's volcanic or a bit of glacier or a fossil, and it's exciting knowing them things.

'And it's not only rocks either. It's cathedrals and things like that. When you go round with her she talks about the architecture and you listen to it. And you'll even go and put sixpence in that little box at the end of the church and buy one of these little books and read up all the history of it all. Now at one time, I'd never have done that. Aye, aye, aye, there's lots of things like that and you get very excited about them. Now, when our Mary went to college, it was down in London and you mightn't have heard about this, but there's one of these here big music composers and he's called Benjamin Britten. Well, this here chap, Benjamin Britten, he writes these big operas. Na then, when he had his first go at this, the Queen comes and watches it, and he doesn't want it to be a flop and a farce does he? So he goes to one of these colleges and all the students work it out for him. They sing and dance it on the stage. Now they had a go at

these operas of his before the Queen saw them, at this college where
our Mary was. Now you wouldn't find out things like that if you
hadn't had children who went to school, would you? There's this
here Royal Festival Hall in London that's one of the best places in
the world for this here music, and as I say it's only since our Mary's
been going to school and college that I've ever thought about this.
Last summer the wife and I went on a trip to London. We went to
the British Museum. Now at one time that's the *last* place we'd have
gone to, but I was filled with wonderment in that British Museum.
We went into one big room where it was all about the civilization
of Babylon, and there were these great big statues that they'd
fetched all the way back from Babylon. My! you should go and see
them! Great big things they were, made them to last in them days,
didn't they? Aye, and all that civilization gone—you get to thinking
about that. All their civilization has gone but ours is here. Now how
does all that come about? . . . Education brings all kinds of things,
doesn't it?—same as the people round here, they just think you go
to school and then you go to work, but its not like that when you've
been educated. You can see big things like a civilization, you don't
just think about the job you're going to do.'

Not all the parents had been roused in this lasting way, but
in the first two years of grammar school there were very few who
were not touched by the excitement of knowledge in some way.
Parents who had not opened a book for years began to read their
children's set texts, and fathers settled down to maths and
physics homework alongside their sons and daughters. Whereas
the middle-class child looked to his parents for help with homework, there was here rather a co-operation in learning. This lasted
only a year or two, and for the fathers the emphasis was heavily
on the more obvious skills of science and mathematics. 'When he
started at the college, I was very interested, indeed, especially
in these mathematics. He'd bring these problems home and I'd
look at them with him, and I'd get fair excited. That first year I
really enjoyed it, looking at his sums and trying to do his homework with him. And then the next year came a lot of this
algebra. Now this algebra stuff's a bit tricky, if you've never had
it before, but you can get the hang of it. I liked that year too.
But afterwards seemingly the problems got a bit harder and our
lad couldn't be bothered to show them me. I'd have liked to do
a bit more with him, but no, he wouldn't let me. We couldn't
keep up in the same kind of way.'

It was commonly thus. After a year or two the children's natural respect for their parents lay uneasily alongside their own clearer mastery of the new skills, and alongside many other doubts that school and early education promoted. There was the beginnings of a split, or at least of a growing sense that the child was out on its own, moving into worlds to which the parents had no access.

But as such awareness began to develop, as the school and its work took on unexpected turns and became both more demanding and important to the child, many of the parents sought to reassert control over their children's education by demanding some clear statement about the kind of job this was leading to. And this voice was generally the father's. Sometimes, as with Mr. Bottomley, there was the consciousness of having been misdirected themselves by a father living out his ambitions through them; and here advice came slowly. Was he asking his son to decide on a suitable job? Or was he really urging his son into the job that he himself would have liked? 'I often thought of that. It's very hard is that. If your lad wants to do something that you want to do, should you influence him or shouldn't you influence him? I thought about that a lot.' Fathers as scrupulous as this were balanced by the small number like Mr. Sadler who had decided very early on that his daughter was to be a teacher—'a nice soft job, with reasonable holidays and plenty of pay.' To any other suggestions from her he reacted by 'taking her down a peg or two', and despite his almost complete lack of understanding of her school and university courses thrust her right through into teaching—a job which she still pursues in what seems a mechanical and highly dissatisfied way.

In between these extremes the central pattern—though it was often broken and sometimes reversed—was one in which the mother protected and pushed the child, whilst the father raised the awkward practical questions as to where it all led. As mentioned earlier the fathers often found it hard to see what kind of training it was that the grammar school offered when technical and commercial subjects found no place on the timetable. To what end all this history and geography, French and Latin? It all seemed to contradict their often 'technical college' vision of education and to lead only into misty nothingness. 'I always wanted education for myself, and then I thought our lad would have it. But what I thought was the technical side, something that I could understand. That was what I thought education would be. I never thought about that Arts side, literature and language and all that stuff. That was new to me; that didn't come into my reckoning about education at all.'

By the third and fourth year questions about future jobs were becoming insistent. This was of course the age at which the parents themselves had taken their first jobs, and it seemed unnatural to some that a young boy or girl had not yet come to terms with the future. There was more than one voice suggesting at this stage that perhaps a commercial or a strictly technical course might have been better, might have been surer than the grammar school. And it was perhaps natural that there should be this early anxiety about a job, from men and women who knew only too well how much secure work mattered. Besides this, some of the parents badly needed that their children manifestly succeed in life, where they had made so little impression themselves: and for almost all there were the neighbours whoes embarrassing, sceptical questions could be so hard to answer.

'Many a time you'd be out and the neighbours would say, "Eeh, is your lad still at school? What's he going to be then?" and I'd have to say, "I don't know what he's going to be yet." And they'd say, "Doesn't *he* know yet?" and then I'd come home and I'd sit opposite our lad in the chair, and I'd say "What do you think you'll be when you leave school?" "I don't know, I don't know at all, don't bother me," he'd say and that was it. When the neighbours bothered me, I hadn't got an answer and I felt soft. They'd look at you as much as to say, "staying on at school all that time and don't know what he's going to be, well!"'

Most children were as unsure of the future as their parents, and as uninformed about possibilities. By the age of 15, only a small minority of our sample had made some decision (not always realized) about a future job. How was it that the number was so small, and how was it that so many of the parents did not get more advice? (We do not suggest that children *ought* to have careers neatly mapped out at an early stage).

Clearly the obvious place to get this was the school. The schools usually offered an annual opportunity for parents to consult teachers, and of course it was always possible to make an appointment with the head. Yet it was clear indeed that these opportunities were only taken up by the more prosperous, and by some of those who had had grammar school experience themselves. And even in these groups it was often only one parent who visited the school. Many families made only sporadic contact with the staff, sometimes giving up after the early years; and there were a handful of instances in which neither parent had ever visited the school.

We have seen that the parents were on the whole peculiarly anxious that their children do well at grammar school, and we have seen too how worried and full of problems some of them already were. And yet there was this failure to take advantage of the teacher–parent relationship. Only very rarely could this be put down as simple neglect. We asked the parents why they did not go to school more, and their answers were so various, and sometimes so barely sensible, as to be merely sketchy rationalizations. Some said they were always working late or the bus journey was a difficult one—despite the fact that their children had managed it daily since the age of eleven. Others felt their attendance would upset the child, others still reported how uncomfortable they felt in the presence of the teachers and further parents. Some felt that one visit a year was worse than no use at all, and complained of the hurry and the big crowds on that night. Others again spoke of the teachers as not being interested in them or their children.

No doubt many of these charges are unfair. But some of these statements made more sense than others and ran true to the rest of the interview. There was for instance no doubt why these parents so seldom belonged to the formal parent–teacher organizations. These groups were run, and often very ably run, by professional-class parents and it was sheer social discomfort that kept working-class parents at a distance. There was no bad feeling over this, rather it was recognized that in a sense the school 'belonged' more to the professional parents and it was only natural that they should also 'own' the parent-teacher body. Besides they clearly did the work well, and gave generously of their time and talents. But this feeling of intruding into an alien world 'belonging' to others, spread over the whole school, hindering the interested and worried parents and hardening the few careless and idle ones. 'No, I've never seen the teachers,' said Mrs. Keith, 'perhaps I should have done, but somehow I never got round to it, and I thought that as long as everything was all right there was no need for me to go. I've never had anybody that I could ask advice from. I would have liked advice sometimes, I got very worried. But there was nobody that I could ask.' Some parents, like their children, put on a bilingual act for the school. Mrs. Proctor observed this in a neighbour, 'she was talking right posh to all the teachers, but when we got out of school I walked her down and the language she used! "I'll flatten the bugger!" she said.' Or the tension might come out in angry scenes with the staff. It was not so much a case of the school being 'right' and the parents 'wrong', or vice-versa. It was again these two touching worlds, and the brittle contacts between insensitivity and hypersensitivity. One parent asked for an interview with the head. 'He wrote me a letter to say would I mind being prompt because his time was valuable. Well, that put me off straight away, because I'm always prompt at keeping appointments, and so I got up to the school at twenty past two though the appointment wasn't until half-past. And do you know what time he came—he didn't come until twenty-five to four! Twenty five to four! So I had an argument with him straight away.' Other parents came away bitterly disappointed with their meeting. For them the grammar school undertaking was such a venture in the dark, and there seemed so many doubts about it and no clear future. What they sought on their visits was above all information and reassurance. 'I don't know why we went. I expect that what we wanted was encouragement,' said Mrs. Teasdale. But what they reported and resented was the meagre opportunity of seeing teachers, and the irrelevance of the comment and advice they did receive. The last things they desired were either sharp little pep-talks urging their child to work even harder and take more marks, or any sign of lacking interest. Yet (to them) this was how school could seem: all parents were unimportant, but they were the most unimportant.

'Well, we can't tell you much about bloody schooling because they didn't tell *us* so bloody much about the job! They did not! Once a year you went to that bloody college, a great big bloody queue, two or three minutes each. They don't know your lad in it, you talked to Spierpoint, the head, didn't you Mavis? And he didn't know who

our lad was. No, he had no idea under the sun, he just looked up
there into the sky, like he does, and said yes and said no. I don't
think it's bloody right. They should either give a lot more time
or let you go up more often. You should have it six times a year.
But we never knew owt. You'd see this bloody Glen-Smith fellow
and he'd look at you and hum and bloody haw and he'd give you no
encouragement at all, none whatever, not a bloody bit of encouragement. And me and Mavis, we'd go down the steps of that bloody
college and we'd be right depressed, right downhearted. We never
thought the lad had a chance, and there in the end he gets a scholarship to university. There it is! . . . aye, don't come talking to me
about Marburton bloody education, it's time that the bloody rate-
payers went and shook them buggers up. We're good citizens,
aren't we? We might be poor folk around this way, but we've as
much bloody right as any other buggers in this bloody town to get
the job done properly.'

A flood of language like this shows well the misunderstanding
of needs, the anxieties, the sense of 'us' and 'them', the social
unease and the bewilderment that we encountered so often.
It is hard to estimate how much this failure of contact between
school and parent tells, but clearly it could have been decisive in
many of those cases where able children have left at 15 or 16.
And especially so when we remember that the parents least
likely to attend school were the ones whose children were
in B and C streams: and most of the working-class entry went
that way. There was a vicious circle here, for when the children
found themselves graded as 'C's the parents felt ashamed, felt
it was for all 'of no use' and communicated this feeling to sons
and daughters. In so far as they understood unfavourable
'streaming', they did not, like middle-class parents, contest it;
for them it was an absolute judgment by the experts in the
field.

As already shown, most of the children who survived were
A stream children, but even in these cases the lack of flow between
parent and school became critical, and especially so when one of
the parents was sceptical, reluctant now about the whole scheme.
'Whenever I used to go and see Miss Woodall,' said Mrs. Holdsworth, 'it wasn't comfort for *me* that I wanted, it was a story to
keep *him* happy when I got back home.' And so on top of this,
one parent's doubts might be directly reinforced by the child's

discomfort. He might be painfully reluctant about his parents presenting themselves. 'Oh no, we never went up to the school. We took him on the first day, of course, but we never went after that. He used to bring invitations home, but he'd say, "I don't think you'll be bothered about that," and so we never used to go.'

These touches of detail suggest in what various ways working-class parents felt the grammar school to be peculiarly alien, and how it was that so few of them—though clearly excited and anxious about their children—turned successfully to the school for advice and explanation. Before we move on, two other effects of this situation need to be noted. First of all, it meant that the working-class child at school carried his own fate in his hands far more than did other children. He was conscious of being on his own, and the habit of taking educational decisions came to him early. Secondly, the parents' failure to come to terms with the school, and the frustration of their anxious questions, sometimes became a part of the background of home tension which helped to widen the gap between the parent and child at a remarkably young age. It took its place amongst those many small details (such as Mr. Holdsworth giving up smoking in order to pay for the 'extras' of his daughter's schooling), which made some parents over-conscious of their children's obligation, and so quick to resent any design of 'uppishness'. Again we touch on a vicious circle.

Two aspects of the parents' attitude have been recorded—their delight in a new extension of their own knowledge, and their failure to engage with the schools over the nagging questions of careers and choices. Along with these goes a third, whose incongruity we must refer back to the irrationalities of human nature. Together with the pure delight in learning and the sensitivity towards 'uppishness', went also an urge for their sons and daughters to mix with 'better' children and pick up a new polish for their manners and accent. They both hated it and liked it when their children spoke and acted differently. None of the fears of snobbishness nor the resentments at change really blunted the original desires to push their children further on, to win for them cultivation in all its aspects. Sometimes the two attitudes were found in opposite parents, but equally often they were held by one and the same person.

For example, some of the children were taken home by middle-class friends, and many parents were delighted at this, at the same time as they pressed charges of 'uppishness'. Here again we pause to catch one full picture. Mrs. Hornby is a proud Socialist who was in service with an employer called Mrs. Montgomery. Mrs. Montgomery took a benevolent interest in her child, and the young Irene Hornby said:

'I'd come up and play with the Montgomery children, and now of course I had to pick up their ways and their manner, and mother liked this very much. After that nothing at Ash Grange could intimidate me. I knew just the time to come in for nursery tea, I knew just how to sit at table, I knew that when I was offered the third piece of cake I must say, "No, thank you," even though I wanted it. I didn't know everything though. For instance, once at nursery tea Mrs. Montgomery was in and I was offered the third piece of cake, and I said, "No, thank you, I'm full." Now that evening I was having my nightly bath and Mrs. Montgomery came into the bathroom and said, "Irene, during nursery tea today you remember saying 'No, thank you, I'm full?' " and I said, "Yes, Mrs. Montgomery." "Well, Irene, you mustn't say that again. In future you must say, "No thank you. I'm *quite satisfied*' Do you understand?" And so I always said "I'm quite satisfied" after that. It was like that all the time, I wet the bed there once. That was awful. When Matilda the maid came in, I said, "Oh Matilda, whatever shall I do?" And Matilda said, "Never you mind, dearie, you must go down first of all and tell Mrs. Montgomery." I did, and no more was said about it. Everything was handled like that, very coolly, very calmly. It was quite a different life from anything I'd ever known. Well, I had two solid months of that, nightly baths, nursery teas and Mrs. Montgomery, before I went back to the yard down Crossley Road. Always afterwards they kept up a fairly close contact with me. They advised mother about my education and Mrs. Montgomery bought me my first smock when I went to Ash Grange, because of course it was quite difficult getting the money since father wouldn't put himself out and mother was having to work quite hard to earn some. But Mrs. Montgomery took the same kind of interest in me as if I'd been their cook for twenty years.'

Girls like Irene Hornby resolved the dilemma of having to change and having not to change by becoming unusually tactful and accommodating at home. 'I always did exactly what I was told at home. I never put a disagreement into words until after I was married.' Many tended to be very quiet (though not necessarily at school), retreating into themselves and hugging their own problems. 'I could never take home a problem,' said one girl, 'If I felt that I couldn't do anything, I didn't dare say anything to them.' Another way out—more frequently the boys —was 'not to be bothered', to be always absorbed in work and other tasks and to 'never have the time' to engage with their parents on more difficult ground. In all this, as a later section shows, they were remarkably different from their brothers and sisters who had not gone to grammar school.

One final point remains. The parents' desire to thrust their children onwards seemed in the end to move from deeper centres than the doubts that were raised on the way. Despite any dissatisfactions with the grammar school course, some parents were paradoxically going out of their way to buy more 'extras' for their children. One of the results of the abolition of fees by the 1944 Act seems to have been that those parents who could, promptly released more money for piano lessons, elocution, classes, violin or singing masters.

So to many, the education of their children seemed to be slipping away from their control. To begin with there had been their own rediscovery of the delights of learning and, in a sense, some began the grammar school course alongside their children. But after the first years came the worrying doubts and frank ignorance about what it might lead to, and when the reassurances and the knowledge did not flow back from the school, a dormant father might awake into a more sceptical life. Those families in which the aspirations were very strong continued to encourage their children to adapt themselves to a new kind of life, and they were not too depressed by unfamiliar problems in their relationships to child or school. They were pleased by the newly acquired polish, and had some sense of what the future held. Parents below the top fringe of the working class were much more bewildered by the to-and-fro relationship with their children, and by their general lack of contact with school and future. By the time the leaving age was reached and the General Certificate taken, many wondered whether there was much to be gained by leaving their child at school. And cutting right across all categories was that small group of parents fiercely living out their own ambitions through their children, and tolerating no obstacles to their path.

The end of the 'O' level course was a moment for pausing, for reconsidering the whole venture—even in the case of highly gifted children. This of course is the point at which very large numbers of working-class children abandon the grammar schools. The Crowther Report showed in detail that in the case of grammar school boys reaching the age of 16, 38% of those whose fathers were of professional or managerial ranking had left. But for the ones whose fathers were skilled or less skilled manual workers, the figures were very much higher—72% and 85%.[1] Nor was this simply a case of the less able children leaving. We will return to this huge leakage several times and test it from different angles.

The children take the General Certificate at 'O' level.[2]

As the pace quickened and the 'O' level examinations drew near, most of the children registered particular excitement and elation. They felt themselves in command of the knowledge to be tested, and markable success had become peculiarly sweet and important. Its satisfactions replaced the vacant areas of the social life and compensated for the tensions and perplexities of home. Yet the confidence was crossed by all kinds of elusive anxieties, difficult to draw out. It was felt much depended on the quality of the 'O' level result and some spoke of a near-obsessive desire to 'collect' as many subjects as they could. There were those, for example, who were not content with even the testing eight subject course but regretted not being able to draw in still more subjects ('I'd have liked a bit of paper for another two. They'd have been no good, but. . . .').

In retrospect a few protested at the fragmentation of knowledge, the superficiality of training, the over-emphasis on time. The course on Literature was particularly open to to sardonic memories. 'You had these set books, and then had to answer questions like "What is it that so-and-so found on the sole of his left foot?"—a fact from page 327!' But this was very

---

[1] 15 *to* 18, Vol. 11, table 5, 17.

[2] Some took the former School Certificate, but throughout this report we use 'O' level and 'A' level as a shorthand for both examinations—unless the distinctions become important.

much a minority reaction. Most were well satisfied with the course and had not much thought about it, then or since. But alongside this there were the number already mentioned, whose anxieties expressed themselves in distinct physical symptoms. One girl would come out in a nervous rash; John Barker roamed the house in his sleep. 'He got up the night before he took that examination and he was wandering in the cellar. We couldn't keep him in bed. After we got him back he was up again, and inside the wardrobe!' On another boy there was a delayed effect, and he suffered from 'these violent stomach pains—but always after the exam, not before.' Anxiety was marked in children who were at the top of their class, and apparently fairly assured of success. 'I was *always* anxious, always a bit worried—worried in case I *didn't* come top, that bothered me a lot.'[1]

The results of the examinations are printed on Tables XXIX and XXX. They show quite plainly what constituted the core of the grammar school course as interpreted by these schools. The central emphasis falls on a line of studies which either specifically trains logical thought, the ordering of available facts, the sharpness of rational analysis, or are especially open to this approach. The line moves from Latin, and the structure of the English Language, to Physics, Chemistry and Mathematics. Few of the children, for instance, took Art or Music, and this was because the schools felt such studies should only be offered to 'C' stream children. We were unable to turn up any evidence which suggested either that 'C' stream children were unusually gifted in this direction (a type of 'compensation' theory) or that 'A' stream children would find such work less rewarding or central. In view of the emphasis on cognitive training and with all the hints of underlying stress that have been thrown up it is

---

[1] Though many doctors are only too aware of the physical symptoms promoted by the examination stress, in our time, of the G.C.E. and the eleven-plus, the evidence is hard to come by. Some doctors detect it, others do not. We suggest that the peculiarly medical question can be illuminated by placing it in its social setting as we (in passing) do here. For example, in the Annual Report on the Derbyshire School Health Service (1959), nine out of 13 doctors speak of having met 'no evidence'; and yet the others can write urgently of a higher incidence of functional nervous disorder (nail biting, bed wetting, tics and behaviour spasms, asthmatic children relapsing, and eczema increasing) at the time of the eleven-plus. They mention also mental and physical strain for some children during the first year of grammar school, the communication of anxiety by the parents and certain psychological upsets at the approach of G.C.E.

recalling those odd touches of the art and music rooms as some-times being havens and points of release. The issue suggested may be worth more attention than its numerical importance implies.

The results then cluster together around a close group of subjects, and this both permits general comment about the examined course and allows for comparison between this candidate and that. Other points will be drawn out later, but a mere glance of the eye down the page goes some way to illuminate the entry into the sixth form. Whatever that entry may depend on, it is clearly not the quality of the 'O' level certificate. Certificates range from just above the pass level to rows of eight distinctions. A certain minimum level was necessary—none entered the sixth after failing more than two subjects. (A study of the records around our sample suggested that the 'minimum' was distinctly lower for middle-class children, and was getting lower every year.) To explain why these children stayed on, we must point back to our analysis of the parents' ambitions; and for some explanation of why other children left, refer to our section on boys and girls who declared against the school. But of course these are only general truths: the patterns were not that crisp. There were quite a few instances in which there was some talk of leaving school. These ranged from homes with financial worries and divided parents, took in a body of homes where dissatisfactions, ignorance and bewilderment had already been recorded, and extended to situations in which a child was merely being 'tested' by a shrewd parent. 'When he got to be 15,' said Mrs. Bleasdale, 'we were out in the back garden and his father said to him, "Now then lad, all your mates will be working. They'll be going into trades—what about you?" But Stanley looked him right in the eye and answered, "I'm working, too."'

Four boys and two girls actually went and tried for a job. Whether this too was more 'testing', or whether it was the parents' desire to cut down a difficult commitment, it is no longer possible to tell. Subsequent success colours the past. But all of them were uncomfortable at the prospect of the offered post, and exceptionally glad to return to school instead. Perhaps these illustrate as well as any the quite unusual need to hold on to school work, and all the vital securities that it had come to represent. Rita Watson tried a job for a few unhappy weeks and then in company with her mother met an Ash Grange sixth former on Marburton High Street. The conversation in town clinched the decision to return to school, and Rita raced home 'went upstairs, and got all my old togs out of the wardrobe—that shiny satchel, the old uniform and everything—and I put them on right away and felt really happy to be in them, and all right.'

A sixth form course was decided on, but not all knew what this might lead to. Ten had a distinct job in mind, and a further 35 imagined themselves moving in the direction of teaching. Fourteen were hoping for a university career without having sense of the following job. And this still left 28 who by and large had few ideas for either present or future, no underlying sense of purpose and only limited knowledge of how to obtain ordinary facts about courses and careers. From them came comments such as 'I'd have been going to school still if they'd let me', and 'I didn't want to do anything except not leave school.' Eric Watson said: 'There was no thinking about a job. I just wanted to go on at school. I don't think you ever do think about leaving—it's so secure at school. You can't imagine leaving so much security—that's why it's so hard a break when you do come to leave. I think there was a general atmosphere that you just went on to university. It was nothing definite, it was something that filtered down from further up—you just got this impression that you went on and on.'

Brothers and sisters

We have not the space to fully report on what happened to the brothers and sisters of our 88 working-class children. But a few general details inserted here, and one suggestive instance, may be helpful. There were only 55 families with more than one child. Out of these only seven families had a boy remaining at a secondary modern school, and only 11 families had a girl there. So most of our children had their brothers or sisters at grammar school with them. The situation of the child who had a brother or sister at a secondary modern school was very much a minority one. Or to put it another way, the selective process in the schools picked out and held not just gifted *individual* children, it selected *families*. Because of this, families were not usually divided through differences in children's schooling. But what happened when this *did* take place? One of the most suggestive instances that we met was the one of Jean Ash and her sister, Margaret.

Jean Ash was the only girl whose sister went to a secondary modern school. In the acuteness of her discomfort and her feelings of loss and abnormality, she became articulate precisely *because* her family situation was so unusual. She experienced in her relationship with her sister a much more intense form of the same discomfort that she felt with many of her day-to-day working-class acquaintances. And her separation from her family and the life of which they were part made it easier for her to talk about them, even though she still complained of feeling disloyal.

Her sister, Margaret, was two years older. During the early years the two sisters were close playmates; and they played together with the many other children nearby, went to parties together, and slept in the same bed at night. Jean felt very keenly the separation when Margaret had to go to school at the age of five, and two years later when her turn came to go to the same school she was disappointed to find herself in a different class. But it was the same school and they still had friends in common. When the scholarship examination came Margaret was away ill: Mrs. Ash said, 'I don't think she'd have passed. She's not the type.' Jean, when her turn came, passed out top and went to Ash Grange, leaving Margaret behind with only one year further to do at school before she left school.

They no longer had school matters to talk about: Jean was reluctant to talk about Ash Grange at home in case she was thought uppish, and she seldom brought her few Ash Grange friends home. Her sister's friends visited regularly, but Jean did not know them now. Margaret went to work in a shop. 'She started going out with boys a lot sooner. She was working, you see,' said Mrs. Ash, 'and you do when you're working. Jean didn't really start going anywhere until she was 17.' To Jean, 'She was always two years older, but just then she seemed to shoot away from me. Whilst I, well I was still a schoolgirl. She did seem very old. She was older really at 14 when she left school than I was when I was 18. She was much more adventurous. She'd come home and say, "I'm *going* to do something," whereas I'd say, "*Can* I do so and so." '

The sisters see each other once or twice a week, but this does not indicate any close sisterly feelings as much as an empty formality. 'We've just got nothing in common. When I go round to see her I've got to *think* of things to say to her. It's a bit better now we've both got married because we've got household things to talk about. Perhaps when we have some children that'll bring us closer together.' Jean's mother said, 'They're as different as chalk and cheese.'

Several parents, faced with these very obvious differences between their children, seized upon the same phrase, 'As different as chalk and cheese.' The differences were so bold, so fixed and final, that it seemed that they had always been there, inborn, clearly visible from an early age. Investigating at a fixed point in time, as we were, it would be rash to say that what parents see in their children now is the result of educational separation and moulding. But we felt that parents were continually readjusting their sense of a child's innate 'personality' in order to fit changes in the child's temperament and abilities due (to a large extent) to differences in schooling.

Sixth form

In the sixth form, four took a mixed course and the rest divided themselves fairly evenly between Arts (47%) and Science (48%) sides. The emphasis fell more heavily on Arts for girls (57% to 34%) and on Science for boys (59% to 41%) This compares well with a national sample collected by the Oxford University Department of Education. (Table XVIII). Was there much difficulty in making this either/or choice? The survey from Oxford[1] suggests that many sixth formers resent the close specialization and the clear choice between art or science. 39·9% of their sample of students would have *preferred* some kind of broader 'mixed' course in which both modes of knowledge might be pursued together for a while. The Oxford survey may

---

[1] *Arts and Science Sides in Sixth Forms*: a report from the Oxford University Department of Education (1960). The report showed that in the sampled population in England, 39·9% 'would choose to present at 'A' level some combination which includes both Arts and Science subjects.' In Germany the figure was 60%, and in France 36·9%. In actual fact, only 5·8% in this country *do* follow 'mixed' courses. The report argues persuasively that the sixth form course might well be centrally based on mathematics and the engagement with our literary heritage, instead of decisive specialization.

well be right. But its findings were not reflected in our sample
of working-class children. This does not mean that the Oxford
survey was 'wrong'; it rather suggests that working-class
children may look at this question differently from others. The
majority of those who stayed on were in this, as in all other
matters, very ready indeed to accept the status quo. And the six
who objected to the clear cut Arts/Science division did so on
grounds quite different from those reported from Oxford.
They were not concerned about choosing between two 'cultures'
at a stage when their grasp of either was only tentative. Their
dissent stemmed from a wish to continue into the sixth form
studies which should be 'logical', neatly factual, 'mechanical'.
This was the spirit in which they had been trained for the 'O'
level certificate, and they found themselves much more uncertain
when sixth form studies turned on questions of response,
evaluation, judgment, imagination. 'Let me tell you, what I'd
really have liked to have done would be Latin together with
Maths and Physics. That's what I wanted to do. It was the
logical mechanical aspect of Latin that appealed to me, and
similarly with Maths and Physics. That's what I felt to be good at.
But the timetable didn't allow that—it was Latin, History and
French. It was a damned awkward course—what could you do
with it? None of the universities accept it as a course except
Cambridge (I think Oxford might now). So that was where it
led to—Cambridge.'

Against the number who regretted the weakening of the more
'mechanical' aspect of study, there was that body who responded
to the change in the nature of learning. This was especially true
of some who had not done very well, and had perhaps only
scraped into the sixth form. For them acute difficulties were
sloughed off with the ending of 'mechanical' knowledge. 'I
would put it like this,' said Ronald Turnbull, 'I would say
that I didn't become intelligent until the sixth form. Up
till then I hadn't really thought about anything—I wasn't
what you would call intelligent! A master called Daye had a lot
to do with it. He was just utterly different. He taught you in a
completely different kind of way. After we'd had a few lessons
from him, he stood in front of the class one morning and said
he was shocked at our knowledge of English. Absolutely shocked
that boys could have learned so much literature off parrot-like

and understood so very little of it .... it was with him that I began to *understand*.'[1]

There was then this shift in the fundamentals of study for some. It set back a number, but there were many cases in which undistinguished children responded to smaller classes, to being treated like adults, and to being invited to understand rather than memorize, and they suddenly blossomed into promising university candidates. But it would be easy to over-emphasize this. There was not always a change on entering the sixth form, nor were most of these boys and girls very ready to forsake the old skills in favour of new and more elusive ones. By and large they divided up into their Science or their Arts groups, and continued methodically on their way seeing less than might be expected of the other side. Boys and girls made most friends in their own class, so that specialization first of all induced and was then reinforced by a new social life. Scientists were close friends with scientists, and 'Artists' with 'Artists'. And their defensive hostility towards the other camp sometimes arose from more than a sense of personal limitations; it could occasionally take as its basis the evident attitudes of school and staff. That consistent academic need to divide children sharply into 'types' sometimes operated here, mixing of these two 'types' could worry some teachers just as much as mixing of the sexes or the 'moderns' and 'grammar' worries others. 'We science students used to spend some free periods in the library, where the Arts people were. But Mr. Thinleek often came round and gathered us up to take us back to his own form room and work sitting at the back of his class. He used to say, "Keep away from those Artists, boys!" '

We have already given some attention to those children whose interest in school studies went along with an anti-school spirit. Little more needs to be said of them here, except that their difficulties continued undiminished. Resentment at the formal school orthodoxies was as strong, and as difficult to articulate

---

[1] Interestingly enough, research workers have pointed to a degree of correlation between the more 'mechanical' aspect of the 'O' level course (say the English Language paper) and linguistics at university level—a correlation which cannot be so easily claimed with all university subjects. (A large number of university graduates fail the English Language paper at 'O' level first time anyway.) See, for instance, Hewitt, E. A., 'The Performance in English at 'O' level, of a sample of University Students.'

as ever. 'Somehow it made you *feel* as if you had to be a rebel,'
said Arthur Robinson. 'You'd *got* to go round in ragged uniform
and not shaving.' When the school held a mock election, boys
like Leslie Barron stood as 'Communist candidates'—'They
chalked up Vote Barron! Vote Barron! in red chalk, but the
school suspended us for that, and he wasn't allowed to stand as
a "candidate".' In their leisure time they ignored cricket and
played shove-halfpenny—and the school felt it had to punish
this too. There were the old troubles about having friends
outside the school. A girl might be taken on one side by a teacher:
'Miss Lavinton said to me that a sixth form girl had got no right
to meddle around with things like youth clubs. All her mind
should be on work and on the school. It made me smart and
blush, I resented it very much. I was keen on the youth club,
and liked it.' A boy might be embarrassed when asking his headmaster for testimonials: ' "But aren't any of your friends from
the College," he said to me. "Don't you go about with anybody
from the College?" and I said I was in the Boys' Brigade and
went cycling—but he was none too pleased at this.' These boys
and girls were hardly ever made prefects by the school, nor
appointed by the staff to any other office. And yet when an office
was decided by class voting, an anti-school group might go out
of its way to quite deliberately 'capture' a post. A particularly
illuminating instance occurred at Marburton College. An annual
prize was offered to 'the boy who had done most for the school.'
This was always decided on a sixth form vote. In one year the
anti-school party lobbied this issue and put one of their own
members forward—he had done nothing for the school in the
orthodox sense except criticise it, and get into trouble. Nevertheless his supporters were extremely thorough. They played on all
kinds of latent dissatisfactions and schoolboy awkwardnesses,
until their candidate was elected by a majority of one vote. The
staff were unhappy and demanded a recount. The anti-school
party objected, lobbied further and had their man re-elected by
an increased majority. And then after a whole series of man-
oeuvres, the school took the vote-counting right out of the boys'
hands and declared that the true result was a draw, and that the
prize must be divided with the 'orthodox' candidate. The end
result was that the anti-school group was left one degree more
'anti' than before; and the vicious circle operated again.

But of course most boys and girls were not in this position and had little sympathy with it. Those who had identified themselves with the school, taken pride in its uniform, joined its scout troop or O.T.C., now came into their own. They became the formal leaders of the school community. Forty-eight of our sample were made prefects. Fourteen became either head or deputy head of their school. The proportions are high. (We tried analyzing these prefects against home background, but nothing important emerged.) In Early Leaving[1] the committee touched on the difficulties of working-class children in the sixth form. They analysed the number of working-class children on their samples who became prefects, and discovered that working-class children did rather better at winning office than middle-class children in the sixth form. From this they roundly concluded '. . . .nothing should be done which could give the slightest impression of favour towards children from what might be regarded as better homes. We are quite confident that no such favour is shown at present. This may be illustrated by what the heads have told us about appointments as prefects . . . .the evidence clearly shows that. . . .no favour is shown on social grounds in the appointments. . . .' Our figures agree with their findings; bias, if any, runs the other way. And yet this is another case of figures revealing only a fraction of the truth. The evidence drawn up here suggests that figures of this kind are nevertheless reflecting a social process in a curiously inverted way, and that 'findings' or 'conclusions' of this precise arithmetical nature can, in a sense, be irrelevant to the issues that are affecting young peoples' lives.

The orthodox children did not offer those vivid accounts of school life that we grew to expect from others. For them school was such a smooth process, once they had learned to fit in. They had their difficulties and tensions all right, but these hovered around the life at home. Previously at school they had taken extra care over their accents. In the sixth form this was bearing a certain fruit. Many schools had readings or speeches from their sixth formers at their annual public prize giving. And here again working-class children seemed to do not only as well, but a little *better* than others. On the public platform the orthodox

[1] *Early Leaving,* p. 40 and table Q.

working-class child spoke the idiom better than the native born. It was worked into the very grain of their ambitions. 'In the sixth form we were always talking about "the cultured man". It was really exciting, we'd listen and we'd want to be "cultured men". And when it came to Speech Day I was given the chance of doing the "English speech" and that was from Eliot's *Notes Towards a definition of Culture*: that shows you I spoke very well even then.' When they intruded into a school 'election' it was from quite a different angle. 'He loved his school, did Raymond. I think they made him deputy head boy after a mock election. He'd worked so hard on that, preparing his speech. They had him as a Fascist candidate and he read up all Sir Oswald Mosley's speeches, until in the end I think he came to believe it almost. The headmaster was so impressed by his speech, that was why he made him deputy head boy. He said to him at the time, "If you put as much effort into it as you did into that mock election, there'll be no need to complain." ' Most of them put a great deal of such 'effort' into all aspects of school life, and where other children were sullen or resentful, these were sociable, friendly, tactful, ready to attend to the school's point of view. 'Oh I never had any trouble with the school,' said Bernard England. 'I've always been the kind of person that's—what's the word?— establishment. I'm always the kind of person that's with the establishment. My face always seems to be liked wherever I go —it's funny, but it was like that at college, it was the same at university, and it's just the same at work.'

At school they worked hard, played hard and were rewarded for it. Their dress was smart and correct, their accent was good. Sometimes classmates forgot such a child's working-class origin, and only rediscovered it, to their surprise, in later life. Outside school, links with neighbourhood life or non-grammar school children had largely gone. One girl came across her former elementary school companions at a Sunday school; 'But I stood out. I felt different. I know I talk Yorkshire but they talked, not "broad", but slipshod—not grammatical. I only went along to play the piano. You can't blame them, I know, but—I *looked* different.' A boy might become friendly with a non-grammar school girl, only for his *parents* to end the relationship. ('I played pop with him about *that*.') Other less aspiring parents felt their child ought to have more of this social life. 'I thought all that studying wasn't good for her, so I pushed her into something at the chapel, because she never went to youth clubs or anything like that,' said Mrs. Morley.[1] There were two large exceptions to this lack of contact with non-grammar school children. First of all, it applied to a much lesser degree to those children who came from the outlying villages. Where there was a distinct and isolated community, the old roots were preserved to some extent. More important than this, and rather paradoxical, was the fact that the orthodox child tended also to make and keep connections with a church or chapel—and these lasted through into adult life. The number who had this strong church connection (choir, Sunday school 'teachers', etc.) was as high as 48. And there were amongst this group, churches or chapels which drew together, in a loose way, children from different schools. Some of the few and light social links across the educational divisions are due directly to a local church.

But if neighbourhood ties were lost or weak, relationships at home were also changing. We have already touched upon this insofar as it affects brothers and sisters in a following section. But the fuller context of home life demands continuing mention. The social life of school and the particular fields of study were both now out of the parents' reach. Together with this had gone changes in tone, manner, accent, friendships, which often troubled home relationships. The boy or girl knew that the important educational decisions must be taken by himself not his parents, and his sense of 'life' and 'knowledge' was often such that fathers and mothers began to seem very dull and limited indeed. 'I thought my parents were terrible, and very badly educated. They were always doing the *wrong* things.' With some this was no more than a passing hubris, but there were others

---

[1] One side effect was that many boys and girls were much 'later' than their non-grammar siblings in approaching the other sex. The situation was often weighted against exploratory adolescent courtship, and though this didn't too much trouble the majority, the more shy boy or girl found an unnatural gulf between the sexes which got harder and harder to cross. They irresistibly measured their own sexual development and activity against their working-class background rather than alongside their middle-class colleagues. When we interviewed them, of those who were caught in this recurring human dilemma, a few had widened the gaps still further by covering their shy self with a hard and repellent shell—and others, lacking an adolescent apprenticeship in love, had released the feelings of the years by marrying the very first person with whom they at last achieved relationship.

perceptive and candid enough to admit that these things could bite down to the very roots. 'My parents and I had got nothing in common. I'd got nothing to say to them, except what I forced myself to say. It's dishonest to pretend anything else. Really, we'd got *nothing* to talk about.' The imbalance could be established in many ways, but the orthodox child belonged to two worlds —school and home—and sometimes developed two identities to match. 'And then I had these two personalities. At school I was extrovert, confident, full of life. I knew what I was doing all the time. I was heroine in the school play, first violin in the school orchestra, captain of netball, captain of the school, captain of the house, top of the class, sometimes. "Miss Ash Grange", my husband calls me. But at home I was oh, so quiet, so timid, never said a word out of place. I just shrank inside myself and mother ruled the roost.' Behind the assurance of the school personality was frequently this lack of reciprocal flow between parent and child. Their assured and successful school identity was in a kind of suspension, almost disconnected. And this vacancy counted more and more as they entered adult life.

As the sixth form course drew to an end thoughts began to concentrate on university or training college. The middle-class children had a fairly clear idea of where they were going, and of how to get there. The situation with working-class children was much more mixed. There was the small number whose parents were intent on thrusting them through to university despite all obstacles, and there was that larger number who drew from middle-class connections a much clearer sense of possibilities. But by this stage many of even the most ambitious parents had, in a sense, been left behind. They might originally have hoped for their children to get a good grammar school education and then move in a local bank or office: university was a strange new thought. To some it seemed so remote that it had never previously occurred. Mr. and Mrs. Rushworth had a talk with their son: 'We'd said, "Do you want to be a draughtsman?" and he said, "Yes, I think I'd like that," or "Do you want to be an architect?" and he said, "Yes, I'd like that too." And then he said, "But I'll tell you what I'd really like. I'd like to be a maths teacher, and that means I'll have to have a university degree." Well, I could have fainted! I could, honestly. I nearly dropped through the floor! "University,"—that was the very first time that word was ever mentioned in this house, and as I said I could have fainted.' Others too were just making the discovery, but for some it came rather late in the day. The Latin qualification diverted some from their desired course or centre. 'She didn't find out till she was in her last year that she needed this Latin. She'd no idea before then,' said Mrs. Giles of her daughter. 'Now we thought he might go to university,' said Mr. Abbot of his boy, 'and we went along and saw one of the masters. But the master said, "He can't go because he hasn't got the Latin." Well! Nobody knew owt about that till right at the end. He couldn't go, flat!' Others were slow off the mark in putting in applications and knew nothing of closing dates and waiting lists. 'I wanted to go to London,' said David Ingleby, 'but one day Creed walked in and said, "It is now too late to apply for the following," and he read out a list including London. That was the first thing that anybody said. I rushed off and immediately applied, but it *was* too late, and I had to look elsewhere.'

University and college were approached in a mood in which elements of sheer ignorance, general perplexity, or mere lack of initiative were hard to disentangle. Lack of initiative there certainly was, and this may have had something to do with the 'automatic' nature of education so far. Everything had always run along smooth lines, once you accepted the school's ways, and a few had realised that a stage was now reached where they were expected to fend for themselves. But it would be misleading to leave it at that. Sheer ignorance was also there to a startling extent. Two girls were thinking of Oxford or Cambridge, but 'didn't know it was possible to stay three years in the sixth form to do this. I know it's silly to say this, but I just *didn't* know, and I went feverishly looking around for a place, and in the end got into the School of Tropical Medicine and Hygiene—and it turned out to be absolutely the wrong course for me.' We went very carefully over this, and it was perfectly true. Neither girl— their qualifications were excellent—knew when she left school that she could have stayed longer and prepared for Oxbridge. Again, neither Mr. and Mrs. Lynch nor their son had realized that there were grants above a nominal sum of £10 or £20 for university courses. The boy left under this misapprehension at 18 though he had a perfectly reasonable chance of going to university. Rita Watson and her parents had heard of State scholarships and Borough scholarships, but again thought they were mere prizes worth some £20 only. They were determined to get their girl through university and had drawn on their life savings in preparation for the expense. Mr. Clarke wouldn't approach the school for information because of its 'tone', so 'I went down to the education office to see what there was. I saw a fellow there and I asked him what grants there were. But he said there was a book which told you about them things. I said, "Oh right—I'll have a copy," but he said, "Nay, we haven't got one here." And I said, "What do you mean, you haven't got one? That's your job, ain't it?" And that was the way it was—nobody knew anything.' Another boy also 'knew there were State scholarships and things and I knew they paid for your fees and your books, but I didn't know they'd see you through. It seems daft now, but you *don't* know. I think they should get all these kids at 15 and tell them in black and white just what grants and scholarships and universities mean.' We were careful to check these instances so far as we could. It had not occurred to us that ignorance of quite that elementary kind could be common, and we had asked no systematic questions on this point. The cases we record were thrown up spontaneously and there may well have been others. We probed behind them, and it was plain that the school was being perfectly helpful, in its own way. Other pupils and parents received the advice they needed; and there was certainly no animus against these children, or any failing of that kind on the part of staff. Simply, the channels of communication were not open: nor was the need for clear primary information recognized. So much that was naturally *assumed* by the middle-class pupil or teacher, so much that was part of the 'normal' atmosphere of growth, needed to be discovered by, or explained to, the new working-class pupil.

Together with the element of ignorance and the lack (in some) of initiative, we must add a note on financial unease. First of all some of the parents were under very real financial stress. This was especially so in the case of large families and of widows. In nine families either the mother was widowed or there were at least four children. Only an unusual degree of determination, and a trusting readiness to do without, kept these boys and girls at school. Most children who might have come under this heading had already left. Secondly, some parents whilst not under this degree of stress, were making major sacrifices of which the child was deeply aware. Chief amongst these were those homes where a mother was going out to fairly hard manual work, at an age when her energies were diminishing. Now in both cases, though money may have been just sufficient, the boy or girl felt daily that their parents' lives were being governed and narrowed by his needs. This, added to so much that had gone before, promoted the most acute sense of debt, of dependency. And this takes us to the other side. Just as the parents might hide from the child some part of their financial difficulties lest the child tried to give up the educational advance; so the children turned down courses of study because of their parents' money troubles, without consulting those parents. The act of generous deprivation and concealment happened on both sides. An illustration of this would be those instances (there were some here) in which a boy or girl with a reasonable chance of entry at Oxbridge never made the attempt simply because they didn't want to bring their parents to the expense of paying for the *rail fare* and the short stay necessary to cover interviews and orals. This immediate need for £5 or £10—and not the cost of a three-year course—could be decisive. Or this situation may be complicated by a hostile parent: 'There was this time when he had to go to Leeds for an interview, and do you know, we hadn't a halfpenny, for the rail fare. I couldn't ask his dad because I knew he'd fly off the handle, so I said we'd borrow it off Aunt Mary. And we did, and when he came back he sat there with his dad all night and never said a word about it.' In this state of half-knowledge they were very impressionable, ready to grasp at any advice offered. Those who resolved the dilemma best were the orthodox pupils who had not only given all they could to the school, but had come in the sixth to identify themselves with a particular attractive teacher. The influence of one master at Marburton College and one at Thorpe Manor is evident when the applications to university are examined. Each seemed to cut through the haze of wavering and doubt and send a steady line of students to read his old subject at his old university. The other area of bewilderment lay in the social aura of university. Many felt that universities belonged to the upper and middle class, and were extremely sensitive in approaching them. Janet Rawnsley was considering trying for Oxford and obtained application forms. But when she discovered a space on the form asking for 'Father's occupation' she abandoned it. Others felt this acutely when they were asked up for interview. One girl at such an interview had been requested to read aloud a passage from *The Times,* and that for some summarized their sense of the gateway to university and college. Unorthodox interviews left them confused and (such was their respect for the sheer body of facts they had painfully acquired) scandalized. 'They accepted me at the university,' said Norah Clark, 'but the interview was ridiculous. They made me read a poem—I never read poetry—and then they asked me how much my train fare had been—and I couldn't remember.' Nor could they accept that there were other roads to university besides their own: it came as a surprise. Eric Weston was interviewed at Oxbridge. 'They offered me a place in two years' time and that was not too bad, but then I met the boy in the next room and I discovered that he'd got very poor qualifications, had only just applied but had been given a place right away. I was furious when I thought of all I'd been through, how hard I'd worked for years to get there!'

The final approaches to university and college were full of many kinds of confusions. They found their way through application forms and such like, not by pestering the school but by tagging on to a middle-class friend, or following someone who had gone in an earlier year. Thus one middle-class girl or boy might draw to a particular university a small group of 'uncommitted' working-class friends too. Or one working-class boy or girl being accepted at a Cambridge college might tow behind him, for two or three years, a line of similar applications. It is important to distinguish this pattern from the school's strategy of entry, for it *is* something quite different. What boys and girls *did* and what the schools thought they did, were not always the same. 'I'd set my mind on going to Oxford,' said Geoffrey Thurston, 'I didn't know anything about it. It was just the name. It sounded good, and I wanted it. I'd no ideas how to get there, and in fact I don't suppose I would have got there except that there was Relfe in our class. He went to Balliol to do history. Well, I knew him quite well, and he seemed to be up in all these things. He'd found them all out somewhere, so I just followed his footsteps. At every stage I went to him and asked him about the papers, how to apply, when to go, what to do.

He told me all these things, and I just did what he said. And so there I was—in Balliol with him, doing history.' Behind the canny 'imitation' lay the long hours of hard and determined work. 'All the time he was studying in his bedroom,' said Mrs. Gledhill, 'and so I said to him, "Where's it all going to get you, love?" and he said, "I'm going to Cambridge," and I said, "You're not. You can't go there. It's not for working-class folk. We could never afford to send you there." ' Another mother described her son 'sitting there, and he used to say, "I *must* get a State, I *must* get a State!" and he'd bang on the table with his fist!'

'A' level and leaving school

It was by passing their 'A' level in two subjects (a fair basic standard for college or university entrance) that these boys and girls had qualified for our sample. Thirteen children now left school for work in pharmacy, the civil service, accountancy, laboratories and the forces. We meet them again in the next chapter. The rest continued with state education for at least two further years, at college or university. In order to get a grant for a university course an 'A' level candidate must also sit scholarship ('S' level) papers and pass sufficiently well. This is not altogether true, for there are other ways of gaining Ministry grants. But only one member of our sample even knew this; he went to university on the Ministry's teaching grant scheme. No one else was aware of such a possibility. It was nobody's fault, for it was again nobody's responsibility to circulate answers to unasked questions about unknown possibilities.

This kind of ignorance could be overstressed. It was certainly there, but the momentum of the educational process solved many people's dilemmas. They may have had all kinds of doubts about grants and universities, but if they entered for 'S' level as well as 'A' level, and gained an award, these matters sorted themselves out. And indeed 74% of the boys did take both papers, and 67% took an award. For the working-class boy who had survived in the grammar school up to 'A' level, the road to university was much easier. There were obstructions, and some were defeated by them. But for the majority the way, though not clearly seen, was discovered to be wide open—and the automatics of the process drove them through.

For girls this was not true. Only a third of them entered for 'S' level, and all gained awards.[1] The diversion of talent had taken place before the point of university entrance. And the diversion was, of course, in the direction of the teachers' training colleges: 20 of the girls entered them. We were not able to establish the reasons for this, and can only record notations. First of all it had something to do with considerable ignorance about what a university course was. Boys shared this ignorance, but with them there was no well-established alternative—they just carried on. Girls reacted from the unknown by simply lowering their sights and aiming at training 'college. Secondly, having reached this decision, many began to rationalize it by claiming that since they only intended to become teachers, there was little point in training for four years at a university rather than two years at a college. All had the impression that a year at university would cost more out of their parents' pockets than a year at college. This, we understand, is not true—but no one had information as opposed to opinion on the subject. Thirdly, the failure to reach for university was connected with a lack of knowledge about the range of jobs open to a woman, after her degree. Little else besides teaching came into people's minds, and hence permitted the mental reduction of a degree course (four years with an education year) into no more than a needlessly-long teachers' training scheme. Fourthly, we were unable to establish whether pressures from the girls' homes were pushing them on to the shorter commitment, though we believe something like this was sometimes at work. On the other hand, there were just as many homes where the parents would have been enormously proud of their daughter going to university. The crucial decision arising out of this old dilemma of the working-class child was not, we think, one dictated by the parents ('You can't go because. . . .'); it was one silently made and privately pursued by the girl herself ('I'd better not tell my parents because. . . .'). Had it been brought into the open the parents might often have strongly urged the longer course: but they seldom knew much about either. And finally the feeling that 'education doesn't matter for women' froze the wilder and more generous ambitions, and hardened the

---

[1] Mrs. Heaton for instance averaged 63% in her 'A' level papers, another girl 69% Neither entered 'S' papers.

smaller ones to the point of decision. Nobody rationally believed this phrase about the education of women—neither the teachers, nor the parents, nor the girls themselves. It was always 'they say. . . .' And yet it had its effect, for after all it sucked its strength from the most primary kinds of ignorance. All these notations are connected, and do something to chart a clearly defined gap where gifted girls from working-class homes are diverted from that fuller education which others take. Obviously more should be known of the abilities of girls entering training colleges, their social background, the kind of frustrations they introduce, and the kind of satisfactions they find in training for secondary modern and primary schools.[1]

There were interesting differences in the final choice of university or training college. We have seen how haphazard some of those individual choices were; yet over the whole sample the pattern emerged differently for boys than girls. If we except the group of boys who went to Oxbridge, then the great majority of the rest seemed to 'cling' to their home area. Two-thirds entered a university not 30 miles away.[2] Girls spread out much more widely, only a quarter of them kept within the 30 miles radius. This was no doubt partly due to the distribution of training colleges, yet added to this there seemed a distinct movement by some girls to put a distance between them and their home. For many, as we later show, it was only a temporary 'break'; nevertheless perhaps there was a certain truth in Mr. Bleasdale's laconic comment, 'It's the mother that educates them, and it's the mother that drives them away.'

Ideas about careers had now begun to precipitate more generally. Those who left school had come to some terms with the future, though often not very satisfactory ones; and of those who went to college or university a large number were

[1] McIntosh, D. M. also remarks that 'There is evidence to support the view that there is an increasing tendency for girls to prefer the shorter approach into the teaching profession through the training college rather than by way of university.' *Educational Guidance and the Pool of Ability*, p. 173.

[2] In 1955/6 55% of students at Liverpool University were drawn from within 30 miles. At Manchester the figure was 48%, at London 43%, at Leeds 40%, at Birmingham 38%, and at Bristol 26%. The figures decrease each year as the 'provincial' universities more and more become 'national' universities, and their local functions are assumed by smaller institutions. Halsey, A. H., writes illuminatingly on this in *The Harvard Educational Review*, vol. 30 No. 2.—from which this data is drawn.

thinking of teaching. The way in which the education system produces its teachers would require a special study in itself. And at this particular point we merely record the fact that it was the 'drifters' who began to make up the bulk of the future teachers. We must state too—the pattern plays all through this report—that they turned to teaching not because, deep at heart, they wanted to do it—but because they did not want to move away from the academic succession (eleven plus—O level—A level—college—teacher) which had become so entwined with their very sense of who they were in society. This is not to pass judgment (the glance is too hasty) or to disregard that number whose need to teach was moved by very different pressures. But it is to mark, on the tantalizing edges of this survey, some fragment of that social pattern by which an educational system tends to staff itself. The whole impetus is reconsidered later.

One final note on careers. Towards the end of the school course there were some who felt disinclined to pursue an 'intellectual' training further. Some girls preferred nursing to college and had their way; but not without a distinct feeling that they were stepping out of line, that they 'ought' to pursue a more exclusively academic line, and that this was what the school expected. Nursing was 'inferior' to teaching. Ambitious parents might support this feeling ('. . . any girl who can go to Ash Grange and do as well as you in exams is not going to waste their time nursing'). And a variant of this was a desire to be a P.T. teacher rather than a normal school master. Jean Barker had expressed this hope and was rebuked for 'wanting to waste her brains'. Peter Trafford had a similar feeling, but when his parents consulted the school: 'We said, "Well, we're thinking of his being a games master." "What!" he shouted and banged both hands down on the desk. My goodness! I wish we hadn't said a word. "A games master," he said, "very well, very well, very well. . . ." and he carried on like that. By the time we got back home the games master idea was quite written off.' Peter then trained as a maths master, and never practised it. It was with a touch of a similar revolt against a fully cognitive training that we ended the section on the middle-class child. But in that instance it was successful; in these it usually flickered out. Is it worth wondering if this total emphasis on the intellect, to the neglect of other areas of the personality, doesn't have something to do with a few of the doubts and dissatisfactions that we later record?

Training College and University

Though this was a most important stage in education, we are only able to handle it very briefly here. Twenty girls and one boy went to training college; 16 girls and 38 boys went to university.

The sheer number of training colleges seemed to permit a form of social sorting-out. Many of our sample sought entry but only a few gained it, at the top-flight colleges. The ones they attended seemed to cover only a limited social class range. They generally reported colleges full of girls from upper working-class or lower middle-class homes, in training for primary school teaching. Girls from much further up the social scale were either grouped together in the top colleges or they were rare birds of passage anyway, or they were toned down and lost in the mass. To pursue this point would be outside our province and it is only relevant when we look at training college from the social angle and attend to it as a *finishing school*. Girls emerged from training college with better accents, some new manners, fresh expectations —but with little social poise, for they led little social life, and with few friends much above their own social range. Social tensions were certainly there; ('I was curling up with fright in case anyone asked me what my father did.') And many who had merely half imitated the accent of their teachers now made a fully conscious effort to eradicate all trace of their origins from their voice, and emerge into a new kind of educated neutrality. But some of the major strains (relationship to neighbourhood, relationship to family) were both behind them and at a distance. An odd girl here and there moved backwards rather than forwards, and with a kind of inversion, spoke steadily more 'Yorkshire' as her companions became more 'B.B.C.'

But smaller matters drove some social dilemmas temporarily into the background. Energies often centred around a whole host of regressive rules and regulations on meals, manners, punctuality, dress, and above all boy friends. It is no part of our brief to develop the host of almost laughable stories that went with this heavy weight of restrictions. Some training colleges were in remote and fairly inaccessible spots, but they nevertheless had their monastic rules and their fiercely matronly assemblies. One principal, we were told, forbade her girls to wear red 'because it inflamed men's passions', and on another occasion girls were exhorted always to wear stockings because bare legs apparently did the same. Patricia Wimpenny was ill-advised enough to speak to her principal about her boy friend: 'Young lady, you have no *right* to be thinking of social life while you're on teaching practice.'

All the same, for most girls this restriction was more severe than anything they had yet experienced, and in some ways a distinct step backwards from sixth form life. There could be regression in other ways, too. Some girls spoke of certain college courses not offering that training in thinking and judgment which had begun to open for them in their sixth form. They recorded instead mechanical study, factual mass and received opinion as being all too often substituted in its place. Both these subjects—the social and the academic side of training college—move off-centre from this enquiry. We were not seeking or measuring this kind of information but it bulked large enough in free conversation to require mention. All students passed their course, and most became primary teachers.

As for the university, here the figures tell their own story, and summarize the enquiry so far. The city of Marburton with a population of 130,000 and possessing schools and teachers of more than common distinction, managed in a four-year period to send 38 working-class boys directly from grammar school to university. A mere glance through the incomplete school records shows that very many more boys from middle-class homes entered university with them. The case of girls is even more striking. In the nine years ending in 1954 the city had sent only 16 girls (but upwards of 51 girls from middle-class homes). 10 of these 16 girls came from 'sunken middle-class' families. Even at this stage of the survey, before the many threads have been drawn together, it is clear that the explanations for this are extremely complex, and not to be crudely translated into terms of 'blame' or 'praise' for either schools, children or parents. (A caution: some children had been disqualified from the sample for other reasons than social class—as explained in Appendix 3).

The final choice of university also adds something to this story. First of all, almost a quarter of the boys went to Oxbridge. One quarter of all students entering university in the 1950's did this. On the other hand, no girls reached Oxbridge at all. The girls were scattered fairly evenly over the northern and midland universities, except for two who reached London. They did not go too far from their home territory, but they did not cluster around Marburton anything like so tightly as the boys. For example, only one girl but 13 boys chose Leeds University and indeed, as we mentioned, most of the boys found a university not 30 miles from home.

A certain number did not go into residence in any full sense, but either came home every weekend from Friday to Monday, or lived at home and travelled up to lectures daily. They were never drawn fully into the university proper, hovering always on its edges; and for them university merely called up memories of miserable digs, long train journeys, and hard work in libraries or labs, occasionally broken by bouts of drinking. At home they had lost their neighbourhood friends, and their colleagues from school had scattered or were at work. It seemed, in one sense, the most barren period of their lives. They made no wide social contact at university, obstinately refused to pick up new social habits, and in speech sometimes regressed into a Yorkshire idiom. One or two joined working men's clubs. Yet it was a contorted and unhappy attempt to strike back roots into neighbourhood and working-class life. Nothing did or could come of it; they met the worst of both worlds.

At university the bias towards the scientific studies increased. Twenty enrolled for Arts degrees and 34 for Science. Again the beginnings were full of doubt, some had no more idea than their parents what precisely a university was and did. There were those who were dazzled by the surface sheen of the cultural life, but that soon dimmed. 'When I went to read English,' said Brenda Sadler, 'I'd hardly read anything; I was afraid I wouldn't be able to talk about books or music, but you soon found that you don't have to know very much about anything to talk about it.' And there were those who struggled again with the old problem of accent. This ranged from strident over-imitation of upper-class timbre to straightforward discussions at home in which the natural shift to a more educated accent was plainly argued out. ('Mother, I shall have to start speaking correctly. I can't lecture to them unless I speak correctly.') There were those who reported living through waves of feeling in which they spoke broader Yorkshire at home than their parents and better English at university than their lecturers. Some began to make friends with students from much richer homes, and some had their first genuine acquaintance with students from the public schools. They could be very admiring, like James Wood. 'Most of my best friends were public school boys—very interesting and amusing characters. You can always tell a public school boy. Later on you find them going to the same parties as you. They always seem so relaxed—and they fit in so well, they know just what to say.' But though many shared this admiration, their unease frustrated such contacts, and they tended to bunch in groups from similar backgrounds. It was often easier for them to become intimate with an American or Persian student rather than develop a relationship with a fellow Yorkshireman from Giggleswick.

Right from their first vacations all the students worked for money. Even for the group at Oxbridge it was clear that the idea of vacations as pauses during which to store up reading that might be deployed over the coming term, was a myth. There were very often good financial grounds for this. Many of the homes were short of money, and an ageing or widowed mother might be working long hours to keep a boy at university. Some students worked in order to buy their own clothes or extras, others because they felt they had a duty to contribute to the home. But though money difficulties were real and important (almost everyone complained about the large regional differences in local authority grants), more than this was involved. Some worked to justify themselves in their parents' and neighbours' eyes as people who could not only study, but also attempt *real* work. Keith Mountain put it like this: 'I got a job on the railway, and enjoyed working with my hands. I felt quite proud, and when I came home at night, since I wasn't half as tired as I thought I might be, I used to say to my parents, "There you are, you see!" Because it's funny, my parents have a queer idea of "work". Reading a book, or anything like that, isn't work: only doing things with your hands. So I suppose in their eyes all the "work" I've ever done was in those vacations.' But the need could go one degree deeper than this, could become an attempt to actually *be* a workman for a while, rather than play at being one. Some took vacation jobs as if they were casual labourers and tried to hide their identity as 'students', smothering it in a fuzz of matiness and strong Yorkshire, until a casual remark showed that no one had been deceived. And indeed coming to terms with working men at their jobs proved harder than they thought. There was the feeling of remoteness as if workmen were a quite different kind of mechanism. 'It was an experience, and I felt I'd got a real insight into the way those men's minds worked, quite differently.' There was a revulsion from 'the never-ending sexual chatter and jokes', and there was horror at the demands a life-time of hard manual work could make—'as if their whole lives were submerged in the work and they had no time for living.'

Difficulties with vacation work were associated with their struggles to come to terms with their parents and their background. Resentments and irritation at the coarser streaks in working-class living, that they dare not introduce into the discussion of home problems, could be exercised on this safer ground. Some mothers and fathers found difficulty in even physically imagining a university which their children never invited them to see. 'When he went to Cambridge, I thought it must be all big classrooms.' or 'I would dearly have liked to go there and look, but he never encouraged that. He didn't seem interested in our going there.' And yet for those who were encouraged, university proved much less intimidating than grammar school. There were rapturous comments from parents, ('Oh, I never thought it would be like that, oh it's smashing, it's lovely!') of a kind that education so far had seldom aroused. And for those parents fiercely living out their own longing through their child, university was a strange mixture of pleasure and pain. There was the delight already mentioned, but at times of crisis the parent too could be deeply involved, just as during schooldays. 'Sometimes,' said Mrs. Holdsworth, 'when she was having exams, I couldn't sleep at nights. It was terrible, I think I suffered more than she did, and when she got through I used to say to myself, "Well!. . . . *we've* got through again!"'

Oxford and Cambridge

The group of boys who went to Oxford or Cambridge are worth describing separately, because they bring to a momentary focus many of the divergent lines. It was hard to decide whether they did represent the most gifted section of that working-class entry at the age of 11, or not. We were unable to come by measurement here, but (as a personal impression only) we were disinclined to accept this supposition. Glancing over their histories it is quite clear that there was a special impetus coming from their home background, quite independent of native intelligence; and further that for many of them their Oxbridge ambitions had come to a fierce intensity or fallen into a lucky vein, whilst they were at school. They had gone when others had not, not always because they were more intelligent, but because they were more determined, more single-minded or more fortunate. And yet this does not take us very far. A look at their degree results shows that there were no firsts here, and indeed seven of the nine took thirds or low seconds. But more remarkable is the way their results plummetted after their opening year. Henry Dibb came up with an Open Scholarship, took a first after one year, failed in his second year and ended up— working hard—with a third. Richard Beckworth also came up with an Open award. took a first in Latin and a top second in French after one year. His next year yielded only a second class, and he too ended up with a third. Ivor Gledhill similarly won an award, and took his first after a year, but after three years he could only command a second, and when he stayed on for a fourth year he failed altogether. Eric Western had taken eight distinctions in School Certificate, three at A level, and gained an Open Scholarship, yet extraordinarily hard work saw him finally through with a low second.

Plainly the vagaries of the Oxbridge selection system cannot this time be held wholly responsible. There is a curious element of 'pattern' here, and this small group seems to be sensitively recording a crumbling away felt through much of the sample. To begin with it either had something to do with specialization —or specialization was a symptom of it. Henry Dibb protested vigorously against the over-cultivation of his mathematical abilities in a rawly competitive spirit since the age of 15. Eric Weston said, 'I just couldn't absorb any more facts. I think I was burnt out after so many years. I'd begun to lose interest, I'd been going on for all those years and I began to think about it. Yes, for the first time I began to think what was it for?—and I couldn't absorb any more.' So it was not simply specialization as an educational theory, nor all the narrowing of horizons that can go with this when it is pursued with a driving, competitive intensity—for others triumph over this. Yet specialization carried with it certain *social* consequences. One man reflected over his friendships to find when he had last known on close terms someone who was not, like him, a physicist. 'Yes, at university you get the chance of mixing with people from all walks of life, but none of my friends were like that. They were all doing physics. It's hard to say when I really knew anyone who wasn't doing physics. Back at school in the sixth there were a couple of arts types I argued with—but no, I didn't *know* them. Still perhaps they were the last two.' There was this also then; close specialization from an early age was not only recorded in terms of academic theory and choice, it was *felt* in terms of personal relationship, and in competitive strain. And yet the question that Eric Watson and others began to formulate— 'What was it for?'—had more than specialization behind it, though this might be the area in which it developed. It was a question born of the difficult and the obscure social rifts and struggles which for them had become part of the process of education itself. Did they, after all, want to move forward as successful middle-class citizens? Or was the temptation to try some return? Or was there a way out? The plummetting of academic results (and the Oxbridge group are taken as a pointer to waves of disturbance that were felt over much of this sample) seemed related at the deepest levels to a lost feeling for source, means, purpose; a loss heightened by an absence of the sustaining powers of social and family relationships.

Degree

Yet though a few found themselves looking into an abyss (it became no less here and there), the general movement forward was one of success. It was flecked with the doubts and stresses that gathered with peculiar concentration around the Oxbridge group, but the momentum of the years, if not so easily buoyant, carried them on for all that. The least troubled areas were those where the family, as it were, rose with the child back into the middle-class; and there was something special (the tensions were different) in those instances where a very tight relationship had held between parent and child.

With the degree ceremony the long climb was celebrated by a new flood of feeling entering the vacancies of recent years. These were lovely moments, scenes of fresh sentiment that for a moment washed over all other difficulties.

'I didn't ask for time off work. I took off—I wasn't going to miss that. I was real proud of our lad. . . . .'
'Where he got his degree is an awkward place to get at—there, where the gate is, right by the road. There was such a crowd of people waiting outside that you hadn't time to itch! And there he was right on the edge of the crowd, by the railings, and I went up to him and congratulated him, and gave him a pound that his Aunt Lilly had sent him. I said, "I'm sorry I can't give you any money, love," and he said, "Never mind about that, mam, you've given me help and confidence and . . . ." it was three words he said. . . . Aren't I silly?" '
'. . . . and when she came down from the platform with her scroll, she flung her arms right round us, and all she could say was: "Oh mum, oh dad." I was laughing and I was crying as well. She's not one of the kind that forgets.'

Five failed their degrees. Each felt it as an enormous blow. 'I failed. I'd never failed anything before. It was such a shock— I thought that it just couldn't be, and it was all wrong, and it was a mistake.' Their whole being had rested on the passing of exams, and they felt it as a collapse, a huge vacancy out of all proportion to what it meant. It broke open fissures in the personality that do not seem to have healed since. One man immediately left university, and deaf to parents and friends, worked for a year as a labourer. He took the exam again, failed once more, and abandoned all work of every kind for several years. Another girl left, took a junior post in an office, tried again a year later and failed even more badly. A third left and immediately took an unskilled job in a factory and held it for several years. All connection with the world of education could be suddenly snapped. Tutors and school teachers played no part. With failure they threw up (at least for a time) everything, and went for help not to the university appointments board, but to the local labour exchange. For Joyce Teasdale, it was slightly different. After the first shock, she experienced a new sense of release. 'I decided then and there that I'd go and do what I wanted. I'd been doing what other people wanted for so long and now it was time I did what I wanted. I went to the employment exchange, and they offered me all kinds of more academic things—but I had decided definitely that I was going nursing.'

There were three first class degrees, 30 seconds, and 15 thirds or unclassified awards. More of the undecided turned towards teaching as the time came to leave the ladder, and 17 took fourth year courses for Diplomas in Education. Five stayed on successfully for their Ph.D. Four of these had begun weakly at the age of 11, and came from the second-class grammar schools. The fifth had risen from early days at the bottom of his class at Marburton College.

In summary

The children who lasted the full grammar school course came largely from the upper strata of the working class. They came too from small families and lived in favourable, socially-mixed districts. A certain economic 'line' was obviously still at work. Furthermore the majority had home backgrounds of no mean calibre and either one or both parents were strongly supporting the child. Many of these parents were both aspiring yet deferential —and it is perhaps not surprising to find these children to be educationally ambitious and also highly accommodating to the new worlds they meet. The majority who lasted were those who, on the one hand entwined academic ability with a positive orthodoxy and, on the other hand, had pressures behind them bearing on the school. Most accepted the new school with its different values and became some of its most hard working and worthwhile members. In turn they became its prefects and its leaders. But there was another side to the orthodoxy. At times it softened into something not simply 'positive', but emollient and over-accommodating. And further it had meant a rejection at conscious or unconscious levels of the life of the 'neighbourhood'. This mattered less for some than others. But when the new manners, new friends, new accents, new knowledge, heightened the adolescent tensions of home life, security and sense of purpose shifted from any wide emotional life and located itself narrowly in schoolwork, in certificates, in *markability*. A minority of the survivors came from those children who had declared for the neighbourhood and against the grammar school. The detailed texture of day-to-day life was marked by local strains and conflicts which began to throw up the most radical doubts about the direction, quality and social nature of the education they were receiving.

At home the working-class parents were faced with a situation in which their children became stranger to them, and this was intensified by their lack of information about school, careers and the possible future. On the one hand were intelligent, ambitious and anxious parents; on the other capable and hard-working teachers. Yet there was little flow between the two. The difficulties promoted by this, and previous disconnections, did not break up the momentum of the higher education process; but they did much to shape the people we interviewed and—here and there, if our impressions are right—something to limit or damage them. Despite all this, the path from 'A' level to college or degree was very much less treacherous than it had been up to eleven plus, or between selection and the sixth form. There was a diversion of gifted girls to the training colleges, and amongst those at university were some who were undercut by social doubts which, playing upon a sensitive or flawed personality, could have distressing results. But most of the 88 completed their education happily and successfully. There had been moments of stress, but most grew through this and accepted both the way in which they had been trained, and the world for which they were being prepared. They are now middle-class citizens.

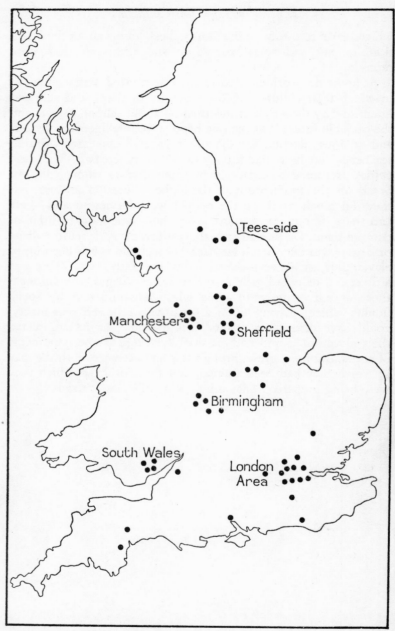

Homes of 61 working-class children who have left Marburton.

5

MEN AND WOMEN

THE members of our central sample were men and women with homes, jobs and children of their own. So far they have been reflecting back on their school and college days, and we have observed them developing into the adult citizens whom we might meet today. We now move into the present and place them in that social setting. How different are they from their fathers and mothers?

First of all, they are not citizens of Marburton at all. Geographically they are very scattered, as Table V shows.

TABLE V

GEOGRAPHICAL DISTRIBUTION OF CHILDREN
(88 boys and girls educated in Marburton to 'A' level:
see map opposite)

Now living	Girls	Boys	Totals
Marburton	15	12	27
North of England	13	12	25
Midlands	5	7	12
London area	2	10	12
South and S.W...	2	2	5
South Wales	1	3	4
Abroad	0	3	3
Total Nos.	39	49	88

Twenty-seven still remain in Marburton, and the figures for girls are higher than those for boys. (A further scrutiny showed that this is not a case of the unmarried remaining near home, or vice-versa.) We might take this as a pointer to the resilience of the mother-daughter bond, even under the many stresses explored here. But after allowing for this important qualification we see that 61 have, in fact, left Marburton. Almost always they have left it for other industrial centres—Birmingham, Cardiff, Newcastle, Leicester, Manchester, Nottingham, London. Indeed the pull of boys towards London stands out. Of course, this mobility can be 'explained' in terms of jobs, though most could, if they wished, find equivalent posts in or near Marburton. That can only be a partial explanation, for the whole relationship with the Marburton of their youth is now much more complex and disturbing.

Secondly, they hold quite different jobs in society from their parents. 82 falling in the Registrar General's Class I or II— whereas their parents came from Class III, IV and V. (Table XIX). This is the rough measure of their social mobility: though what this means to the person involved is again complex and in need of closer attention. If we consider the kinds of jobs they hold, then the lines of mobility become clearer. (Table XX). The most striking thing is that 46 of the sample have become teachers— they themselves are now staffing the educational services. There is no other category so large as this. Eleven are involved in research work for industry, and seven have entered industrial management. An equal number belong to the civil service. Of the remaining 17, two have become doctors, and three ministers. Three are in the navy, air force and colonial police, and there are three laboratory assistants. The rest is made up of a pharmacist, a nurse, a draughtsman, a cookery demonstrator, a social worker and one unemployed man. For women at home with young children we have counted the job they last held; otherwise the job they were pursuing on the day we interviewed them has been recorded.

Thirdly, their homes are quite different from those of their father or mother. A few began married life by thriftily buying old working-class property after the manner of their parents, or they are in temporary lodgings, and here the material differences are not so apparent. But the more characteristic instance was the new three-bedroom house on a new private estate a few miles out of the city. ('I keep telling you, this isn't an "estate"—

it's a "suburb".' said Mrs. Sutcliffe.)[1] Outside the garden was newly dug and if there was not a small car by the kerbside, then there was an empty garage awaiting the day. Inside, the home was not yet completely furnished, and could seem a little sparse after the crowded furnishings in their parents' home. There were tiles and bright rugs on the floor, and the interview took place in the through-lounge. Since they lived away from home they had not inherited furniture from their parents, and most of their possessions were new. They were new in a rather safe way—G Plan or Ercol—and not too 'modern', not too much in the forefront of design. It was 'fifty-fifty' whether there would be a television set yet, but very often there was a portable gramophone, with bright record covers from *Oklahoma, Beethoven's Eroica, Bing Sings,* and *Tchaikovsky's Fifth*, piled around it. Lines of books from college days found a place somewhere, and these were supplemented by the library and fiction buying that we discuss later. A magazine rack held the daily paper, women's magazines, baby books, *Amateur Gardener,* and *Do it Yourself.* Many of the husbands were experiencing the unusual pleasures of working with their hands—building a new wall, repairing the car engine, painting the hallway, planting a first crop of early potatoes. Sixty-three were married, and children were appearing. The eldest ones were at the infant school stage, and a new cycle of educational problems had begun. The children had names like Jane, Christopher, Ralph, Patricia—though many were reaching out to names one degree less familiar: Fiona, Noel, Vivian, Karen. The television set was switched off as we came in ('I say "rubbish" but I'm watching it all the time, and I can't get away,') and we were offered tea and biscuits on a small neat tray, with a napkin. Many times there seemed an element of insecurity about the interview—and though this is difficult to communicate rightly, it needs to be recorded. Some had nervous mannerisms, were halting in speech, inclined to argue rather than discuss. This was less so with the women but most marked indeed with the men. Others were very knowledgeable about interviews and surveys, and soon began discussing problems of method. Mr. Weston considered all the questions carefully, but rather than

---

[1] In this section on adult life, it seems only proper to change the convention, and from now on to refer (generally) to people by their proper title, i.e., not Brenda Sutcliffe but Mrs. Sutcliffe.

answer them, doubted the refinement of their methodology, and pointed out the dangers of asking question x unless factors y and z had previously been taken into account. Mr. Todd met our initial request with a note suggesting that he be taken out to lunch, and informing us that he was 'very much against taking random samples', that the aim of this enquiry 'seems to be odd', and that there was nothing to be said about grammar school education except that intelligent people got through and the rest got out. Others treated the interview ironically, and others still laughed a lot and tried to make the whole thing a joke. Mr. Williamson said, 'Of course I'm a very confident person. It's just the way I am. I'm on a par with everyone, socially or intellectually. I'm perfectly at ease, perfectly at home. I'm not frightened of anyone.'

If we go behind the figures about jobs, and explore the individual human situations, we can understand a little more why the interviews often had this nervous edge. To begin with, the picture of social mobility was not as easy and triumphant as all that, when examined closely: the figures do it only a rough justice. We had noticed in following the school and college days how late many were in deciding on a career. This was partly the penalty of their unusual position (though considering the large numbers of working-class pupils in schools the 'unusual' can paradoxically be taken as the 'usual'). As we have seen, their parents had not the knowledge of the professions with which to help them, and their schools did not assume the need for early and detailed advice. But, of course, it went deeper than that, for college and university did provide specific guidance—though those who most needed it still felt the differences between 'us' and 'them' and turned instinctively to the Labour Exchange in preference to the Appointments Board. We have seen too that it sometimes became involved with early specialization, with letting the arbitrary tyrannies of the timetable decide the direction of the adult career; and there have been hints that it connected up with the kind, class, and quality of the social world for which they were being prepared. But none of these are full explanations, they are but movements in that direction.

The ignorance of the school child had turned too frequently into an adult malaise, into a drifting, rudderless existence. The question of pursuing a chosen career assumes an attitude, a state of being that might be called living to some purpose. This living to some purpose is, for most of us, nourished from the affective securities of family life and the social strengths of the neighbouring community—just those supports and potencies which were increasingly strained or lost to sight during the process of growth. None of our tools of measurement or numerical analysis can hope to probe the depths: we can only chart the surface—and register, for what the reader finds it worth, the impressions received by that most delicate and yet irregular of instruments—the social observer himself.

Staffing the educational system

One part of the surface area that is relatively easy to chart is the choice of teaching itself as a profession. As we have noted, over half of our sample entered it. They are mostly primary and grammar school teachers with a mere scattering in other branches, as is shown in Table VI.

TABLE VI

DISTRIBUTION OF 46 FORMER WORKING-CLASS
CHILDREN IN TEACHING

Type of Teaching	Men	Women	Both
University	2	nil	2
Technical College	2	1	3
Grammar School	6	10	16
Secondary Modern	4	2	6
Primary	2	17	19
Total	16	30	46

One or two suggestive notes can be added to this table. First of all, only nine girls did *not* become teachers. Secondly, 'sunken middle-class' children did not usually become teachers, but went instead into management, scientific research, the church or the armed forces. Thirdly, the grammar school teachers were mostly Conservative voters, whereas the six men (but *not* the 19 women) in secondary modern and primary schools, voted Labour.

Fourthly, and not surprisingly, 13 out of the 19 primary school teachers lived in Marburton still.

It is very hard to do justice to this large number of teachers. Manifestly there were some for whom teaching was an inevitable and natural activity, an overflowing of the self in an unforced desire to share delight and knowledge with the young. But the major emphasis did not fall here. Far more frequent was the man or woman who had drifted from certificate to certificate, and then, lacking any decisive urge to strike out in a chosen career, had let the automatic nature of the educational process take the decision for them: they had stayed on as long as they could, adding a teacher's certificate to their other certificates, until they found themselves back in the classroom. It was as if education had never nourished in them any other capacities except those needed to score high marks in academic examinations. This comment stretches beyond the actual number of teachers, for even amongst those who did take up other jobs there was a number who felt they had made a mistake in leaving the academic life, and looked back with longing to teaching as a 'safe' career. How often we heard, from parent and child alike, that Alan or Margaret, or Peter or Ann, would be at school still if only it had been possible. To our mind there was often something disturbing, sometimes regressive, about it. What kind of teachers will they become, shaping other working-class children?

Some of those in industry were half considering moving across into teaching, and there is indeed a certain amount of shift between jobs on our sample. Over two-thirds (62) have held only one *kind* of job (e.g., teaching), though they may naturally have moved from post to post. This number is swollen by the women who married during their first job and have partially resolved any of these dilemmas by giving up outside work and running the home. Eighteen have tried at least two distinct types of job (e.g. teaching and police force). And eight have attempted three distinct types, or more. Since the members of our sample are aged between 24 and 33, there seems to be some restlessness here. Again it is a case of charting the surface, but there are some points to be made. First of all, the question of specialization obtrudes itself once more. Five who felt that they had specialized wrongly from too young an age, now broke away from their formal qualifications into a new field. John

Bolton had concentrated on English in the sixth form and read an English degree at university. But at the end of it he felt that his really vital interests were in practical engineering, and he began again from the shop floor in a steel mill. He worked during the day and studied alongside 15-year-old boys for his Ordinary National Certificate in the evenings. He followed this with his Higher National and promotion in the junior ranks of management. But this speaks for decision and character that were not common: and Mr. Bolton, in a sense, enjoyed the best of both worlds. Others too broke away from their qualifications but most lacked the opportunity or courage. And some of the dissatisfactions about careers either arose from, or was blamed on, wrong specialization.

But all this concerned only a small minority, though an important one. Another motive for the chopping and changing had to do with the possibilities of advancement in industry. Some who tried a two-year graduate apprenticeship scheme found their talents unused: and worse than that, believed that there was little chance of promotion for their kind. As they sensed it, there was mobility from the working-class home through university into the junior ranks of management, but there the line ended. Mr. Beckworth reported first the frustration: 'I took this two year training course for works manager. At first the men were a bit suspicious of me. They thought who was this young man coming to tell them how to do their jobs. But by and by they saw that even though I had ideas, nothing was ever done about them. I wasn't allowed to do anything by myself, all my ideas were passed to my superior, who passed them to his superior, who referred them to his—and that was the last you heard of them.' But he also felt the lines of promotion were not as open for him as for others: 'There were two kinds of graduates that they took. There was me and my kind. But there were others that joined at the same time—right regiment, background, right car, knew how to handle a pair of guns and a fishing rod. They got on like houses on fire. Up and up they went, just like that—they'll be on the board of managers now. But I felt that I was being left behind in a corner, just neglected. No matter what I did. No matter how good the ideas. Nothing happened. After two and a half years they offered me a job that I could have done when I was sixteen. That I could have done quite *well* at sixteen.

Nothing more. So I wasn't going to start at the *bottom* again. Not after two and a half years. It was like playing at snakes and ladders, only my kind being the kind that comes down the snakes. I gave my notice in.' Others, too, spoke like Mr. Beckworth, but we have no means of offering closer judgment on their situations.[1]

Another aspect of the world outside school and college that could be unusually troublesome was the handling of working-class men. 'Man management was my trouble,' said Mr. England, 'looking after all those drivers, fitters and mechanics. It's very hard, I can tell you. Much easier to have a problem on the desk in front of you—even if it's a very difficult problem—and to work through to the answer, until it's all clear and finished.' Mr. Linley was a surveyor who similarly expressed relief to get back to his drawing board and office, and out of the situation he hated most of all—supervising men who were digging the roads. Mr. Pollard worked as a trainee in the mines: 'I was deputy, but I was between two fires. The under-manager on one side and the men on the other. When the manager said to me, "Get that face shifted," and when I went to the men and said, "Let's get that face shifted," they'd say, "All right, but we'll need an an extra hour's by-pay." And if I didn't pay the men, I didn't get the work done, and if I did pay them then the manager would come and play hell with me. When you've been to university, you want to treat the subject as a science—so I transferred to the planning side.' Now of course no one would argue that every graduate ought to be able to handle men directly, as well as figures and books. But two comments are required: first of all, this desire to get away from personal relationships and leadership into the securities of the desk does perhaps hint at something we have touched on before—a radical failure to develop other than the narrowly academic faculties. But secondly it indicated that here again we are moving into questions of social class and background. When these managers order their workmen about, they are giving orders to men who might be their own fathers. These difficulties are inlaid with those other problems about background and class, which education seems not to have resolved at all. The young manager was always caught 'between two fires'.

[1] cf. Clements, R. V. *The Managers: a study of their Careers in Industry.*

So far we have been placing the main emphasis on the dissatisfied and unsettled, and though it is a minority situation it does need developing. One third of the sample said they were dissatisfied and unsettled in their work—though this could be sometimes a very mild remark. The figure was higher for men (18) than for women (11), for whom marriage and the home had solved some problems. This dissatisfaction seemed more to us than the natural restlessness of youth, and sometimes suggested a gross waste of human vitality and talent. It is probably helpful to offer a few individual situations, from this third, in order to show the doubts that they promote.

Henry Dibb ✗

Mr. Dibb has already been mentioned. It is illuminating to look at his full history. Mr. Dibb's name is prominent on the Honours Board of Marburton College. He identified himself with his grammar school, and was placed in the 'A' stream. He joined the school scouts, and indeed became a Queen's Scout. He was head of his house, and deputy head boy of the school. He won an Open award to Oxbridge. At Oxbridge he took a first in his exams after one year. Thus far it looks a success story, and perhaps this is the Henry Dibb that Marburton College remembers. But at university Mr. Dibb began to both doubt the special development of one side of his personality (he was a mathematician), and to have specifically *social* doubts about the direction of his education. The Appointments Board sent him a list of jobs but he accepted none of them. He wanted nothing which had only to do with his mathematical faculties, and he could not face going into industry—a world out of which he thought he had climbed. The university was unable to do more than offer him further lists, but this was not the kind of help that he required. 'My tutor had more or less given me up and when we met we merely embarrassed one another. He was no bloody help at all.' After taking a third class degree he returned to Marburton and took a job as an ordinary working man. He began as mill worker. But the attempt to work himself back into the grain of working-class life was a failure at this point. 'I used to work such long hours, and then to do that all my life—it would be hell.' He tried his hand as a bus conductor and found that since he could find no social life in Marburton—he couldn't be working class and he didn't want to be middle class. Then he was earning more than he could spend. After a year or so he had £100 in the bank, and almost on the spur of the moment he called in the nearest travel agency and bought a one-way ticket to Canada. In Canada he hoped to find escape from the social perplexities which troubled him in England. But in Toronto and Montreal the story was much the same. He worked unhappily as a clerk, a milkman, a bus conductor. . . . and then he heard of a job on an isolated weather station on Banks Island, several hundred miles north of the Arctic Circle. He felt that out there in a small community of meteorologists and Eskimos his difficulties might be resolved. He stayed there for three years, again earning more than he spent. Time passed, until he got bored with Banks Island and realised that he had £4,000 in his account. He returned to Marburton, 'but really I'm no better off now than I was four years ago; I've got plenty of money but. . . .' His problems had not been solved by either Canada or Banks Island, merely shelved. He spent a year in Marburton doing nothing except sleeping, watching television ('criticising but watching'), and making abortive attempts to find his social place in Marburton life. After 12 months he caught a train to London and decided to tackle his problems one by one. He enrolled at L.S.E. and started his university course all over again, only this time reading Economics[1] and, finding some relief in the return to student life, the need not to decide anything much for another three years. 'I'm just hoping with the passage of time and the extra qualifications, I'll get some idea of what I want to do. I wonder how much of it was due to the school? I often wonder what would have happened to me, say, fifty years ago—if I'd been my father, say, and hadn't been to college.'

---

[1] Eight children finding themselves in the wrong line, meeting failure or hitting their ceiling, enrolled for external degrees in the hope of finding a new way out. But all 8 abandoned this course. It was as if once they came off the ladder, nothing in their power could quite put them on again with the old momentum. And once a line of study proved to be the wrong one, the tendency here was to start again with Economics. Perhaps this was because it required no special sixth form training. Perhaps it was because it seemed both an academic science and yet 'practical' in a special way—giving command over the true centres of power in society. We do not know.

Geoffrey Lynch

Mr. Lynch was a gifted boy at school, popular and prominent at sport, who got an average of 66% with his three 'A' level subjects. He had not however, realised that grants were sufficient to cover the cost of a university career and, embarrassed at the burden he might become, had not applied to take scholarship papers. He left after his 'A' level exam, and took a temporary job in accountancy as a clerk until his national service began. The forces offered some kind of respite for 'after 18 I was just lost.' He signed on for 3 years in the radar section and spent his spare time polishing up his languages. When he came out he had some savings to live off whilst he found his feet. But he could not hit his level. He tried the police force for six months but then thought that this was starting further down the scale than he ought. He tried teaching but was depressed at the idea of entering training college and being ploughed back into the system. He took another job in accountancy, but built up a social resentment against his superior—a young man fresh from university with bowler hat and rolled umbrella. He left, and considered emigration. But before taking the step, 'I went down to the Labour Exchange—it was a pity I did really,' and there he was offered and accepted a job in a quite different field—chemistry. He began as a lab. assistant and started building on his school certificate knowledge of chemistry by attending evening school and working towards an external degree. But he found it harder and harder going on a rather small salary, and in desperation rejoined the forces in order to get on the Russian course. When we interviewed him he had got himself into a kind of social no-man's land—British interpreter in Berlin: but was no clearer about what the future was going to hold when he was once again demobbed. His parents have begun to accept the situation. His mother said: 'I used to worry a lot. He used to get depressed when he couldn't settle down, and it used to worry me when he started changing jobs and when he was out of work—but now I don't bother as much, I've got used to it.'

Jean Barker

Mrs. Barker was a talented girl, very high in her class, who became a school prefect and seemed set fair for university. She was frightened of the burden she might become to her parents, but was unable to broach the subject with them. Towards the end of her schooldays she heard of the examination for the Scientific Civil Service, and in something of a panic cancelled her other plans and entered, rather late, for this. It seemed a way both of doing herself justice and yet not imposing financially on her parents for a further three years. She left school and awaited the results, but her preparation had been late, hurried, and incomplete, and she was refused. She was lost and without advice, and turned to the Labour Exchange. From them she took a job as a draughts-man in an engineering works. Rather hopelessly she has pursued the job ever since. She cannot come to terms with her colleagues at work. ('It's not snobbery—or if it is it's only intellectual snobbery') and expresses her irritation by correcting their grammar when they speak to her, ('not ridiculing them but just to show them the proper way'). She has lost easy and intimate contact with her family, and in the evenings has pursued a series of quite disparate and unconnected courses of study at the technical college. None of these seem to lead anywhere, and she doesn't read at home—but she invests the routine habit of learning with a certain hope. She remembers and privately practises some of the skills she was taught at school. Rather than paper a room in a straightforward manner, she first likes to treat herself by laying out the problem in algebraic terms. She once tried teaching this algebra to her father, but he could not grasp the point. In the evening paper she notices that middle-class school-mates have now become practising doctors, ('Look where she's got to with just the same start as me. I wish I could go back to Ash Grange tomorrow.') More and more she becomes to believe that 'everyone is born into this World with a special purpose', but that she herself has been 'wasted'.

Such is the kind of situation that we mean by 'unsettled' and the type of human particular that we have in mind when we discuss the losses in home and neighbourhood life, the automatism of learning, and the slackening of direction.

Normality and the 'Orthodox'

But this sort of disturbance was not the major emphasis in the sample. Two-thirds of the people that we saw seemed to suffer no strains of this kind, and, of course, many of the remaining third were less dramatically affected than the three cited. It is in the nature of this kind of enquiry that the damaged and the disturbed throw up the most vivid kind of detail, whilst the normal, the contented, do themselves less than justice.

Mr. Ross, for instance, came from a submerged middle-class family, and was one of the only two members of the sample to become doctors. He has joined the R.A.F. medical service, and speaks with assurance of ultimately rising to Air Vice Marshal rank. His bearing is easy and untroubled, he is good at his work and cares very much for it. He enjoys the social round, and his wife makes an excellent hostess. Many others, too, are making a positive contribution to society in a wholly contented way: there is no aura of disturbance and frustration around them. Indeed it is hard (if at all possible) to distinguish them from some of the middle-class children that we interviewed. And this gives something of a clue to the 'top' two-thirds of the sample. It is here that we find most of the children from the 'submerged' middle-class families. But not these alone, for with them go many from the more traditionally working-class homes. Indeed, we felt the two groups could still be distinguished a little, but knowing no way in which we could measure this distinction, we have tried approaching them from one or two different angles, believing this will suggest something of the differences. It is necessary to move very tentatively, but looking at these former working-class children in adult life we believe there are three emphases to record.

First of all there was that group shading away up to a third of the sample, whom we term the 'disturbed'. Secondly there was a group of hard-working, contented professional class people, many of whom came from 'submerged' middle-class homes. They included some of the most positive people we met, positive in the sense of being men and women wholeheartedly and gen-erously ploughing their talents back into society, as they ran their homes or pursued their careers. This is the group and the emphasis that we have in mind as 'normality'. But alongside them, shading in and shading out, there was another body of professional people who yet require a slightly different marking. We have termed them the 'orthodox'—the word has constantly forced itself into previous discussion—for one of the main impressions of the survey was of a group of children from (often) aspiring working-class homes who had fully identified themselves with

167

their grammer school, who were proud of its uniforms and traditions, who soon picked up its tone and accent, and often became its prefects, captains, personalities. They impressed by their readiness to accommodate. Where others kicked back, grumbled, remained dissatisfied, this body was tactful, positive, hardworking and for the school. After school the men sometimes took commissions in the forces, when other working-class children were unable (or unwilling) to rise even to the rank of corporal. In their professional life the same ease, tact, and friendliness is evident. We term them the 'orthodox' because along with all this there was yet a certain rigidity about them, an astringent dislike of any form of 'nonconformity', and an eager concern to engrain themselves in 'established' society. This is a clumsy and general way of putting it, but particular examples on the way will give it a local life and colour. Mrs. Rushworth knew their kind of ready sociability. 'They're all socially very pleasant they get on with people—they get on with *everybody*, like John here. John always gets on with people. There's *never* any awkwardnesses, *never* any brushes. He can talk to anyone. And then there are wider interests, horse riding, polo or sport—something a little wider.' It is when this ready and aspirant sociability hardens into an over-concern with the status quo that the word 'orthodox' pushed itself forward.

Marriage patterns make their own comment on social mobility. Ten people had married the son or daughter from a professional or business family, and 13 had married into homes where the father's occupation was clerical. In a crude kind of way this represents the up-current. The remaining 40 had all married former children from other working-class homes. So in most homes that we entered, both husband and wife had a working-class background. Further light is thrown on this when the wife or husband's education is considered. It is simplest to take this at the secondary level. Three had married someone who had been educated outside the state system. Eight had married someone who had attended a secondary modern school. But again the great majority bunched together—52 had married someone with a grammar school background. So perhaps the characteristic home was the one in which both husband and wife had been born into the working class, received a grammar school education and had now set up home together as professional-class people, perhaps teachers. And maybe this explains a little the 'enclosed' feeling that we got in meeting couple after couple: the discovery that wife and husband had this similar working class/grammar school background—and so had all their *intimate* friends. The new children moved socially 'up', but as a distinct unit not yet enfolded into society. The unit was all the tighter since over half of the husbands or wives also came from Marburton. There were 20 marriages in which each partner had had a grammar school education, after being born into a Marburton working-class family. Twice a boy on this sample had married a girl also on this sample.

Education then dictated marriage. Not altogether, and not exclusively, but that is the emphasis one wants to make. When we asked those who were unmarried what qualities they were looking for in a partner, they tended to begin with an educational 'qualification'. If the woman had her 'A' level, then she wanted a husband who had his, or more. If she had a degree, then this was her minimum. Perhaps it was good sense, but it could seem a rather odd insistence. There are, need it be said, many other valuable human qualities. The note, however, was distinctly there, heightened perhaps because this was an interview about 'education'. Some had tried boy or girl friends who had only gone to secondary modern schools, but felt they were too far apart. It was hard to find a point of contact from which to broaden the relationship, and raw attempts to 'educate' were disastrous. 'As a matter of fact the girl I was engaged to hadn't been to a grammar school and she broke it up. The educational differences had a lot to do with that. I tried to get her to broaden her ideas and improve herself, but she wasn't prepared to do that.' The educational lines were too firm for most sexual relationships to break through. The modern and grammar school division was reflected and confirmed by married life. And yet eight had taken a wife or husband who had no more than this 'modern' education. They had crossed the lines in a somewhat different spirit from the above quotation, not to 'improve' but to love. And they were amongst the happiest of these marriages. 'Tom hadn't a grammar school education or anything like that. But I don't think that matters. He's very kind and he's very gentle. And he loves me and he's not frightened of showing it like some men are, and that's what I like. Education never got between us, it never did.'

Such marriages were possible—and they seemed good marriages. But they were not usual, and all the major pressures were towards preserving the educational stratifications into adult life.

Those who married 'up' had their own difficulties to face, special stereotypes to break. When Mrs. Beresford declared her intention of marrying a member of our sample, her mother was most distressed about an ex-working-class boy moving into the family. 'She said to me, "Do you think you'll be happy? I don't see how you can be happy married to a man that eats his bread with two hands." And I said, "Does he? I haven't noticed it." She meant he'd eat his bread with two hands—as if he were playing a mouth organ.' The curiosities were shared by the working class, too. Mrs. Harrop was reluctant to bring her future husband home, because of their difference in class. But he threatened to come up and stay at the Y.M.C.A. in Marburton one holiday, 'and that forced my hand. But he fitted in very well. It was Whitsuntide when he arrived and there were all sorts going on. You know what it's like in this part of Marburton at Whitsuntide. They have the Walk, and the Brass Band, and it was all very interesting for him—because they don't have these down South. He had a job telling what people said at first, but fortunately he could speak Norwegian and that helped a lot with the dialect words! All my relatives were there, and they told him, "We've come to look at thee, lad."' But once the wedding celebrations were over, and the couple had settled down in neutral territory, there was usually little if any further contact between two sets of parents, coming from different social classes. And though the children were scrupulously fair in visiting both equally, the very tact was a recognition of the difference —and of course the more prosperous parents had that extra command of communication and distance which the car and the telephone bring.

Finally, there were a group of unhappy instances in which the child had drifted so far apart from the parents by the time marriage was contemplated that they were not even drawn into it at a merely formal level. 'I went up to see the wife in hospital and she was trying to tell me something. I could tell she was getting excited but she couldn't get it out, and then the woman in the next bed said "She's trying to tell you that your son got married today." So I said, "That's the first I've heard of it. How do you know?" And she said she'd got to know it off the ward orderly who knew an auntie. And so when I get back home and he comes in I said, "What's this about you getting married today?" And he said, "Who told you that? I can't keep anything secret!" ' Further implications of marriage are discussed in the final section of this chapter, on the parents and the grown child.

What class are we?

Education, marriage, and a profession: there is no difficulty in putting these men and women into a social class according to any of the common measures.

They are almost all 'middle class', if we use the Registrar General's classification as our guide. And yet this is only the crudest approximation to the situation we met, for when we asked them what class they thought they were we met very different answers. Table VII is a somewhat arbitrary statement of the class they claimed for themselves. It is arbitrary in the sense that these statements were qualified in very many and very important ways, which defy such simple summary. This we will try to bring out, but for a beginning we can consider the immediately 'measurable'.

TABLE VII

CLASS RATINGS BY FORMER WORKING-CLASS CHILDREN

	Self	Parents
Middle Class	58%	31%
Working Class ..	30%	69%
'Classless'	12%	nil
Total %	100%	100%
Nos.	77	67

Of those who answered this question only 45 considered themselves 'middle-class', despite their possessions, income, education, or profession. Almost one-third graded themselves as 'working class'. How could this be? The surface mechanism was quite simple. They extended the working class drastically upwards so as to include their parents and themselves in the same grouping.

They spoke not so much about 'the' working class as 'my' working class. Mr. Barker argued: 'Now my working class is a big one. I should say that it goes right up to the people who earn £1,000 or £1,200 a year. I'd put myself in that— the working class.' Mr. Abbot foresaw that he might rise eventually beyond this limit, and put himself out of his working class. So in his case the ceiling was pushed up to an even safer level. 'Anybody that gets less than £5,000 a year is working class. I don't see how they can be called anything else.' Of course, this device worked the other way too. We also asked them what class their parents belonged to. According to our criteria all the parents were working class, but again almost one third of the sample put their parents in the middle class. There was a certain truth in this as our references to the 'submerged' middle class have shown, but more than this was being asserted. Mr. Melton repeated baldly that 'we're all middle class now.' Mr. Williamson assured us that 'there's no other class at all in Marburton except the middle class.' Mr. Beresford distinguished between his parents' view and his own. 'My parents would call themselves working class. They'd be proud to. But in my opinion they'd be middle class.'

A glance back to a small sub-sample of parents confirms Mr. Beresford, and yet shows the same device at work there. Seventy-nine of the parents called themselves 'working class' and seven 'middle class'. They distinguished shrewdly and directly between the station they held in life, and the station they desired or had lost. But when we asked a group of them what class their children were, the same process of 'stretching' the classes set in. Over half claimed their children were still 'working class'. This device requires one or two comments. First of all a basic truth beyond the reach of our measuring tools was sometimes being affirmed. 'Class' could be something in the blood, in the very fibre of a man or woman: a way of growing, feeling, judging, taken out of the resources of generations gone before. Not something to be shuffled off with new possessions, new prospects, new surroundings; to be overlaid perhaps, or felt in new ways. A few of the parents and a few of the children had this in mind when, by their weight of qualification, they protested against 'objective' measurements. 'We are working-class.' said a school-teacher, 'you've got to be what your parents are—we *can't* change.' But class was not generally spoken about with just this kind of seriousness, and so we discuss this 'stretching' as a device. 'Device' because it was often being consciously done. One part of the mind acknowledged stratification, change and difference, but was overtopped by another part not wanting to know and recognize these things. As we say, they did not speak altogether of 'the' middle or working class, but of 'my' middle or 'my' working class. A tiny illustration catches the point. Six men answered the question by saying they were working class, yet at a later stage in the interview all six said quite clearly that they were middle class.

The device of 'stretching' is obviously enough a means of denying the changes brought by education, of re-affirming the solidities of family life. And yet it does not of course speak for the existence of any such solidities, though it may do. We show clearly enough in other sections how, for very many, the most vital connections between the child and his working-class home were atrophied or severed. So the question is: who is the audience to whom the device of 'stretching' is addressed? Plainly, it is partly the stranger asking for an interview which might touch on private and disturbing questions. But clearly enough it was just as often addressed to the self, an inner colloquy to soothe the doubts; a last protection.

Nine of the children had avoided some of this by simple contracting out. They said they were 'classless'. This possibility was not offered to them in the questioning, it was forced by them. Had it been there as an invitation no doubt many more would have taken it up. Mr. Eyre said, 'We often talk about class. Irene and I are the two most classless people we've ever come across.' Mr. and Mrs. Bleasdale maintained that 'Of course there are lots of classes, but we aren't in any class. We're disenfranchised. We've been disenfranchised for about ten years now.' Mr. Rippon said, 'It's interesting, all this business about class. I sometimes think about it, and I think we're not in a class—we're just waiting to go into a class, perhaps.' And another, a minister, asserted that 'Well, in my position, I'm not allowed to be in a class.'

Many strongly wished to be outside the whole English class system, against which they addressed so much of their energies. The idea of 'classlessness' did not just 'happen', it was actively sought by some. A number had considered emigration, and amongst its attractions was precisely this. Several, already mentioned, had temporarily achieved something of the sort. Mr. Dibb at a lonely weather station on Banks Island, Mr. Barron unemployed for four years, Mr. Proctor sailing the seas and planning to marry a wife in Hong Kong, because Chinese girls were 'civilised' and English ones generally were not. Mr. Lynch interpreting between East and West in Berlin. They found themselves in different situations for different reasons, but this desired neutrality they shared in common. 'I'd like to live in a society where there aren't any such barriers.'

What are our politics?

Many of the parents thought that to talk of class and to talk of politics was merely to approach the same subject from a different angle. How did their children relate education and their new social class to politics? Table VIII compares the political opinions of parents and children.

TABLE VIII

POLITICAL OPINIONS OF PARENTS AND CHILDREN COMPARED

	Parents	Children
Labour	50%	27%
Conservative	34%	50%
Liberal	16%	15%
Other	nil	8%
Total %	100%	100%
Nos.	128*	88

* Not all the parents were asked.

We recall from an earlier section that the main bulk of the parents were Labour, though the Conservative interest was high. With the children there has clearly been a considerable shift of sympathy—65% to 73% were *against* the Labour party, the traditional political voice of the working class. The Liberal support is similar in both generations, though its kind is, we believe, very different. With the parents, Liberalism is an old

loyalty fostered by the particular conditions of Marburton.
With the children it is, as we will illustrate, quite another thing
—a statement of political rejection, rather than the assertion of
a political positive.

The 24 who supported the Labour party came from homes in
which both parents tended to be vigorous Labour believers.
A very small group of them were no less vigorous in the pursuit
of a Socialist ideal, not much different from that which their
parents had followed. But most of them had moved 'rightwards'
in their party. 'Well, at school I was an unthinking Socialist, and
I'm still a Socialist, but I don't think the same way as those
crack-pots like Zilliacus and Crossman. Those fellows still think
we live in the days of Keir Hardie. I've got no time for that set.
The Labour party has got to be an entirely different thing. It's
tempting to turn Liberal sometimes.' With many their continued
support of the Labour party seemed very doubtful. Mrs. Harrop
had voted Labour at the last election out of old loyalties, but she
was more relieved than otherwise when her party was defeated.
'I don't think I was sorry that the Conservatives had got in.
I don't think they had finished what they were doing, you see.
It would have been like changing horses in mid-stream. I think
the Conservatives should be allowed to carry through their
policies, and if Labour had got in I don't think they could have
managed.' With Mrs. Mitton these doubts had nearly carried
the day, until she confided in her mother. 'At the last election
I was a bit worried. I'd always voted Labour but I went to see
my mother and said, "Mother, Tom is a Conservative, and it
doesn't seem right the husband and wife voting against each
other. Shouldn't I vote Conservative now?" And my mother
said, "What! Who are you talking to? You work, don't you?"
"Yes, mother." "Well then, you're working class, aren't you?"
"Yes, mother." "And the working class sticks together and
votes Labour." And so I did, but I wonder . . . .' Their political
support of the Labour party was argued generally in international
rather than domestic terms. Africa and disarmament came to
their lips more readily than the extension of the Welfare State
or further assaults on the 'commanding heights of the economy.'
But instability of commitment and the drift towards the right
seemed dominant.

Mr. Mountain's father was a Trade Union officer and Labour

candidate in local elections, but he himself is a Liberal. 'When I was younger I was much more of a hot-head Labour supporter —adolescent idealism, if you like. But I grew tired of the Labour party. I think the Liberals are the new party, the new radical party. This slogan of theirs 'People Count', well, it seems to me the same thing as Christianity.' Few Liberals were as positive as that. The more usual Liberal on this sample was the one who had drifted out of the right wing of the Labour party and was still moving rightwards, or the one who had contracted out of politics altogether. They were *against* the Labour party, but they were not much *for* anything at all. Mr. Abbot considered 'Politics are a thing of the past. Whoever gets in they haven't much control. It stands to reason that everything's controlled by world-wide booms of trade.' And Mr. Keith had never got around to expressing his Liberal sympathies by voting at the polls. 'I've never bothered. It doesn't seem worth while turning out to vote. What's the use of me voting?' These Liberals, as distinct from the parents as Liberals, shaded off into those who had contracted so far out of politics that they would admit of sympathising with no party. 'I don't know that any of the parties appeal to me very much,' said Mr. Beckworth. 'United Individualists, that's who I want to vote for—only there wasn't one standing last time.' The contracting out was a movement away from the Labour or the old Liberal positions. The United Individualists did not have Conservative upbringings behind them.

The most politically articulate section were the Conservative voters. The Conservative backgrounds had almost always retained the support of their children, and when there had been division between the parents, the more right-wing one had tended to hand his loyalties down. And there were quite a number who came not only from Labour backgrounds but very active Labour backgrounds. It is perhaps indicative that the only member of the sample who had Parliamentary ambitions wished to be a Conservative M.P. Both his parents vote Labour. Those from traditionally Conservative homes carried on their parents' easy belief in the superiority of the Conservative idea, Conservative politicians, and Conservative supporters. 'You think of the cream as being Conservative,' said Miss Edwards. They were now joined by former children from Labour homes, 'disillusioned' by nationalization or the Welfare State, who spoke a similar language.

'I'll tell you something. I once thought I was Labour,' said one, 'but these public schoolboys, they know what they're doing. They know what they're talking about, and how the job ought to be done.' Others who had swung from early Labour leanings pointed to particular issues. 'I was disillusioned by nationalization,' said Mr. Ross. 'I know the arguments on both sides—I could argue on both sides quite easily. But I feel more and more that the chaps who know how to run a big business are the chaps who know how to run the country.' Mr. Weston explained his change on these grounds: 'It wasn't so much what attracted me about the Conservatives, as what I was against in the other party. I vote for the party that will serve the country best, and I think the "philosophy" of the Conservatives was the better one. They don't have this tendency to merge people into a vast herd.'

Some of the Conservative voters had a nagging sense that they *ought* to have been Labour. They handled this by relegating voting to something off-hand, flippant. 'I'm not interested in politics. I'm right out, I don't bother. I voted Conservative last time, but I only did that to walk down with Elizabeth—she was going down that way.' Sometimes they took pains to define themselves as 'left-wing Conservatives', or as Conservative voters who had 'socialist principles' as distinct from Conservative voters untroubled by such. Mrs. Naylor was an extremely talented woman who had been fiercely Labour when she was younger. 'Really, in theory, I'm Socialist. But I vote Conservative. I didn't like nationalization, I'm all against that. It won't work. It's true I did feel a bit guilty doing this. I think it's disloyal. But we treat politics very lightly in this house—we just laugh about it and joke about it. We treat it like trifles.'

But others had subdued their past and their doubts more successfully, and spoke with passionate hostility against the haste, the disturbance, the non-conformity they associated with the Labour party. 'I dislike all extremists,' said Mr. England. 'I don't like the fitters at work for example. I don't like these nuclear disarmers and people like that. They don't know what they're talking about—they're like children. It's the same with South Africa. You've got to go out there and get the experience and see what the conditions are like—and then you'll understand why it all is. Lots of people are too ready to jump in the scale and weigh it down without thinking. All these extremists! I'd like to send a lad of mine to public school.'

The Conservative families then successfully handed on their traditions, for education and the national scene only confirmed the rightness of the parents' judgment, in the children's eyes. And towards this steady centre there was a general pull over the rest of the sample. The drift rightwards was most often a statement of rejection. A vote not always so much for the Conservative or the Liberal party as *against* the Labour party. The particular issues most quoted were nationalization, taxation for more welfare, nuclear disarmament and South Africa. On all these the Labour party was faulted and felt to be 'extreme'. The general phrase that many of the parents had used was 'the Labour party is for the working class.' The children disliked this. In their view the 'Conservative party was for the country'. There was insecurity behind all three voting patterns, but the whole sample had a built-in impetus to the right, which seemed as if it might come out even clearer were they questioned again next year, or the year after. For the former working-class child, a high regard for the Conservative élite ('the cream', 'these chaps from the public schools') over-mastered feelings about 'disloyalty' to their background ('socialist in theory'). A number had postponed or eluded this kind of choice, becoming a new kind of Liberal, or taking the lonely stand of the 'United Individualist'. The 'built-in impetus to the right' was all-evident with the 'normal' and the 'orthodox', but its magnetism seemed to be felt more strongly each year even by the 'disturbed'.

'The Uses of Literacy'

As another approach to position and values in society, we asked questions about reading. To what use was the hard-earned literacy put? We enquired first at the level of daily and Sunday papers. There emerged here a certain similarity to the political statements (though of course the concentration of the press on the 'right' makes difficulties), for on the whole there was a hovering in the centre and a push towards the right. Of the 60 people[1] we asked about dailies, the largest single group read the *Guardian*, (20), 13 read the *Daily Express*, and 12 the *Daily*

---

[1] Unfortunately we did not begin to use these questions until after the survey had started, and answers are quoted for their suggestiveness, not their completeness.

Telegraph. The *Daily Mail* (4) and *The Times* or *Yorkshire Post* (5) were the only other ones to draw much attention to themselves. Four read no dailies, and one read the *Daily Herald.*

Sunday choices showed the same balance, with the *Observer* (at 20 out of 49 people) well in the lead. The *Sunday Times* took 13, and the *Sunday Express* ten. Despite the high level of formal education, the attraction of the 'populars' as opposed to the 'quality' papers was very much there. It is hard to reconcile the number of *Guardian* and *Observer* readers with some of the social views expressed; or at least it suggests that many readers on the sample did not fit the usual 'image' of these papers.

We were interested in literacy in a more demanding sense than this: literacy as one of the supreme skills handed on by education, not simply to facilitate the everyday activity or open up new realms of light entertainment, but literacy as a means of discovering and enlarging the readers' sense of life. How true or false was this? We limited our question to books read in the last six months, and only put it to 54 people. Sixteen had done no reading at all. The largest group (22) had read some light fiction. Under this head we included Penguin detective stories, paper back Westerns, Romances from the public or the Red Circle Library. Ten had read something from a book club, or a circulating library such as Smiths. John Buchan, P. G. Wodehouse, Jerome K. Jerome, figured here. Eight had read 'professional' books—for their work as scientists, doctors, ministers. A final, and even more arbitrary grouping, we term 'serious'. By this we mean reading unconnected with work but of a somewhat more testing calibre than P. G. Wodehouse or Stephen Leacock. It included a touch of Dickens, of Lawrence, of Conrad, of Dostoievsky, but the bulk was quite elsewhere. Here were the modern novels (C. P. Snow) likely to be found in Penguins (in one way or another, Penguins *directed* so much of this reading, in the absence of lasting impetus and tips from college or university days). It included a little of the new fiction on working-class life, such as Alan Sillitoe's *The Loneliness of the Long Distance Runner* ('but, oh no, it's not the same working class as I come from,' said Mrs. Rodgers). But perhaps its most distinctive section—and one of the most distinctive sections altogether— was the one which touched the borderline between modern history and eminent biography of our times. The admiration we touch on for the status quo, the interest in, and sometimes identification with, the 'top', that we found to be such a consistent trait in these ex-working-class children is caught a little here. Mrs. Argyle had just read Sir Winston Churchill's memoirs of the second world war. Mr. England was reading Sir Winston's *History of the English Speaking People*. Mr. Raines had recently finished it. Mr. Ross had finished Sir Winston's war memoirs and found them 'splendid'. He was continuing with A. L. Rowse's *The Earlier and Later Churchills*. Mr. Southcott had turned aside to Sir Anthony Eden's memoirs, and Mr. Dufton to Lord Montgomery's. All of this last group were very enthusiastic about their reading.

Education: looking back and looking forward

Attention here is given to the men and women reflecting back over their education, and considering the adequacy of the present system. How good did they now find it? There was no doubt but that the majority were well satisfied. Mr. Robinson is an exception and is utterly against the principle of selection and rejection. He was highly sceptical about grammar school education and by no means convinced that it selected, held, or developed, intelligent children. He is himself a primary school teacher, teaching seriously not for, but against, the eleven plus. Mrs. Sellers, another primary school teacher, had grown assured of basic impossibilities in the present system, and took her stand on direct experience. To her understanding, for instance, 'late developing' was an empty phrase, since so much potential development was stunted by the initial act of rejection, that only the child with a strongly compensating home ever succeeded at a second attempt. These voices. however, were lonely protests. Mr. Ingleby, another teacher, considered 'the eleven plus to be a most effective exam. It's a well known fact.' Mr. Kingsley, again a teacher, said, 'I think it's all right, this dividing up at 11. Take the intelligent ones away from the unintelligent. They might make some mistakes, but those come on later—late developers.' Mr. Raines did not see that there could be any more intelligent children in the population than the grammar schools now took from the selection exam. 'In these places like Merionethshire where 60% go, they're not really *grammar* schools—they're *comprehensive*.' Mrs. Nichols thought the children who failed the selection exam. were quite content and she had voted largely on the issue of comprehensive schooling; 'I think you never will get equality, and I don't think children want it.'

The few who mentioned comprehensive schooling (they were generally teachers) were hostile. The majority of the sample, however, had little or no idea what comprehensive schools were, and not much to offer on the subject. And though some had claimed that it was a 'political' and not an 'educational' concept, the Labour minority was in fact just as unaware, or as unconcerned, as the Conservative or Liberal majority. One man had met some comprehensive school enthusiasts when he was in the army, and in his view they summed up all that he found regressive and lunatic in education. 'I don't want things changed. I like it the old way. Why change? We got through all right. Now when I was in the army there were some teachers in the billet, and they were talking about these comprehensive schools. They'd got comprehensive schools on the brain. They're the kind of people who cause all the trouble in the world—idealists! Leave it as it is, that's what I say—and these crackpot psychologists with their ideas, they're behind it too.' Another man caught almost the same phrase. 'I wouldn't want to see it changed. I think it's all right, as it is. You'd say that I'd an interest in it, like it's seen me through all right, hasn't it? Why change it?' Despite the details of previous sections, most felt that the educational road for talent could not be more widely open. Mr. Gledhill considered that intelligence stratified itself naturally. 'If you're brainy in the working class you rise automatically. I don't think there's anything to stop you these days.' Mrs. Hare spoke about an absolute correlation between intelligence and education achieved in our time. 'They are the same really. They are both the same. The people with intelligence always get the education they ought to have.'

Other recent changes in education disturbed them. Mr. Beresford disliked the Crowther Report and was of the opinion 'that most of the changes since our day are for the worse. I don't like the G.C.E. The way they can get a certificate now in one subject or two subjects—just the subjects they like!' The process of selection at the end of the fifth form hardly troubled any. 'The people who left were intellectually inferior', said Mr. Spencer, and that summed the matter up. The children who entered the grammar school before the 1944 Act had a particular point to make. They were often hostile to the abolition of fees and considered that this change too was for the worse. Mr. Southcott was 'half-way up the school when they changed and you got free places. Well, I know this sounds a bit snobbish but you got a different kind of boy then in the top half of the school from the bottom half—a different kind of boy altogether.' Mr. Williamson confirmed him. 'Abbeyford was a very good school. You got lots of boys who came from good homes there. You got boys coming to school in cars—take Peter Impling, for instance, and lots more too. But later on, when we got further up the school and you didn't have to pay any more, it changed a bit. Not much, but you began to get all those boys from the estates.' Mrs. Hillaby wanted fees brought back. 'I think you should still have to pay to go to grammar schools. It became much worse after they let anybody go who wanted to without paying. They got girls who didn't care, girls who would leave at 15—all these girls from the slum areas coming. I think we should go back to what it was before and charge everybody and keep it select.'

Main dissatisfaction was with the grammar school as compared with the public schools, which so many admired. Mr. Waite feels this at work. 'I've often said in the past that I wouldn't send my children to public school, but when I think of the lack of self-confidence in myself I think that perhaps I will. I was having a discussion about this confidence at work with a man the other day. There's two men there and you hear them on the phone, and you'd think they knew all about everything. And sometimes *you* know that *they* know absolutely nothing, but there they are on the phone, 'No, no, old boy, you've got that absolutely *wrong.*' And then if anything does go wrong, it's never *their* responsibility. They may make an awful blunder but to them it's just something out there, the great irresistible force. It's drilled into them as soon as they go to public schools. They're born to rule, and all the way through it's drummed into them and they come to believe it.' Mr. England feels like this often. 'Perhaps I'm going to somebody's house and I've got to meet some new people. Perhaps I'll walk round twice before I go and knock on the front door. And all the time I'm saying to myself, "If you were a public schoolboy you'd walk straight up there and you wouldn't worry." It only dawned on me after I left university, the big difference that education makes. It's very good this public school education, you can really go ahead—it's leadership they say, they can train you for leadership. I don't think I'll ever get that confidence. It's got to be done right back in the schools.' It was the same with women. Mrs. Hadfield argued. 'I could never vote for the Socialists, because of their educational policy. I don't approve of scrapping the public schools. They're a very valuable tradition, they teach you to lead and carry out your own ideas. The grammar schools spoon-feed you and teach you to be led. You've got to have the public schools to provide the leaders.'

But though ideas are turning frequently in this direction, it is still largely a matter of respect, not participation. Either the money or the contacts are not there readily enough for the new generation to be schooled outside the state system. All children who were of age were attending state schools. Until the day the new families enter the public schools, the old unchanged grammar schools would suffice. 'I've started a tradition, going to Abbeyford,' said Mr. Agar. 'I've started a tradition and I want my son to carry on. I would have liked to send him to a public school —but he'll have the chance of carrying on the tradition after me at Abbeyford.'

Looking back on working-class life

As already indicated there were a number who either wished to return to working-class life, or to open up a new relationship with it of the affirmative kind. They found the task much more difficult than they had at first thought. They might join a working man's club, but since it was not quite like any club at a university there was a temptation to size it quickly up and then demonstrate how it should be run. They might interest themselves in dialect and working-class speech, becoming more particular about the remoter points than any working man. Or they might go around collecting 'characters'. 'This old chap said to me, "Never trust a Christian." He was right in his own way. He didn't mean "Christians"; he was talking about hypocrites. He said to me, "You see yond feller, he's a union official, a methodist preacher and all, but yond's the sort that when he sees the manager coming he'll grab the shovel out of your hand and let on he's doing all the work!"' There were many false starts and illusory relationships. The ones who had most success were those who remained true to their own skills, such as teaching, or medicine, but accepted a particular responsibility to the world from which they came.

But again the majority had no such interests, and responded and judged quite differently. They were hostile to such working-class movements as the Co-op or the unions. 'Unions were a good thing in their day,' said Miss Coates, 'but they've out-lived their usefulness. They've been taken over by the militant people and the communists. We're getting far too many strikes.' 'I read history,' said another woman, 'and I can see that they were a good thing once, but I don't think there's any real need for them now. They're out of date.' And Mr. Proctor announced the difference between his own judgment and his father's. 'I've got some very strong view on unions. They're organised associations to ensure that slackers can get a minimum wage without working. Those are *my* views, not my father's. He's been in a union ever since he was 14.'

They were concerned to distinguish between the strata of working-class life they had come from (often, as we saw, it now transformed itself into a middle-class background) and the rest of the working class. 'There are two kinds of working class— the ones who swear, and the ones who don't, in the 'bus queues. My father was the non-swearing kind.' For the class as a whole they might have little sympathy. 'I'm glad to get out of the working class,' said Mr. Kingsley. 'I should say by and large that the working class are those that lack abilities, those who can't get on, that's who they are.' To Mrs. Sutcliffe, they are 'the people that don't bother, people that's poor and don't bother.' To another, 'they are the *Mirror* people, the dead-beats, those who don't take pride in themselves and never do a solid day's work.' A young mother is shocked that people like this and without her education, should earn more money than she does. 'You read about these miners, and you hear about them getting £20 or £30 a week. And they can hardly write their names! I think it's a shame. I don't think it should be allowed, I think that should be stopped. People like that shouldn't be allowed to go and earn £20 or £30 a week. And lots of people do that. Like all the people round here, the level of intelligence is very low—I could diddle them all ends up if I wanted to—but they earn a lot of money. They earn lots and lots of money. I don't think it's right.'

The emphasis can be caught by listening to the boy whose

father wished him to be Labour's Prime Minister. He is talking about possible marriage to a working girl. 'In my last job I was supervising hundreds of girls, and they could gossip about nothing except all kinds of rubbish. Lord, I couldn't marry one of those. No chap in my position could. I call them all "girls", but some of them were 40, 50 . . . .'

To Marburton their attitude is ambivalent. On the one hand, they consider themselves mobile, rootless, and delighting in that condition. 'I must have a car,' said one. 'I must be mobile so that I can get away to places. I've got to be able to get away. I used to go off in the car every week with two friends. And when we went to a place, one of them would say, "I don't like this place, I don't know anybody." And I said, "that's funny, I like this place *because* I don't know anybody."' On the other hand there was an understandable desire to return and show that they'd made good. 'I've just paid £2,200 for a little maisonette out in Barking. Well, if I was back in Marburton I could buy the Town Hall for that price. You'd feel you were more than somebody. I think the time's come when I'd like to go back.' The trouble with going back was that the new prosperity might not protect the new persona. Some made the discovery that a spell of Marburton life called back an old, a lost identity that they didn't welcome. 'I can't explain.' said Miss Fox, 'but here in Leicester it's very enjoyable—friends, tennis, car rallies. But when I got back, well I'm just like I was at school, not like I am here.' There was a loyalty to Marburton, but it had to be defined in new ways. They liked a certain touch of the 'north', spoke well of the frankness of the northerner against the subtlety of the southerner, and now and again objected to the metropolitan centrality of English life. 'As if everything happens in London and the rest of the world doesn't matter. Every paper you pick up, every time you turn on the television or listen to the news, it's London, London, London, all the time. You come home from work, turn on the news and the announcer's there, and he says the temperature on the Air Ministry roof is such and such. And there you are! Buses can have been blown over in Newcastle and people killed —but the temperature on the Air Ministry roof is such and such!' The popularity of the *Guardian* was not unconnected with this measured degree of old loyalty ('It's strange but I find that the *Manchester Guardian* is quite a respected paper down here.')

It was a looser loyalty, purged of class, of the 'neighbourhood', and not unlike their politics. 'I support Marburton at sport,' said Mr. Turnbull. 'I always turn up the sports page in the *Guardian* to see how they've got on. But I'm not Marburton like my father is. He thinks Marburton is the be-all and end-all of the world, the most glorious place on God's earth. I'm not like that, I'm just not local. I don't like being local this or local that— I don't like being local anything. I often talk to my friends about this, and I put it to them like this. I say I'm not Marburton, I'm British.'

Our parents and ourselves

These men and women were usually grateful that the grammar schools had pulled them out of working-class life, and fed them back into society at a different level. Many spoke with harshness about the life they had left. It could not be expected that they would use this tone about their own father and mother; and it may be that difficulties and irritations with that relationship were projected into general statements of working-class life and attitudes, as a mode of indirect release. We do not know. And indeed of all the very difficult ground of human relationship that we have covered, this final report on parents and children is the most difficult. So far we have illustrated education tugging the child away from neighbourhood and then family life. A gap of non-understanding opens between child and parent, and education fails to foster those human impulses which could bridge the gulf. Something like this, qualified this way and qualified that, is very near the centre of this report. But we are of course aware that many of the difficulties and changes that we touch on are not exclusive to the working-class child. Some matters that we quote are experienced in other areas of society, some are close to the inevitable perplexities of growth. In adult life, then, do the former children reach a kind of maturity which re-opens the affective flow between mother and daughter, father and son? Have we been concerning ourselves with a passing phase of growth?

Certainly such a positive note needs to be sounded somewhere. Some did grow out of a strangeness, a hubris of late adolescence into a surer and equal relationship. It is beyond our abilities to say who and why these people are. Some notations can be made, but tentatively only. The major one is that the great healer was the new grandchild. Marriage might or might not call out a celebrative rush of affection that made for momentary understanding, and the 'union' within the family. But more turned on the birth of grandchildren. Not so largely for the father and the grandfather (though much was sometimes gained here) as for the mother and her mother. We pointed out earlier how a third of the daughters still lived near home, whilst the sons were much more scattered. It is a crude measure, but it says something about that relationship; about the triumphing mutuality, the discovery of 'natural' placing within the cyclic pattern. No doubt at all but that this was true for many, and that it closed the cracks of adolescence. Differences of formal education, of information were still there. But 'knowledge' was accepted as wider, richer than this. And the very real differences in training and outlook were recognized yet, as it were, suspended above a basic security of relationship. 'I got quite far from my parents. Not the money —it's the education and things like that that make the difference. Until the baby was born—and now I'm much nearer my mother. I don't know about my father. I think my mother understands this, but she mightn't like to admit it. But it's true.' (Consider Table XXI).

But given this, the larger picture was altogether different. There were more homes in which the situation shaded off or bleakly announced itself as being otherwise. It is hard, and perhaps unwise, to be more precise, for the 'shading off' was various and elusive. Still something was picked up when we simply asked the parents what their children did for a living and got this from Mrs. Kingsley. 'He's teaching in Stoke, but what he teaches I don't know. I think he'll be teaching in the grammar school, or maybe it's the council school, or. . . .' Or this from Mr. Thurston. 'I don't rightly know, he never mentions. He works for the Steel Company though.' Or this from Mrs. England. 'He works for Vickers but I don't know what it is. It might be aeroplanes. I never bother myself.' Or Mrs. Gledhill. 'He's a "second mathematician." What's that, do you think? Will that be a good job?' Or Mrs. Clark, 'I don't know.' All these replies were given good faith and meant to be helpful, and they could be too much insisted on. Still they do suggest breaks in communication when, after this whole process of education, a mother does not know whether her boy teaches in a primary or a grammar school—or even what her daughter does at all.

There were sometimes open rifts between children and parents, and we could not possibly assess the many things that had gone to make such a split; if matters had gone wrong, not everyone would speak of it to a stranger. The children were the readier. 'There was a programme on television which said something about not being able to converse with your parents after you'd been educated. And we were all sat round the television set, my father, my mother, some aunts and an uncle—and they all said the same thing, just the same reaction—"snobbishness!" But it was right, we all knew it was right, because that's how it was with us.' Indeed many of the children were extremely clear-eyed or candid about the change. 'I don't think you realise,' said Mrs. Dyson, 'how narrow the interests of your parents are until you've been away and you come back. While you're at home and brought up with them you don't realise it, it's when you come back you realise how narrow they are.' Some experienced a curiously 'external' feeling, as if they were looking 'in' on something. 'The way our parents do things and look at things, the way they set about living—that's altogether foreign to us. We look at it from the outside, and it seems strange,' said one son. And a daughter pondered, 'I like to go back and I still like visiting. I like to go round and hear relations talking about themselves. . . . but I'm not sure. . . . I'm not sure whether it's quite the same interest as I used to have, or if I regard them more as. . . . well. . . . specimens, in a way.' An astringent honesty might revolt at a pretence of relationship where no relationship existed. 'Lately my father's taken to kissing me, and I can't stand it. It turns me over inside. I wouldn't know what to do if he started talking to me intimately. I'd be embarrassed.'

The major and the final stress falls somewhere on this side, the side of change, breakdown and loss—and we do not pretend that the situation is peculiar to the working-class family. The parents ponder it, at different levels. At the very simple level of curiosity about income. 'I think he'll have a good job, judging by that house of his. But he won't tell me how much he gets. I asked him last time but his wife said I shouldn't know.' Or at a most testing level, where the words are hard to find. 'We often talk about this, don't we Mary? His ways aren't our ways. Our

ways are moulded, if you follow me, they're moulded in the old
ways. But his ways are altogether different. He doesn't tell us
much, he doesn't tell us as much—so we don't talk. It's as if
when we talk we don't talk on the same level, you see. His way
way of putting things isn't the way that I can understand. Or
perhaps I'm too much of a nit-wit! I can follow the words, if you
get me, but I can't follow his ways of looking at things— do you
see?'

The parents' pride in their children's 'getting on', their
readiness to accept small returns, momentary contacts, made
them less prepared to put the failures into language. There were
other things to dwell on, or to speak to strangers about—the
new house, the second-hand Jaguar, the framed degree photo-
graph. But the children were more open-eyed, more ready-
tongued. With some, the acts of rejection were harsh to hear.
And even for those, like Mr. Barron, who wanted to find some
passage back, the task was too often a hard and defeating one.
'I feel more akin with them when we're silent. I can get on with
them better when we walk silent together. It's when we start
talking that we notice the difference.'

In conclusion: a précis

In *Chapter* 1 we saw that in the prosperous city of Marburton,
records showed that very few working-class children stayed in
the grammar schools to pass their final examination at 18, and
move on from there to college, university or the professional
life. On the other hand, the proportion of middle-class children
who did so was very high. Neither the removal of school fees,
nor a long period of local prosperity and high employment had
been enough in themselves to release large numbers of working-
class children for the full sixth-form course. These observations
from local records agreed with the national picture documented
by previous educational research.

In *Chapter* 2 we studied the school lives of ten middle-class
children. We saw that they began school with an educational
inheritance. It was not just that their parents had often had
secondary education (this applied to some working-class parents
too), but rather that their families had interpenetrated state
education in Marburton from its earliest days. It was for families
like this that grammar schools were conceived and built; it was

by men and women with similar habits of evaluation that they have been directed and staffed. To the middle-class child the prevailing grammar school tone was a natural extension of his home life. Nevertheless problems arose about the potential abilities of some of these children. When this happened, parents and teachers usually co-operated, and the children moved successfully onwards. On other occasions teachers pre-judged a child's limits, only for parents to interfere and see to it that their child received the full course—and (usually) at the 'best' level. In the instances we recorded the parents were right: their children's abilities flourished and multiplied when favourable conditions were secured. The children became capable and independent citizens, and we considered that this very minor enquiry threw some light on the quite different situation of the working-class child.

In *Chapter* 3 we drew a sample of 88 working-class children who had passed their final grammar school examination. We visited their homes, and measured or grouped our impressions. The successful children were usually born into small families. Over one-third were only children. Often they also lived near to a successful primary school where the pace and tone were influenced by middle-class parents. Further, over a third of the parents had connections with the middle class themselves, and shared many of its aspirations—if not its secure knowledge and modes of communication. This group we discussed as the 'sunken middle class'. Most of the remaining two-thirds of the homes also came from the uppermost levels of the working class. We considered the foremen separately, and looked at their desire to break open the closed ranks of management through the education of their children. We also grouped those parents who had been selected for a secondary education themselves, and who now (often enough) tried to live out their obstructed longings through their children. We also recorded a body of parents who were the leaders and organizers of their local communities. Our whole discussion went to suggest that behind the majority of the 88 children was a home where, for different reasons and in different ways, considerable pressure was put upon the children to do well, and to survive at school. This pressure may not have been quite as powerful as that behind the middle-class children —it was not reinforced by that assured confidence which knocked on the head teacher's door and demanded this information or that, and got it. It was a different force; but it was strong enough both to encourage the child to accommodate himself to the new worlds he entered (if that was to be the price of survival), and to support him in the grammar school venture if the schools failed to recognize or meet the needs of working-class children.

In *Chapter* 4 we followed the children as they remembered their schooldays. Primary school seemed local and familiar in many ways: it was a special continuation of normal neighbourhood life. But grammar school marked, for most children, a sharp break with this former world. Now they spent almost all their time with similarly selected children in a middle-class atmosphere. Neighbourhood life and any relationship with the majority of local children disappeared or diminished. As more and more of the 88 children adapted themselves to their new school, their rejection of neighbourhood life became more than a matter of simply not having the time: gradually it became a conscious and articulate rejection of a way of life, and of children whom they did not think were of anything like equal ability with themselves. Meanwhile a minority had held out against this way of adapting themselves. They were distinctly against the school and for the neighbourhood, and preserved their own codes of judgment and behaviour.

For both kinds of children there were gradual changes in home life. Few homes were divided because one child had gone to grammar school whilst another had gone to a secondary modern school—for this was very much a minority situation. But parents who had become excited at the new ranges of knowledge to which they were introduced through their children, became more and more perplexed as their sons and daughters developed new ways, and as they themselves failed to get adequate information about the nature of the course and the adult prospects it led to. The heavy burden of homework and the crises occasioned by long competitive preparation for competitive examinations further complicated the stresses in family life. All this held generally true even for parents who had some connection with the middle-class—unless that relationship was strong enough to bring knowledge and confidence as well as aspiration.

At the end of the grammar school course the majority of the 88 children, now taking their own place as prefects and leaders ot school society, had become orthodox pupils. Only a small minority (largely a self-supporting group) remained dissident, trying to gain the education the school offered without the social emphases that went with it. Then, despite the difficulties in getting vocational information, most boys and girls went on to college and university (gifted girls being diverted in some numbers to the former). But this was often because they had been carried along by the momentum of the educational process from certificate to certificate, rather than because they had made a series of informed and personal decisions.

In *Chapter* 5 we considered the 88 men and women as they are today. Almost all are professional class people. Over half (30 out of 39 with the girls) became teachers themselves. They live in industrial areas up and down the country, and often they have married husbands and wives from similar backgrounds or with similar education. The educational stratifications determined at eleven plus are often preserved and confirmed in adult life. Up to a third of the people report themselves dissatisfied with their work and position in society, and one or two instances considered in detail suggested that this was sometimes more than the natural discontent of ambitious young men and women. Some were doubtful about the society for which they had been trained, and doubtful about the social nature of that training. Others felt the losses in family and neighbourhood life which education had sometimes compelled. But against this, most of the 88 were satisfied with their education and the social rise that had gone with it. Gaps between themselves and their parents had sometimes closed with the birth of grandchildren. On working-class life in general many expressed harsh opinions. With their own education they were pleased, and most wished to see no changes in the present system, unless it be that grammar schools should become more selective still, and penalties be imposed to prevent lower working-class children from entering them in any numbers. They were sure that eleven plus had separated them merely from 'the dim ones' and 'the future teds', and they saw no reason to be troubled about working-class boys and girls who left grammar school at 15 or 16 ('intellectually inferior').

Today most of these 88 children have developed into stable, often rigidly orthodox citizens, who wish to preserve a hierarchical society and all its institutions as they now stand. Back in Chapter 3 Mr. Bleasdale spoke of the Jack London novel he read nearly 50 years ago in which 'there's something like this. The deck hands are around and there's Jack the cabin boy and he's going to be something like the midshipman in the end. And they say to him "Now you won't forget when you're in the high places." ' These working-class children now find themselves much nearer the 'high places'. But it would be sentimental to report that the majority of them, though discharging their duties to parents, wanted (in any testing way) to 'remember'. Most wish to forget.

PART TWO

6

SOME NOTES ON STATE
EDUCATION AND
WORKING-CLASS LIFE

OST of the working-class children felt that all was well with their education, and they wanted the system that produced them preserved intact. But like all other research workers in this field·we have our doubts. From the evidence we collected, there was good reason for concern—and there are improvements and suggestions to make. Perhaps the smaller ones are best handled first, and we begin by drawing to a point a series of local suggestions that may well have formed in the reader's mind.

1. *The possibilities of good records*

Fortunately for us, Marburton schools kept quite good records of their pupils, and generously allowed us access to them. One of the most interesting entries was the one under 'father's occupation'. Often this was helpful and showed us whether the child was roughly working-class by background, or middle-class. But sometimes it was missing and sometimes it was the baffling word 'clerk' or 'engineer'. This last could point to a parent who was director of an engineering plant and earning £3,000 a year, or it could mean a semi-skilled mechanic earning £8 a week. We had therefore to check all the entries by tracing the home and making direct enquiries. The results turned up in this way somewhat altered the picture given by the records. Nevertheless school records provided a real and illuminating start. Marburton, however, has now abandoned the custom of asking children for a record of their father's occupation. In this it has fallen into line with other education authorities. It is felt that such questioning is rather 'impertinent' and no business of the schools.

This seems to us a setback, and a false propriety. Any head teacher is in a stronger position for knowing, in some detail, the social composition of the school. If working-class children are leaving in large numbers at 15 or 16, if they are sinking into the B and C streams by 13 or 14, then the knowledge of what is happening is at least the beginning of reform. And this seems even more important if the intellectual potential of the children is also known. Just as the head should know with some precision the social background of his children, he should also know (we contend) such of their potential ability as can be measured by non-verbal intelligence tests. He can then tell, not only that working-class children are sinking in large numbers, or escaping at the first opportunity, but also whether many of his potentially gifted boys and girls are lost this way. This looks obvious and neat and rational on paper. But it needs to be said; for one of the obstructions to fuller education in our schools lies in the assumptions of the teachers themselves. What teachers *think* is happening in their schools, and what actually *is* happening can be two different things.[1] The proof of this lies in the Crowther Report. That Report demonstrated the vast size of the wastage in our schools. It showed that over half of our most gifted children were leaving by 16. Yet grammar school teachers of considerable intelligence and experience were steadfastly denying that there was more than a trickle of loss. The Headmaster of Watford Grammar School wrote in 1953 that 'the huge majority (of those who leave after taking the ordinary level of the General Certificate) have approached their academic ceiling, and to ask them to continue (with sixth form studies) would be a waste of time. There are very few potential graduates leaving the grammar school at sixteen.'[2] He could hardly have been more experienced or more wrong.

---

[1] For example, Dr. J. C. Daniels of the University of Nottingham in an unpublished Ph.D. thesis demonstrates that when a sample of teachers was asked about the effects of 'streaming' on children they taught, they were quite uncannily wrong in instances (such as the number who had moved up or down from their class) which could be accurately measured or recorded.

[2] From a letter to the *Times Educational Supplement*, 16th October 1953—quoted in Floud, J., Halsey, A. H., and Martin, F. M., *Social Class and Educational Opportunity*, p. 125.

Similarly we spoke to a grammar school headmistress about gifted children leaving early from her school. She was an intelligent, sensitive and very capable teacher, and tried hard to answer our questions. Glancing back over her time at the school, she recalled *four* such cases. They were all vivid, even dramatic events which could hardly have been overlooked—one girl collapsed on the speech-day platform, in another case there had been a murder in the family, and so on. Nevertheless as far as we could see, the wastage in her school was just as large—and perhaps larger—than elsewhere. It was so big that she had not seen it! And this is a fair case; for it is as if everyone recognizes the size of the Crowther Report's findings, but everyone thinks it applies only to other schools, not their own. The problem is of such a size, and so masked by social habits and assumptions, that it takes the record card and the sample to reveal it—for to our established generations of good grammar school teachers, it has become 'the normal'.

It is then more than a research worker's grouse to plead for the keeping and reading of records, especially in relation to potential ability and social class. It is an absolutely necessary check against social illusions and stereotypes, for which no amount of experience is an adequate substitute.[1] It is apposite to recall that in the 1920's Bradford was far ahead of many other education authorities because it consistently took the trouble to check what was happening in its schools. It steadily recorded who was receiving the education offered by the city, and this in itself was impetus enough to fashion a system of schools not easily equalled in the country at that time. The keeping and reading of records is not to be left to investigating committees or casual research workers. It is properly the direct responsibility of the authorities, the head

---

[1] The importance of simple factual data as being something that 'experience' should build on, rather than despise, is illustrated in an article by Pape, G. V. (*Education*, November 16th, 1956). Mr. Pape was head of a very large and streamed primary school. He took the trouble to study the dates of birth entered in all his class registers. A very straightforward piece of addition soon showed him that in each year the older children tended to be in the A class, and the younger ones in the B and C streams. Indeed it was quite obvious that children born between September and December in any year not only tended to be in the A class, but also to pass the eleven plus! This factor, which had clearly got nothing to do with intelligence, but rather with age on entering infant school, may well be at work in very many primary schools. But again teachers (good and careful ones) taking children every day, may not observe it.

O

teachers themselves. It can no more be divorced from the quality of education than can the recording of standards attained in national examinations. And it is surely reasonable for an authority spending the community's money to know which sections of the population are using the opportunities offered. For it is from a lack of such skeletal facts that a whole myth about English Education since 1944 has arisen. A myth about the lavish financing of education in the Welfare State (questioned by Vaizey, J. in *The Costs of Education*), and a myth about the achieved education of the working-class child (questioned by *Early Leaving* and the Crowther Committee). Such pieces of research do much, but the major responsibilities are better taken nearer home—by the education committee, by the head teacher. Is it too much to ask for such knowledge to be gathered and used at the working face? Advance in English education has often been made on a local front. It would not be hard for any local authority to learn more of the harvest that we still don't reap. Perhaps some of the attention focussed on the gilt-lettered Honours Board could usefully be given to a box of humble cards?

2. *The Extended Sixth and the Junior College.*

Secondly, something needs to be said of the great exodus at the end of the fifth form when gifted children, glad to get an Ordinary certificate, turn with relief to work and the adult world. For it is interesting to note that many of the children who stay on— perhaps merely entangled in a mesh of friendships which pulls them into the sixth—find a strange change not only in schooling but in their own abilities. Among the middle class children, we remember Mr. Peters, a C stream boy who came into his own in the sixth and began the road to a Ph.D.; among the working-class children was Mr. Turnbull, who, after an undistinguished middle school life, suddenly 'became intelligent'. Why does school (sometimes dramatically) become more satisfying when they enter the sixth? The end of the mechanical 'O' level run has obviously something to do with it. So has the chance to make a fresh start, and even open up new subjects altogether. But something also has to do with being a sixth former, with taking on some of the responsibilities of the school, engaging with teachers in open discussion and disagreement rather than passive note-taking—with being treated like an adult. A boy or girl's whole sense of importance is altered as they find unused powers called back from fantasy and into a direct apprenticeship for life. This aspect of the sixth form as an apprenticeship, as a testing out of adult capabilities, seems to us altogether excellent; so excellent that it is reasonable to wonder how many of the fifth form leavers might have accepted education for several more years had they only experienced a term or two of good sixth form life.

After all, what many of them forsook school for was precisely this—the chance to move out from late childhood into early adult life, to earn a wage, take on a woman's responsibilities in a hospital or office, wear make-up, nylons, new suits. In the fifth form, boys like Mr. Stevens found themselves unable to reconcile their social role as schoolboys with their new capabilities, yearnings, feelings. They felt there was something wrong with them, not the system; they were 'over-sexed'. Similarly fifth form girls, becoming sexually conscious of themselves, grew to hate the restrictions of school uniform, and took it off as soon as they got home. They wanted their high heels and nylons; and it seemed hard to relate this to life in the fifth form. Out of the perplexities of adolescence it was difficult to know what form of behaviour to adopt—whether to assert, to defer, or to rebel—because it was difficult to know what attitude adults held towards them.[1] We were shown a schoolgirl's essay in which one passage went '....many of the school rules begin to seem petty and childish and we wish that, instead of them being so numerous, we could be trusted to behave as they imply, and not to be dictated to in such a rigid manner. We also wish that the staff would treat us more on their level of intelligence and maturity and not give the impression of having to talk down to us.'

Here are young people whose new elations and ambitions cannot be cramped in the middle school desk, in the middle school uniform. Frustrated of their trial adulthood, their energies turn in upon themselves and are lost in fantasy; or their hope forms around the coming escape from school, or bursts outwards in destructive and rebellious energies which assert their new and

[1] 'Perhaps one of the chief clues to adolescence lies in the fact that at that time the potentialities for many various kinds of behaviour are still present. Mutually incompatible drives and emotions are simultaneously aroused, many of which later become shed or repressed bit by bit as the individual chooses inevitably this path rather than that, and increasingly limits the range of response.' Tanner, J. M., *Growth at Adolescence*, p. 145.

overlooked identity. Of course this is not always true; but it has something to do with the 'blackboard jungle' reports from some secondary modern schools, the recurrent comments on 'behaviour' problems with the 5B or 5C classes in the grammar schools. Boys and girls of 15 *are* difficult to teach in our society. And the explanations for this *are* complex. Obviously enough the rejections, the grading into the second-rate, does much to intensify the problem in the secondary modern school. And no doubt something of this sort applies to the C stream of the grammar school fifth.

An interesting finding from the statistics for juvenile offenders[1] shows that the peak age for delinquency is the last year at school. Up till 1947 this was 13, and then, quite dramatically when the leaving age was raised to 15, the delinquency peak suddenly appeared at 14—and has stayed there since. It is both understandable and pitiful. Understandable that young boys and girls should be lost amongst the 'mutually incompatible drives and emotions' of adolescence. Understandable that many years of second-class schooling should have directly and indirectly bred all manner of disappointment, frustration, carelessness, idleness, disrespect, need. Pitiful that this language of need should be lost upon us, that we cannot turn these bursting energies to better use and that we should seem to fail most dramatically, not with our youngest pupils, but precisely with those to whom we have given ten years' attention. No doubt this applies most largely to the secondary modern school, but something of it spills over into the grammar school—particularly that part with which we have been here concerned. And no doubt something must be blamed on 'home background' or the mass media or the climate of the age or the breakdown of religion. . . . But to strike out at such large targets is merely to parody the headmistress's speech on Open Day. To thrust out great blobs of blame can be a way of evading smaller problems nearer home, under the wing of our particular responsibility.

A further note on the loss from school at 15, before drawing an argument together. It is sometimes said that pupils today 'mature' earlier than did their teachers when young. The point is worth pursuing. Clearly enough there are many possible

---

[1] See 15 *to* 18, vol. 1, para. 63, and chart 5.

measures of physiological maturity, but sexual development can perhaps be singled out. 'During the last hundred years there has been a very striking tendency for the time of adolescence, as typified by menarche or the growth spurt, to become earlier.'[1] Research in the United Kingdom, the United States, Finland, Sweden and Norway shows the same pattern. The evidence from Norway reaches back illuminatingly. In 1850 the average age for girls beginning menstruation was 17; in 1950 it had dropped to 13·5. It appears to be dropping still. So on top of all the foregoing we must remember that young boys and girls are taller and heavier than they ever were, their sexual development is starting much earlier than it has done—at least since the industrial revolution—and yet they find themselves not out in the factories or farms testing themselves alongside men and women, but cramped behind fourth or fifth form desks.

So we have, amongst a net of tangled problems, one that can be taken out of context and examined on its own. These fourteen and fifteen year old children are older than perhaps we are accustomed to think. They are already driven amongst the storms and calms of full adolescence. Possibly on top of other disappointments about their schooling, they are living with themselves not as young boys and girls but as young men and women. And yet they are denied the opportunity to test out their new powers (unless indeed they leave for a good job—the delinquency figures drop when young people get to work). As Dr. Tanner puts it, 'Where society does not permit the adolescent to assume a social role compatible with his physical and intellectual development, but keeps him dependent. . . .adult maturity is come by with more difficulty.'[2]

If we limit our attention to this problem as it affects the grammar schools and look for an answer, we can find one to hand. The grammar school certainly has an answer. Didn't Arnold of Rugby find himself faced with just such juvenile delinquency? Only in that instance the drinking, fighting, bullying, stealing, prostitution, was the habit of much older boys. His solution was the creation of the sixth form. The hooliganism was replaced by responsibility. The boys were treated as 'men', as the young adults they manifestly were. This solution was

[1] Tanner, J. M., op. cit., p. 88, in which most of the available data is summarized.
[2] Ibid, p. 148.

adopted wholesale (with much else) by the new state grammar schools, modelling themselves on the older public schools. It was a good solution, in 1850. What we have been moved to ask during this survey is whether it is still such a good solution in 1960.

It seems to us that Arnold's sixth form must now begin at 15, or earlier. All of the present fifth form must take on the new status. Before the choice of leaving school presents itself, boys and girls ought to have had this second wind, this chance to be in the school as boys and girls no more, but young men and women. There might not then be the general readiness to leave, even amongst the gifted. It can in any case hardly do much harm to treat boys and girls as being many degrees nearer adulthood. The need is to offer responsibility lower down the school; responsibility not only in an organizational or disciplinary sense but responsibility towards learning. We spoke of enquiry, judgment, imagination, suddenly replacing the mechanical memorization[1] of the fifth form—and what a surging release this was. This different confidence in pupils, and this different attitude towards education—though perhaps in part held back by the 'O' level syllabus—should surely come earlier.

To push out a suggestion like this clearly raises many new problems. The size of the extended sixth form is one. We are not, here or anywhere, pretending to offer a blueprint. Our purpose is to set enquiry moving, to arouse possibilities—and hope that vigorous heads or committees will be ready to push forward in practice. But one possibility worth recalling is the idea of the Sixth Form College—a gathering together of all of a city's sixth forms in a separate Junior College: a stage and style of education to lie halfway between school and university. This has been turned over already (by Croydon), and it is to be hoped that one authority at least will show us it in action. The case against it has been largely that it would rob the grammar school of its natural crown, and drain out its leaders. Like so many powerful arguments in English education, it is not only insular (a glance over Russian, American and Continental education points this);

---

[1] Though in a sixth form under our notice, the recurrent, even obsessive, subject for conversation amongst one body of pupils, was the possibility and virtues of having a 'photographic memory'. An interesting reflection on their education.

it is also out of touch with other branches of schooling here. Primary schools also speak of their leaders and their 'crown' (at eleven) and have their very efficient prefects and so on. The Leicestershire System ably illustrates how self-contained a middle school (11 to 15) can be. It seems to us that it is not a problem of spreading the available 'leaders'[1] around, but calling into action the many ones unused. If the organizing of our education is to stay broadly as it is, and yet reach out in new ways, towards present waste and frustration, then that authority which moves in the direction of the Extended Sixth or the Junior College will find itself netting quite neglected riches.

3. Parents and information

One of the perplexing aspects of this survey was the way parents badly wanted, needed, and yet could not easily come by quite elementary information about the sixth form, specialization, college, university, careers. And yet on the other hand, there were schools staffed with able and interested teachers most unlikely to refuse any clear demand for help. Still the gap was not crossed. There were even instances in which parents had not realized that the nominal scholarship award (say, £20) picked out in gold letters on the Honours' Board was not the whole support that the state provided for a university course. There was bewilderment of almost every conceivable and utterly basic kind. Parents were unable to communicate their needs to teachers, and teachers steadily mistook the level and nature of enquiry. Such parents were not wanting to know whether Anne could beat another girl in history, or whether she grasped the second law of thermodynamics. This information was welcome, and often useful—but it hung over a void. They wanted to know what physics *was*, and what kinds of jobs it opened for a girl; they wanted to know whether you could do anything with a

---

[1] The concern with the limited nature and the limited source of leadership is of course one of the recurrent curiosities of English education. There are, plainly, other types of leadership besides the dominative 'public school' kind, and ones perhaps better fitted to our society—but many teachers remain innocent of this.

Educating One Nation reminds us that the Swedes abandoned their old system 'precisely on the grounds that a selection of 40% or 50% was not training all the leaders who eventually emerged,' (p. 72). We of course only let 20% through the 11-plus sieve. Much is lost, but some leadership will out—only as likely to announce itself leading unofficial strikes as anything else.

history qualification except teach more history. They wanted to know the difference between a training college and a university, in nature, quality, time, cost. They wanted to know if their son could even think of becoming a doctor after taking languages in the sixth form. Or what it meant in terms of future choice when their daughter had to abandon chemistry or Latin at 13; or whether there was any difference between the universities at Bangor and Oxford; or any difference between going into the civil service at 18 or taking a degree first. A hundred and one problems of this kind troubled their relationships with school and child.

We saw how often they misfired with teachers, how they were never likely to belong to the prevailing Parent/Teacher Association, how they turned in anxiety to relatives, neighbours, workmates, the clerk in the education offices. The gap here seems to us so large that it is almost impertinent to suggest ways of filling it: obviously there are a thousand. The situation arises because the grammar schools work on the unrecognized assumption that the parent has all kinds of knowledge about education and careers, and will approach the school with specific questions when he has specific problems. This fits well enough with that middle-class public which the grammar schools have always served. They do have sufficient knowledge, if not in their own past, then entrapped in the experience of relatives, friends, business acquaintances. Of course, they have problems too, but problems which can be closely defined and expressed in direct questions. The trouble for the working-class parents was that they knew so little—not even the vocabulary of higher education (physics, university, radiography, specialization, honours course, inter-B.Sc., algebra, Greats)—that they often lacked the raw material to ask the questions with. Instead they asked if Alan was doing well at Latin, were told that he was 2% up in a practise 'A' level paper—and went down the school steps with this new fact floating over the profound ignorance with which they came. And naturally teachers were not giving answers to unasked questions. It all fell into place with the enclosing social dilemmas, and resulted in the lack of flow—of visits at all even—between parents and school. It was not their fault. It was not the schools' fault. It was the way grammar schools have grown up: 'Nobody's Fault'.

What can be done? If education is going to stay very much as it is, then the social gulf and unease between the schools and their new public is going to stay too. That will not be closed by careers masters and such like. Still, some things can be done, and valuably so. To begin with, much clearer explanations about various parts of the grammar school course can be offered to parents. One wonders if the local authorities ought not to be distributing a series of pamphlets on particular subjects, (e.g., *Going to University,* with some very simple explanations, comparisons, figures for cost, and so on). There is no need to elaborate this—the detail is obvious enough once the direction is established. But the factual information has got to be put out there, *whether it has been asked for or not.* It would provide something of that elementary basis for the different kind of parent-teacher relationship that is required if the grammar school is going to concern itself seriously with its working-class entry. Similarly, there is a need to explain every stage to the children directly in class; only it must be done early. Everything must be done *early.* Very many of the people we saw could have benefited considerably had matters of this kind been regularly opened up in class—in time. It would, a little, have dispersed the 'haze'. Were the flow of information set going, in class to the children, through pamphlets to the parents, then the beginnings would be there for discussion. Particular dilemmas might be defined. Of course this would not solve everything. That aura of the grammar school which caused some parents to put on their Sunday-best accents, others to burst belligerently through the classrooms, and others still to go away and never come back again: this would remain. And perhaps not much more can be achieved anyway within the hectic rush of one or two crowded evenings a year. Sometimes during these interviews we felt how hopeless the ten minute annual interview with the teacher was, how stupendously inadequate to the problems emerging. The formal education of the child was continuing day in, day out, whilst only a few hurried minutes could be snatched to glance at the radical anxieties gnawing at his and the parents' energies.

What was needed was an utterly different recognition of the parents' place and the parents' rights. Indeed, often the wiser course would have been to let the child stay at home for a week whilst the parent went to school, gathered his information, thrashed his worries out. And perhaps this *is* the right idea. If we had to make a specific suggestion about the annual or terminal parent-teacher meetings, we would claim that the present position of the parent was quite inadequate. Better by far to give the children a week's extra holiday each year, but let the teachers be on duty all afternoon and evening for parents to come up (and come up more than once, after reflection and the family conference), and thoroughly get to know what was and what could be happening.

A further suggestion: a few of the working-class parents turned instinctively not to the school but to the local education office. They were disappointed; for there was little provision there to help them. We do not need to recall why it was that they preferred an alternative source of help. It was, as we say, 'instinctive' —just as their children's action was also instinctive in turning to the Marburton Labour Exchange rather than the Universities Appointments Board, after academic failure. For one thing they were more conscious that the Education Office founded its authority ultimately on the vote. ("Tha's a public servant, like anybody else.") The Education Office might be strange but in the end it was 'us' who paid the piper. They did not really feel like this about the grammar school: that belonged to 'them'—no doubt at all.

Yet surely there was a rightness in their going to a central office in the city, conscious of their dignity as citizens, and seeking such information? Is there not a place for an *Adviser*[1] in the city offices, whose specific job is to be always available to parents, ready to give them accessible information or ready to arrange that they see someone else? A person to focus more widespread problems of education and welfare; relating, say, the medical aspect of a bad examinee case to its strictly academic side, or offering advice on those financial problems that parents resented opening with a head teacher. There could be a magnificent informal strength here: the strength and position that is often enough unofficially assumed by someone in the city's council housing office, in dealing with the many individual working-class problems that arise there. There *are* ways of opening up a liaison with the working-class public: Parent/Teacher

---

[1] The London Institute of Education successfully provides an *Adviser to Teachers,* supplementary to head masters and head mistresses. If an Adviser to Teachers, why not an Adviser to Parents?

Associations may not be the right way (though they should not, plainly, be neglected), but an Adviser unattached to any school could be part of the answer. These paragraphs locate one of the new problems that state education has thrown up. What is the place of parents? Middle-class parents (rightly) make their voice felt in the education of their children. They pay fees and naturally expect to see value for their money. Or they use state schools and know the teachers personally, or ably run the Parent/Teacher Association. They might even organize themselves nationally as the P.T.A.'s have done, or form a subscribing unit such as the Advisory Centre for Education. But we have still to forge the links with the new working-class parents who are, after all, now the largest group in state grammar schools. Given the present situation, the bridges at least can be built. But do we care to build?

A gathering of loose notes.

It would be possible to go on further in this vein, suggesting this improvement, suggesting that. No doubt such suggestions, if followed through, might improve the 'efficiency' of our education system considerably—perhaps ten, perhaps 20 per cent. A major gain. And yet, even if 'efficiency' were our only criterion, would that be any answer to the loss that research has recorded? Is the waste not on an altogether vaster and subtler scale? Between the two world wars such people as Kenneth Lindsay, Lord and Lady Simon, Leybourne-White, J. L. Gray, P. Moshinsky, R. H. Tawney, Lancelot Hogben, and others, kept the public only too aware of the gulf between educational opportunity and educational ability. They helped make the 1944 Act the great advance that it was. But has the gulf now been closed? Of course, 1944 did a great deal. The final removal of fees made entry to the grammar school at last financially possible for most working-class parents, and crushed the myth that the majority of them did not, and never would want, to send their children beyond the elementary stage. Small pointers show the change that has taken place. In 1926 over half the children of Bradford refused their place at the secondary school,[1] in 1936 Lady Simon reported that 20% of the children of Manchester were turning places down.[2] Since 1944 such a problem has almost disappeared.

[1] Lindsay, K., *Educational Progress and Social Waste.*
[2] In *Education*, September 1936.

(Though as we show in Appendix 1, there are subtler forms of refusal). More working-class children than ever now reach the grammar school. Though the proportion does not seem to have leapt up since 1944; it has increased—but modestly only. Floud, Halsey and Martin showed in admirable detail in their Hertfordshire and Middlesbrough research, that the successful proportion between 1931 and 1941 was about 10%; in 1953 it was 15·5% in south west Hertfordshire—and in Middlesbrough still only 12%.[1]

The crudest economic barriers (school fees, etc.) have been removed, only to reveal subtler ones at work. It is now clearer to see the many small ways in which money and power in society prepare early for a competitive situation. In particular we can note how the middle classes (supported by the primary schools) respond to and prepare early for, the divisions of eleven plus—at which their children do so conspicuously well. We can now understand why, if we have élite education, it does not much matter whether the *formal* selection takes place at 11 plus, 13 plus, or even 7 plus. Middle-class families are in so many ways insured against failure by virtue of their class position; and any form of *nominally academic* selection will, in effect, be a form of *social* selection. Similarly we can now observe more plainly that selection is not an event that happens and ends suddenly at 11 plus or 18 plus. It is a process that is at work all the time from the moment the child enters school to his final leaving: a gentle shaking of the sieve, with now and again one or two big jerks. Even within the grammar school, working-class children are being pushed out of the sieve in large numbers. We have already mentioned the Crowther Report's finding (it is of compelling importance) that 48% of the children with an I.Q. over 120 have left school by 16. The figure is 87% for those with an I.Q. between 108–120. And all these must be ranked as above-average pupils. The ones who leave are predominantly the working class.[2]

This was the position from which we set out, with the aim of

---

[1] Floud, J., Halsey, A. H. and Martin, F. M. *Social Class abd Educational Opportunity* p. 33.

[2] As long ago as 1926 Lindsay, A. D., was writing in terms which could be a review of the Crowther Report, in his book *Social Progress and Educational Waste*. 'As the advantages of money and environment are subdued, the problem becomes at once more hopeful and more difficult; more hopeful because of the evident revelation of hidden talent, more difficult because of the rigidity of civilization outside the school' (p. 161). The words are wonderfully apt: it is just such rigidity which bars our advance now.

catching the feel of the individual human situations behind the figures, and with the hope of judging what kind of men and women these children became after a grammar school education. This final section we deliberately detach from the survey—for just as we adventured there outside the usual limits, so now we want to push out further lines of thought whose suggestiveness does not stem directly and exclusively from the survey behind. That survey merited a few specific recommendations, and yet they seemed, though perhaps valuable, yet small in proportion to the problems raised by the work. No overhaul of the present system (though not to be scorned) will go far enough to meet what we take to be the major problem facing state education. That problem, quite bluntly, is how can we open education to the working class?

A note on 'measured intelligence': the scientist and the bureaucrat

The fees are gone, but the grammar schools are still closed. In this they are not crudely unjust. Their entry can very properly be justified in terms of measured intelligence. A greater proportion of middle-class children score more highly in measured intelligence tests than do working-class children. But of course what this means is hard to know. We can only talk here of *measured* intelligence—not, what we are after all concerned with, 'intelligence'. Because children do less well in terms of measured intelligence this does not mean they are unintelligent; and certainly it has nothing to say about the possession, or not, of the many other human qualities that make the mature man or woman. The whole discussion, which underlies so much defence of élite education at 11, is complex and fluid. But some notes might be helpful here. First of all, no one is in a position to state that middle-class children are *inherently* more intelligent than working-class. The argument is open. Of course the case for a strong influence of inherited ability is well-argued, and is being continually reshaped and refined as it meets new criticism.[1] But the hypothesis that intelligence is distributed at random between the different social classes, and that any measured difference is due to environment not birth, is quite as strong.[2]

[1] See, for example, Conway, J., 'The inheritance of intelligence and its social implications.'

[2] For a very persuasive statement see Halsey, A. H., 'Class Differences in General Intelligence'. This piece also lists the most important recent papers on both sides of the discussion.

'Environment' can be a delicate matter to define and grasp, and 'money' can count potently at one or two removes. For example, much interesting work has been done showing that when we measure intelligence we are very often, directly or indirectly, measuring verbal dexterity. A. F. Watts re-states in the language of our own time what Shakespeare put before us 350 years ago: that language is not merely the reflection or translation of thought—it is the texture of the mind in movement, the process of definition itself.[1] 'We find that we have been thinking only after we have said what we thought.' (*Language and Mental Development of Children*.) The world of language in which a child is reared very much controls his poten-tialities. J. N. Nisbett suggests that the low scores at intelligence tests from large (working-class) families are con-nected with an atmosphere of 'verbal restriction'.[2] When we reflect over the working men and women talking and compare them with the voices of their children, then we can see the point even here. Yet it is *difference* rather than 'restriction' which is caught on these pages. There is a quality about the parents' speech that the children do not possess. Basil Bernstein has shown[3] how working-class speech naturally moves into

[1] As in Hamlet's 'To be or not to be' speech III, i. 56–64, or Macbeth's 'If it were done' (I. vii. 1–12) and 'My thought, whose murder yet is but fantastical' (I. iii. 129–41) passages.

[2] Nisbett, J. N., *Family Environment*.

[3] 'It is suggested that the typical, dominant speech mode of the middle class is one where speech becomes an object of special perceptual activity and a "theoretical attitude" is developed towards the structural possibilities of sentence organiza-tion. This speech mode facilitates the verbal elaboration of subjective intent, sensitivity to the implications of separateness and difference, and points to the possibilities inherent in a complex conceptual hierarchy for the organization of experience. It is further suggested that this is not the case for members of the lower working-class. The latter are limited to a form of language which, although allowing for a vast range of possibilities, provides a speech form which dis-courages the speaker from verbally elaborating subjective intent and progressively orients the user to descriptive, rather than abstract concepts.' B. Bernstein: 'Language and Social Class'. One cannot but respect the tact and distinction of this attempt to catch precisely that which can be measured in the twin speech modes. And yet—as so often with sociologists' work on language—one remarks a certain innocence. Innocence of what is held and defined within our literary culture: the metaphorical and descriptive vitality of language demands subtler treatment than the above. The sceptical mind wonders how much of Shakespeare's most superb verse also 'progressively orients the user to descriptive rather than abstract concepts' and feels again that the 'limits' of language so used are much harder to know than some workers in this field suppose.

description, and how middle-class speech just as naturally turns towards abstract conceptions—and how this can be measured. There is something brave and exploratory about this difficult and continuing enquiry into social class, intelligence and language. The impulse is admirable, and our new knowledge of 'intelligence' (even when, as largely, it is clearer knowledge of our ignorance) is a triumph of patient research.

The tragedy of intelligence tests, and the organization and justification of education in terms of them, is a tragedy of users. The tests are, unfortunately, immensely useful to bureaucracy. Thousands of complex human situations are vastly simplified: situations that were better recognized and left as complex. Under the pressure of mass-produced, mass-applied intelligence tests released from central education offices, children and the problems of their education turn into figures which turn into simple tables—mere fodder for the clerks. No one who works as a teacher and knows the difficulty and delicacy of the work can be anything but shocked to witness some kinds of educational bureaucracy in action, and see 'intelligence' becoming a crude administrative weapon utterly untrue to the situation it stems from. Half-grasped and elusive concepts, fashioned by distinguished research workers, are used facilely by those who have no responsibility back to the work. Intelligence testing is of immense use in education, but this is not that use; as those who won such concepts out of the unknown are the first to announce. And glancing at the difference in speech between working-class parent and middle-class child on these pages, one is reminded again of what it is in language that speaks for quality of feeling, for sharpness of mind informed by generosity of response. It is not necessarily that which can be measured easily. It is not size of vocabulary. It is not number of abstract words to number of concrete words. (We hardly measure language under the pressure of genius in this way.) We need to remind ourselves that 'meaning' and that quality of language which arises out of quality of living is to be defined more in terms of rhythm, of association, of the personal play of words out of the thew and sinew of spoken English: more in terms of these than by width of vocabulary.

Yet it is by such things as 'vocabulary' that we divide children up. And it is this which, if we could but reach 100% 'efficiency', would finally define our process of selection at 11. The test result is far from the full thinking and feeling child, and much more distant still are those same figures when they emerge from the bureaucratic machine. It is worth bringing our literary culture and the culture of our psychologists together like this, in order to point the abuse of both when 'intelligence' tests become built-in to the administrative machine: a simplifying marvel in the office, but an utter distortion in the schools. It sets thoughts stirring: thoughts about the quality of man or woman that we could ever hope to measure, and the quality of what we may well reject. How far should education be concerned with shaping the intellect, and how far should it be concerned with training the quality of emotional response? And how far is the first ultimately dependent on the second when the full stress of adult life has to be met?

A historical glance

So much for entry to the traditional grammar school, the kind of 'mind' it presupposes, and the social classes it supports. But in the survey we took entry for granted, and gave more attention to possible exit. Grammar schools tend to lose their working-class children. Why is this? Some of the answer is sketched above, but perhaps more is added if we look at the history of the schools. There are, of course, grammar school foundations going back many centuries into quite other worlds and conditions than our own; but the grammar school of today is very largely a nineteenth century product. The industrial revolution brought about vast changes in the upper classes. The old aristocracy was challenged by the rise of the coal owners, the railway magnates, the cotton and woollen masters, the steel makers, and all that upsurge of talent and riches that went with the first half of the nineteenth century. The new middle class secured its gains and established itself for future generations in terms of education. The great advance of the mid-nineteenth century was not the grammar school, but the new public school. The new middle class revived the older schools such as Eton and Rugby, and they founded the new such as Cheltenham (1841), Marlborough (1843), Rossall (1844), and Wellington (1853). Private education got off to an immense start.

State education lagged behind, and lagged behind Europe, too. Compulsory education began in 1870, and it was a hard and shaky start. Of course the older grammar schools (such as the Abbeyford grammar school of these pages) were drawn into new life by the local middle class: and fresh ones were founded, such as Marburton College. Then in 1902 the state began to organize secondary education. (At this stage Ash Grange was opened.) But 'the force of tradition was so great that when under the Education Act 1902, the state undertook for the first time the the general organization of secondary schools, the ancient Grammar School, local or non-local, was taken as almost the exclusive model for secondary schools.'[1] The new grammar schools were moulded according to the older grammar schools, which in turn were moulded according to the public schools. The grammar school was a school for the education of the middle class, fashioned after the best examples (the public schools) of current middle-class education. This is and was, of course, a triumph. The history and achievement of the grammar school is a fine one. In widening circles it has spread secondary education through the middle and the lower middle classes, breeding generation after generation of able and cultivated men and women. Only in our own time has it foundered on a rock: the working class. In formal terms the secondary education of the middle class is all but achieved, that of the working class hardly begun. The grammar school has now to address itself to a new public; but could it, even if it so wished?

Its former strength is now its weakness, and may now, if crudely held to, turn to rigidity and petrifaction. The grammar schools are a glory to the English middle classes, and to the *first* stages of state education. Their achievement is an honourable one. They are rich in middle-class values. Often good values, and good attitudes: but not the only ones, and not in our time always the best. Every custom, every turn of phrase, every movement of judgment, informs the working-class parent and the working-class child that the grammar schools do not 'belong' to them.

But how would the grammar schools state their own case?

---

[1] See Banks, O., *Parity and Prestige in English Secondary Education*. And also the Parliamentary reports of the 1902 Act. No one reading that debate can doubt but that the grammar schools were seen as schools for the middle classes, and nothing else. For fuller documentation of the evolution of the grammar schools and the pressures of social class, see for very different perceptions: Peterson, A. D. C., *A Hundred Years of Education;* Simon, B., *Studies in the History of Education*.

P

Some Notes on Education and the Working Class

What do they seem themselves as doing? We were not able in our survey to interview teachers systematically, though we talked with many. Nor did we think this so urgent since all the literature on the grammar school is by, for, and about, the teacher. We found hardly anything giving the pupil's point of view, and very little indeed on the shaping social effects of selective education on individuals. In Appendix 3 we do list some of the books which put the grammar school's case, and stand by the status quo. Perhaps Miss Frances Stevens' *The Living Tradition* is the most helpful of them, since it documents much material which concurs with the Marburton findings, and yet *reads* it utterly differently—as a tribute to the grammar school. (The reader may find this a recommendation). Miss Stevens introduces her book with 'I believe that the maintained grammar school offers the best hope at present of making accessible to a larger population than ever before the best of the qualities and habits of which it somewhat accidentally finds itself the custodian: respect for learning, the encouragement of deep and strenuous thought, a regard for style, and *the tacit assumption of contracts of mutual responsibility between individuals and between an individual and his society.* The grammar school has its defects. But the petty snobbery and priggishness of which it is sometimes accused are in my view much less serious (and in any case demonstrably declining) than are two tendencies: the first, to make the curriculum and the public-examination system a closed circuit; the second, to be increasingly concerned with training—in other words, to think of its pupil-product more and more as an instrument rather than as an end. Despite these defects, at its best it is a place of civilized relaxation, as well as hard work, and an *unrivalled solvent of social prejudices and preparation for democratic living.*' In a fascinating section entitled 'The purpose and character of the grammar school' she quotes, in support, a range of comment from headmasters:

'Has the grammar school ever been narrowly academic? Surely it must always cater for a wide range of ability, *and has always done so.*'
'I would send my own son here, for here, more than in most other types of school, he learns to be a person. There are many ways in which a boy can "find himself", not only through academic attainment.'
'Many marginal boys need to feel *the 'pull' of scholarship and manners*

found in a grammar school. The ideal of the grammar school is not exam.-passing *but finding a niche in the community* (though the demands of universities, employers and society make it difficult to realise this ideal).'

'The grammar-school, whatever its variations, is essentially for those who can learn from books. Those who learn by doing are not really for the grammar school, though they are in fact here and we ought to do our best for them.'

'There is too great a tendency now to concentrate on making learning easy, and to aim at quick impressions. "Flash it on a screen" occurs to us too readily. True grammar-school education is still verbal and bookish, and visual and other aids should be supplements only.'

'We are trying, above all, to give general culture. *I see grammar-school education very strongly as a matter of communicating middle-class values to a "new" population.*'

'The grammar school's main task is to protect children against Vanity Fair. There is a need to create a fortified "society within society". A grammar-school boy must be prepared in some respects *to postpone growing up.*'

'The purpose of the grammar school is *to prepare its pupils for the professions, and to help them to get a good job.*'

'When we succeed best in grammar-school education according to our own standards, are we succeeding according to the demands of the mechanical world? In recent years we have all become servants of the machine. In future more and more jobs will be machine-serving, either literally or serving the machine of State. There is a frightening division between work and leisure which threatens. . . . .'

And then a range of comments from Headmistresses:

'The aim of grammar-school education is service to the community. I am horrified when I hear that the girls are thinking of it as the means to a good job.'

'The aim of a grammar-school education is to make a rounded person, not to concentrate on exam.-passing and jobs. It is concerned with manners (the girls should, for example, avoid dropping litter) and the creation of style; *the public-school virtues, in fact*—though without snobbery.'

'I want my girls to be educated so as not to be part of the sheep-like mass, in such things as their choice of entertainments. The grammar school *adopts the public school's attitude*, that it is the whole person that matters. Though the grammar school *like the public school* cares very much for brains, in the last resort character counts more.'

'Grammar-school education is an essentially abstract form of learning—learning organised in subjects. It consists in the acquisition of a wide moral attitude, first in the abstract subjects, then in life itself. It is a training to use one's powers of thought in any capacity, however humble, and is a preparation of *that part of society* which should have opinions.'

All the above italics are ours. The new pupils have brought new 'manners', and the grammar school seems to have responded in two ways. Sometimes with weary hostility at the entrance of the barbarians: 'The grammar school now includes among its pupils a much higher proportion of children from poorer homes. Some of these children come from homes which are barely literate and where a book is an unusual phenomenon. . . . Others have very low standards of cleanliness and appearance: some seem to have had very little training in social behaviour; even table manners may leave much to be desired. Children like these have very little to give to the social or cultural life of the school, the school itself has to provide much which, before the war, would have been regarded as the normal contribution of the home.'[1] At other times it has shown a calm assurance that all will naturally be well and the working-class will be grateful for such gifts as they receive. 'The working-class father and mother who left school at fourteen tend to accept all that a Grammar School can offer their children and be thankful.'[2] Both responses are protective stereotypes, either re-directing criticism safely outwards ('bad backgrounds'), or meltingly absorbing it within a bland satisfaction at the status quo. Of course there *are* problems of 'background' taken in this narrower way,[3] (though it is the

---

[1] Davies, A., *Bulletin of Education*, November 1950 (quoted in Social Class and Educational Opportunity, p. 27).

[2] Ree, H., *The Essential Grammar School*, p. 15.

[3] The kind of judgments behind much research work and teaching comment makes one look twice. To take a very useful book, *Educational Guidance and the Pool of Ability:* amongst much that is excellent these quotations on 'early leaving' turn up: 'Character weaknesses will undoubtedly prevent a number of young people from developing their talents to the full', p. 118. 'A pupil may have high innate ability but lack the character qualities which are essential for academic success', p. 124. 'Among the factors which cause able pupils to leave school early are adverse home conditions, defective character qualities, and physical defects.' p. 186. One wonders quite what the word 'character' is doing. It is a word that simplifies a complex social situation? Is it really a tailor-made judgement from within the ethos of the old public and grammar school on those without?

secondary modern school which is fighting those battles), and many parents and children *are* only too grateful to accept all that the grammar school offers—though absolute gratitude was not the only note we recorded. But the last two quotations (they are characteristic) go some way to showing why grammar schools can act as if there are few problems here, and why every research worker in the field uncovers wastage and frustration on a disheartening scale. The difference between the grammar school attitude, and the discovered facts requires such explanation: it is in itself one of the most startling and interesting of the facts.

The working-class child who does win entry to the grammar school must accommodate himself to the prevailing middle-class values, or rub up against them. If this survey is any pointer, it seems likely that most of those who remain embedded in working-class family and neighbourhood life leave school before the sixth form. Those who cling to the world of their family and yet survive do so with difficulty and move often into a disturbed adulthood. This does not mean that the quality of their living is less fine than that of their more accommodating and successful class mates. We do not know; but we can scarcely justify a schooling on the grounds that it prepares an early entry into the more troubling dimensions of life. And yet if this conflict between school and neighbourhood at so many tiny, frictional points is perturbing, the situation of the orthodox child is even more so. There is something infinitely pathetic in these former working-class children who lost their roots young, and who now with their rigid middle-class accent preserve 'the stability of all our institutions, temporal and spiritual' by avariciously reading the lives of Top People, or covet the public schools and glancing back at the society from which they came see no more there than 'the dim', or the 'specimens'. Can we wish that our schools offer longer education in exchange for this worship of the conformist spirit? For it seems to us that despite all the formal talk about 'individuals' and 'character', grammar schools are so socially imprisoned that they are most remarkable for the conformity of the minds they train. Highly-inbred institutions, they respond with the talismatic words when challenged—and here and there a gifted and *unorthodox* teacher lives out that older language— but is this, in fact, what *happens*? Schools born out of middle-class needs; schools based on social selection, further refined with each year after 11; schools offering a complex training in approved images of dominance and deference—are these the bases for general 'individualism', for 'democratic living'? Or would not the individual when really present be more likely to be non-conformist (and a candidate for slow expulsion) in the way that some of the working-class children were?[1]

Even the most intimate classroom work must be limited, and sometimes warped by these social pressures. We have no means of assessing the 'knowledge' of the men and women we interviewed. Commentary is speculative: but like ourselves the reader may have attended not merely to the complex interweaving of social strands in educational comment, but also to the oddly *final* way in which education was conceived. Sometimes it was as if education was simply a package, to be considered, weighed and bought.[2] 'That conscious and intelligent incompleteness which carries with it the principle of growth'[3] was generally absent. There was little development when formal schooling was finished, and to take one illustration, we suspect that were the reading habits of former pupils examined there would be a huge gap between the head teachers' claims ('essentially for those who can learn from books. . . .' 'the acquisition of a wide moral attitude'), and the extremely light recreational uses to which literacy was actually put. In pursuing this discussion of social class and education there comes a point when the logic of discussion forces us to consider the quality of the education offered, and a point at which we are noting, side by side, the failure of education to address the whole being, not merely the apt and cognitive self; and the failure to accept that self without divesting it of the most enriching parts of family and social life. This is not the place to make the connections between a schooling which is socially selective, looking to the 'upper' reaches of society, and a classroom training which concerns itself with the

---

[1] No one familiar with the public schools can have failed to make connections, in some respects, between the working-class sample here, and the dissidence and deferences of minority groups (Jews, Roman Catholics, lower middle class) in those schools.

[2] See Halsey, A. H., 'Changing Functions of Universities in Advanced Industrial Societies,' for a 'context' in which to place the growth of 'consumer' education as colleges in a technological age become more democratic.

[3] Leavis, F. R.; 'In matters of essential concern, "knowledge" is not deduction from experiment or the end of a logical process, it is a function of being for, *Quantum sumum scimus*, as we are, so we know'—Knights, L. C., *Approach to Hamlet*, p. 70.

'upper' faculties to the neglect of those subtler modes of teaching —art, movement, music—which make possible the total address. But the connections can, we believe, be made.

An acceptance of working-class life

If then grammar school education is so shaped by restrictive social pressures, if despite our formal legislation grammar schools remain 'closed' to society at large, in subtle but very firm ways which have as much to do with class as with ability —how than shall we break the impasse? On the one hand we have the central culture of our society ('the best that has been thought and known', 'the very culture of the feelings', 'that spontaneity which is the hardest of all') which must be preserved and transmitted; on the other hand we have institutions which do this for the middle class but not for the working-class majority. It seems to us that what we call our central culture and what the teachers call 'middle class values' are by no means the same thing, and the problem is to disentangle one from the other in schools which are truly 'open'. When the head-teacher says 'I see grammar school education very strongly as a matter of communicating middle-class values to a "new" population,' he is surely not saying something akin to Matthew Arnold's classic statement, but something contrary in spirit, provincial and partisan. It is worth quoting Arnold's statement in some fullness:

'Culture looks beyond machinery, culture hates hatred; culture has one great passion, the passion for sweetness and light. It has one even yet greater!—the passion for making them prevail. It is not satisfied till we *all* come to a perfect man; it knows that the sweetness and light of the few must be imperfect until the raw and unkindled masses of humanity are touched with sweetness and light. If I have not shrunk from saying that we must work for sweetness and light, so neither have I shrunk from saying that we must have a broad basis, must have sweetness and light for as many as possible. Again and again I have insisted how those are the happy moments of humanity, how those are the marking epochs of a people's life, how those are the flowering times for literature and art and all the creative power of genius, when there is a *national* glow of life and thought, sensible to beauty, intelligent and alive. Only it must be

real thought and *real* beauty; *real* sweetness and *real* light. Plenty of
people will try to give the masses as they call them, an intellectual
food prepared and adapted in the way they think proper for the
actual conditions of the masses. The ordinary popular literature is
an example of this way of working on the masses. Plenty of people
will try to indoctrinate the masses with the set of ideas and judgments
constituting the creed of their own profession or party. Our
religious and political organizations give an example of this way of
working on the masses. I condemn neither way; but culture works
differently. It does not try to teach down to the level of inferior
classes; it does not try to win them for this or that sect of its own,
with ready-made judgments and watch-words. It seeks to do away
with classes; to make the best that has been thought and known in
the world current everywhere; to make all men live in an atmosphere
of sweetness and light, where they may use ideas, as it uses them itself,
freely—nourished, and not bound by them.
This is the *social idea;* and the men of culture are the true apostles of
equality. The great men of culture are those who have had a passion
for diffusing, for making prevail, for carrying from one end of
society to the other, the best knowledge, the best ideas of their
time; who have laboured to divest knowledge of all that was harsh,
uncouth, difficult, abstract, professional, exclusive; to humanise it,
to make it efficient outside the clique of the cultivated and learned,
yet still remaining the *best* knowledge and thought of the time, and a
true source, therefore, of sweetness and light.'[1]

How are we to reinterpret Arnold's magnificent prose in our
own time? Can it be done at all in an education system which
remains 'exclusive' and not 'national'? Or to put it another way,
can we not begin by accepting the nation, and rooting our
schools and colleges in that acceptance, instead of endlessly
improving the amenities and efficiencies of an élite system? And
is this so impossible; is it at all true, as the head-teachers say,
that the working class (three-quarters of the 'nation') bring
nothing of their own to meet the cultural inheritance? Are they
so 'new', so raw, so blank?

It is not only in education that this line of questions is being
posed. Since the war there has been a whole wealth of documentation of the most stringent nature to refreshen our sense of what
working-class life can offer, and to sharpen our discriminations

[1] Arnold, M., *Culture & Anarchy,* p. 30–1.

in accepting or refusing aspects of it.[1] Two and a half centuries of urban life have established distinct styles of living with very real values of their own, values which are perhaps essential to civilization, and yet which do not flourish that strongly in other reaches of society. Of course working-class life has its limits, its distortions, its raw and ugly patches; and since research has been heavily weighted in favour of abnormality and delinquency we are not short of the record. But as a society are we in any position to neglect our inherited stores of strength, or to obliterate them?

'Obliteration' can be so quick and potent in a technological society; the past can so speedily be lost. The mass media, the central planning office, the bulldozer, are characteristic instruments. So much can be changed so very quickly; mistakes can be so rapid and vast. For instance, when building in brick became more widespread after the great fire of London in 1666 it took many years to alter the face of England and the kind and quality of life that went with it. But a national programme of council estates changes England in a very short time, and again it is more than the landscape that is changed: it is the fineness or crudity of social life. Much of the best work of recent sociology has been directed towards the possibilities of 'inheritance' between the squalid acres of industrial housing and the new estates we now can build. For the same spirit which dismisses working-class life in schools, which evades it in print with a too-simple 'nostalgic!' or 'tribal!' also permits the planning of huge estates and cities in utter ignorance or defiance of the fact that men and women had a way of living before the planners arrived: a way distinct from the planners' own. Others have seen this spirit at work in hospitals, hostels, old people's homes. All that ordinary living might offer is treated as a blank: on this blank we build the Institution.[2] The manifest sources of aid in established family and communal life are squandered. A similar critique must be made of education.

[1] For example: Williams, W. M. *Gosforth;* Mogey, J. M. *Family & Neighbourhood;* Hoggart, R. *Uses of Literacy;* Frankenberg, R. *Village on the Border;* Townsend, P. *Family Life of Old People;* Marris, P. *Widows & their Families;* Young, M. & Willmott, P. *Family & Kinship in East London,* etc. For fundamentally hostile reportage, see: Kerr, M. *Ship Street;* Dennis, N., Henriques, F., Slaughter, C. *Coal is Our Life.*
[2] See Townsend, P. 'The Institution and the Individual' and Turner, M. *Forgotten Men.*

Some Notes on Education and the Working Class

The educational system we need is one which accepts and develops the best qualities of working-class living, and brings these to meet our central culture. Such a system must partly be *grown* out of common living, not merely imposed on it. But before this can begin, we must put completely aside any early attempts to select and reject to rear an élite. They will be the richer and the finer for having come up another way. This does not mean that we overlook the unequal abilities of children. But it does mean that, instead of accepting and reinforcing the environmental limitations, we try to share education with an equality that we have not yet attained. Nothing like this is possible in the present system.

We have come to that place where we must firmly accept the life of the majority and where we must be bold and flexible in developing the new forms—the 'open' school which belongs to the neighbourhood, the 'open' university which involves itself in local life rather than dominates or defies it from behind college or red-brick walls.[1] The first practical step is to abandon selection at 11, and accept the comprehensive principle. An alteration by Parliament is needed to touch off local experiment and flexibility in making new 'forms' within the comprehensive *principle*. No one would wish to see monster comprehensive schools blue-printed up and down the country. They have their place, but there are many other ways, and much still to be discovered. The local variety of English education is, and should remain a strength, within the new principle.[2] Of course this would not solve everything. Social inheritance and deprivation would not be abolished with the abolition of selection and rejection. Social pressures would still be at work, and the middle class child, for

[1] The concept of the 'open' university entails a large new working-class intake. One reaction to this may be the 'more will be worse' cry: extending university education will lower the general standard in an impossible way. Perhaps it still needs to be said that this is not what has happened in previous expansions or in other countries. More entrants have *raised* the standard, when a large number of highly-gifted students have come in to join the many moderately gifted but highly-born students already there. Some evidence for this is summarized in Wolfle, D. *America's Resources of Specialized Talent*. Other American work, such as Warner W. L., Havinghurst, R. J., and Loch, M. B. *Who shall be Educated?* and White, R. C. *These will go to College* bears upon the general themes raised here.

[2] For fuller discussion of comprehensive schools, and for thoughts on variety within the system, see: Pedley, R., *Comprehensive Education,* and Simon, B. *The Common Secondary School.*

example, would do as well as ever (and one hopes, even better). But a huge amount would be achieved by shared schooling in a 'national' society, and the way to richer progress at last opened.

*   *   *

This has been a difficult book to write. A venture largely into territory very little known, and a venture quite outside the usual bounds. No doubt we have made our mistakes. The survey and the notes lie open to judgment: raising more questions than they answer. We have written, candidly, from out of Marburton itself, and out of a large debt to grammar school education, and to those before us who made that schooling possible. And yet we hope our voice is the voice of the last grammar school generations: for something better can be done. State education is a very wonderful, but still very young experiment. These are only the first stages, and it would be hard if we were to rigidify here; and the most enormous waste if that intelligent openness which properly belongs to 'culture' were to recoil beneath the inevitable academic and social pressures, turning softly back to enclose the chosen—but reflecting to most people no more than a hard, excluding shell.

Appendix 1

FURTHER RESEARCH

We believe that much more research is urgently needed into the social nature and consequences of education at every level. Particularly we feel more needs to be known about the experience and needs of working-class people, in order that the next stages of education, the 'open' school and the 'open' university of our discussion, can include them. If good fieldwork were available there is surely no reason why it should not be used in the planning of new schools and colleges, and it seems to us (for example) an opportunity wasted that sociology has not been used in the design of the new universities. There is so much to do in opening education to the working class that we feel no need to be specific or narrow in our suggestions. Regular comparative surveys are needed from 'outside', plus the methodical collection of data *within* the system by local authorities and schools. But this can hardly be done unless we find more money for educational *research**, and it surely demands the establishment of a field research unit in the Ministry. Should this work be left to isolated individuals who come to feel that something must be done, and discover a way of doing it?

Just as further research needs to concentrate on educational deprivations felt by the working class, so it also ought to attend closely to deprivations felt by women. Of course the two are (to a limited extent) related—but it is generally true to say that we have one educational system for women and another for men. Several times in this Marburton study we have taken trouble to disentangle the two skeins—right from the opening stage when we found difficulty in getting enough girls for our sample! Again and again we touched on the under-education of even very highly-gifted girls. Small details give some sense of the discrepancies between the education of boys

---

* In 1959, it is estimated by Sir Cyril Burt (*Brit. J. Educ. Psychol.*, Nov. 1960), we spent £50,000 on educational research of all kinds. That is to say 0·008% of the total expenditure on education: an interesting figure to set alongside industrial research.

and the education of girls. Between 1955 and 1960, Marburton maintained its very prominent place in English education by winning 100 State Scholarships to universities from its four grammar schools. Of these 83 were awarded to boys and only 18 to girls. It seems that this kind of detail can be repeated again and again, locally and nationally. Is this a satisfactory situation? Is it not time we had fuller knowledge.

Thirdly, we feel that much would be gained in the future development of the system if more were known about the teachers themselves. There are very simple utilitarian reasons for this. For example, we ought to know more about the kind of teachers who give the longest service in schools. This known, the training courses could perhaps be designed in some part to attract these people especially. Much of our shortage of teachers—that king-pin of any future advance—might be relieved if we knew *which* teachers gave fullest service. But our own interest does not stop there, important though this administrative level is. We are impressed by the peculiarly in-breeding nature of education: like a machine that manufactures its own spare parts. This obviously has advantages in handing on traditions of teaching knowledge entrapped within the profession. (Which connects with our previous point, for it seems as if much teaching 'knowledge' is entrapped within the *male* profession: men teach boys, women teach girls—and the discrepancies between the sexes are heightened). But it may also make for rigidity and an unthinking complacency. More than once we have remarked on how teachers are the prisoners of their own social assumptions, and felt that it was altogether good that education should be scrutinized from the 'outside'. But little is known, and the whole subject needs opening up. Who are our teachers? What habits and values do they bring to their work?

Finally, as a very small gesture towards encouraging more research in education, we found time to do a handful of interviews on the theme of 'early leaving', and this we print only as a suggestive 'starter' to others. There was a dramatic report on *Early Leaving* in 1954, which included a plea for fuller work on the question. It is hard to know whom the plea was addressed to. Certainly very little was done about it. Certainly too, the report (fine though it was) belonged to what we call the 'unpleasant medicine' tradition, and it too often defined the problems in an antique and unreal way. The forgotten fact is that when good places are available in good schools people will always fill them. Much that concerned the committee has solved itself since: the report showed that the proportion of grammar school children leaving before their 16th birthday had been dropping steadily. This trend still continues, as the following figures show:

Appendix

Age	Number	Per Cent	Leavers
14 in 1949	100,606	100%	18·1%
15 in 1950	82,411	81·9%	
14 in 1952	96,204	100%	11·4%
15 in 1952	85,227	88·6%	
14 in 1958	106,730	100%	4·2%
15 in 1958	102,281	95·8%	

* Calculations supplied by Simon Pratt.

The general educational standard is rising. Now we can talk about
'early leaving' at 16 or 17, instead of 15. But the problem we need to
solve is *not* one of equal advance, not one of a stratified society moving,
in step, upwards. We need to know more about how the huge
working-class population can be *released* into education, and about
how the whole system can be better built at its basis. Peripheral
reforms are all very well, but they must clearly be seen as peripheral.
A study of 'early leaving' might well help us define and resolve a part
of these basic questions, might help us see ways of opening education
equally to the working-class. Perhaps the following small sketch will
help a little to stimulate research bearing upon this discussion. The
method is again retrospective, in order to get the full adult view.
The aim, once more, is to enrich understanding of the social processes
of education, not to provide facts and figures about the immediately
contemporary situation.

Early Leaving
We had plotted on a map of Marburton with coloured pins the
distribution of our successful grammar school pupils. Immediately
large areas of the city were distinguished by their success rates.
Broadbank and Millcross, Woodleigh and Edgefield—'nice residential
areas'—were thickly clustered with pins. Not so the city centre,
where the oldest primary schools in the district still served a population
living in corporation houses built close under the gas-works, along
the by-pass and around the ventilation chimneys of the railway
tunnel. The doctors and well-to-do businessmen had left the district
years ago. Families from here were being rehoused in overspill
estates on the city's edges, but there were few pins on any of these
new estates either.

This was partly a question of the age of the people living in different
districts of the city, but not completely so. The perceptive middle

class parents had shunned such schools as Carthorpe on the pre-war estate and Railway Street in the city centre. So had the more knowledgeable working-class parents like Mrs. Hornby. 'No, I never fancied Railway Street. It *is* the nearest I know, but somehow—I think it was a bit of snobbishness—I always preferred Manor Road.' And the teachers at grammar school would not welcome Railway Street parents, as they had Mrs. Batley when they found out that her daughter had been to Woodleigh, with, 'Ah yes, we always get a good class of child from that school.' For, once at grammar school, the children from Carthorpe and Railway Street were expelled, or they developed behaviour problems, or they slipped into the 'C' streams and left with only a poor G.C.E., or none at all.

We decided to glance over the situation of working-class children who 'abandon' grammar school through such bad behaviour or low attainment. And instead of drawing a sample from the 'C' streams, there seemed everything to be gained by starting from the other end with the local community. We were aware that 'successful' working-class children came on the whole from the 'middle-class' primary schools. Primary schools unleavened in this way had much weaker records. This might show in the smallness of their eleven plus results—though not necessarily so; it certainly stood out when the children's careers were traced up to 18. We therefore had a look at Carthorpe and Railway Street as two 'unsuccessful' districts, yet with certain contrasts. Again we went for a small number of interviews in order to catch the tang of individual human situations (there is after all the official report on the general problem), and taking two relatively successful classes found ourselves with the names of 15 pupils who had gone to grammar school. There were five non-contacts, and we also saw all but three parents. This gave us 22 interviews; ten with children and 12 with parents.

'Refusing' grammar school places

The Education Authority suggested that the rate of refusal of grammar school places was negligible, and the most pessimistic estimate was 5%, given to us by the outgoing educational psychologist. But there were other ways of 'refusing' grammar school places. The mother of one of the Railway Street children (she had five sons and five daughters) had been quite prepared to let her children go to Oxford if they won their way through. But, 'The lad was at home with me when the exam. were on, so he never took it. I were poorly in bed, and then the lass, she'd been off school—it were the same, I'd been poorly in bed again—and they sent for her to take her exam. Well, it was ridiculous. They came across from the school and said that the exam. were on and could she go in for it. She were very clever too and she'd probably have passed. All her friends were surprised because she hadn't passed to go to grammar school because she were cleverer nor them, but she'd been away three month and her mind weren't on it—it were silly her going really.' By the time the boy on our sample came along there were enough older children in the family to run the house, and the school had not quite lost the art of getting children through to grammar school.

This was one leakage which would not show up separately in any official figures. A much more significant bypassing of the grammar school stream was the creaming-off of girls by the 'commercial' school, Howard Court. The Authority gave us the I.Q. ratings for all the children who passed the selection exam. from Railway Street in 1943. The *top* six girls chose to go to Howard Court, and only the two girls at the *bottom* of the list chose grammar school. There were two boys qualified to go to grammar school who chose the technical secondary school instead. These were in effect *refusals* of grammar school places.

School record of children on the 'Early Leavers' sample

Out of the twelve children on our sample one boy was expelled, three boys and one girl left grammar school before taking School Certificate or G.C.E., four boys and two girls left immediately after these examinations; and only one girl stayed on into the sixth form to take a rather poor Advanced G.C.E. which got her to training college. All four boys from Railway Street were very troublesome to the authorities, and there was talk of expelling a further two of them. They were placed in low streams. Of the ten available instances three were immediately put into 'B' forms and seven into 'C' classes.

Their brothers and sisters did little better. There were eight brothers and 14 sisters. Out of these four went to grammar school, three to the 'commercial' school at Howard Court, and 15 to secondary modern schools.

One girl breaks the pattern of 'early leaving' described above. Pamela Royal, who stayed on and went to training college, was the only child of a skilled manual worker. At the time of the interview he had become a smallholder. He knew little of his daughter's education, and remarked that if it had been left to him she would not have gone to training college. But his wife was typical of the sunken middle-class families we had met earlier. She was the daughter of a self-made businessman, and had herself been sent to Thorpe Manor—although she had refused to become a teacher as her father had wished. She arrived from a committee meeting, smartly groomed, made-up and well dressed, and took charge of the interview straight away. 'Oh yes. I was on the Parent/Teachers Committee at Ash Grange. You see at the time I was leader of the Women's Liberal Association and I ran the Darby and Joan Club and I was on this and that, and I think it's very important for the child to be represented at these functions. I think the teachers take more notice of them. We went to everything. Whenever they had a speech day we went, and if there was a school trip we saw to it that Pamela was on it.' This might easily have been an established middle-class parent speaking. There was an absolute confidence in her child's right to a grammar school education, and a determination that she should not be overlooked on the competitive inside of the grammar school. Pamela moved into Carthorpe School from another district at the age of eight and never settled down. It was doubtful if she would pass the eleven plus, but in fact she passed well and reached the 'A' stream at Ash Grange. Once there, after she had 'decided' to become a school teacher all was plain sailing.

The parents of the 'early leavers'

The parents of these successful eleven plus candidates were an interesting mixture (Table XXIV). Mr. Adams was middle class and the only dominant father ('Ted was a very strict man, very strict. In fact in some ways I think he was too strict. . . . there'd have been no leaving school if he'd been alive. She'd have been pushed too'). Ten other families came from the upper working class, and Mr. Firth, a boilerman, would be graded as a semi-skilled workman. Even here children of unskilled workers were remarkable by their absence, and it may be that such children actually have a better chance in the 'middle class' primary schools than they do in their native neighbourhoods. Six of the families belonged to the sunken middle class, (Table XXV), and Douglas Banks's father was a foreman. And it turned out that Mr. Firth, the boilerman, had himself passed his 'scholarship' examination, but had been unable to go (Table XXVI).

Except in the instance of Mary Adams, the mother had been the forceful personality behind grammar school education. Indeed we only managed to see three of the husbands, and the illustration here is generally through the women's eyes. They felt they lived in small enclaves of respectability. Those in older houses treated the estates or massed corporation housing along neighbouring streets as foreign territory. Their conversation looked backwards to the old village of Carthorpe. 'There's been some big changes around here, mostly for the worst. This was the old part of the village, and it wasn't until Donald was a little boy that they started building over there, the big estate then it's gone down a lot.' Those in old housing near the city centre recalled the former 'respectability' of the Railway Street school, where three of them had been pupils themselves. Mrs. Stevens remembered, 'I went to Railway Street, love, same as Ronnie. It was a very good school in those days, a very good school, and lots of children from business people in the town were educated in that school.'

Meanwhile those who lived on the estate were conscious of being slightly 'better' than their neighbours; or if not better, alien in their ways. Two of these families have now moved into their own homes, and another is planning such a move. The boilerman had removed a few years back to the 'half crown quarter', a slightly better part of the estate. Those who remained were particularly sensitive to rougher neighbours, and this led to semi-isolation. 'Mind, it's a bit rough down here. There's a lot here like to go t'club on a Saturday night. I hear them coming back singing, but it's never appealed to me hasn't that. Do you know, I've lived down here for twenty five years now, and I've never been into anybody's house yet. Well to me it's only idle gossip is that. And there's him next door, he's shocking. Shouts and carries on and doesn't care what he says either. Well, I'm ashamed for him sometimes. I'm not bothered for myself you know, but if anybody comes I've to apologise for him. I'm right embarrassed.' Isolation and difference spread over into work. Some were conscious of their superior abilities at the side of workmates and management, and two even spoke of a kind of 'victimization' in which they were 'kept down' or had acute ideas rejected. Altogether they were cut off, outward turning, and in many respects they resembled parents we had interviewed before. If their children had gone into the sixth form and university, perhaps these parents too would have appeared knowledgeable about grammar school. They might have been able to point to grammar school as an important area of their lives. As it was, grammar school remained an ideal; that which might have been. The expressions of this outward-turning ambition were slight, unformulated and not defined as a thirst for knowledge or a practical belief in grammar school as an entry to the higher professions. 'It's always been me that's wanted them to go to grammar school. My husband left everything to me. All the decisions and all the going to see the teachers. I thought how nice it would be—you know how you are when you're a mother and people are always asking you where your children go to school—and I'd be able to say, "Oh, my children go to Abbeyford".' And even this slight ambition was further diffused by other worries: a husband who 'liked the women', or one who would not save, or who was an invalid. 'I had five to look after. My mind wasn't on it. You try your best but you can't really have the same interest in them.' Two of the fathers were invalids; one father was missing altogether.

Fathers who had been hostile to grammar school had previously kept out of the way during interviews, or, wise after the event, had played down their original hostility. But in these interviews such fathers came more into the foreground, feeling they had been proved right. Wives felt uneasily that their husbands' lack of interest had held the children back. In a way these working-class fathers resembled, at a different social level, the middle-class fathers who had not wanted to send their children to a new kind of school: only this time they were poised between modern and technical schools or the grammar school. There was the same sense of a barrier just above their reach— a class barrier which they were reluctant to penetrate. Such attitudes are the direct antithesis of the 'Conservative' working man's desire for his children to 'speak nicely' and 'mix with nicer people'. For Mr. Clough such mixing was not only undesirable but virtually unattainable. 'There always will be three classes and you can't mix 'em. It's practically impossible for t'working man to get out o't'working class, practically impossible. I mean if he won a lot of brass, if he won £75,000 he might buy himself into t'upper class eventually, because that's all that counts is brass up there, but it'd take a long time because they'd be able to spot him. He wouldn't be able to shed his habits and t'way he spoke—which is t'only genuine way o'speaking to my way o'thinking, tha knows; all t'others sound affected to me. All these elocution lessons is trying to be summat tha isn't.'

There was on our sample not a man who had won the pools, but a skilled workman from a council estate who had been lucky in getting a partnership in a growing firm and had become prosperous with the business. He had preserved his affiliation with the working class, and since his success had come late in life without any form of secondary education whatsoever, he had no respect for education. He behaves just as Mr. Clough said he would have done. When we called at his bungalow in a fashionable part of the city he was never in, and his wife said we could not see him because he would not be interested in anything outside his work. She showed us proudly the washable plastic hydrangeas—a more expensive version of a popular Woolworth's line. In the front room was a complete bar with stools, coloured lights and bottles of wines and spirits, the scene of frequent parties. Yet this too, in its way, was only a larger version of the 'cocktail cabinet' which some working-class housewives had substituted in their front rooms for the customary display cabinet. Mr. Burgess would indulge himself in small ways; by buying too many shirts, or by not cancelling the newspapers when he went on holiday. He had kept his membership of the estate working men's club where he was a regular visitor, 'treating' everybody frequently. 'I don't suppose he knows above three people round here. He prefers Glossop Road where he used to live before. Every time we walk down Glossop Road he says he likes it. He says, "It *draws* me".' Mr. Burgess had been away in the forces when his two sons went to grammar school. When he came back he was consistently hostile and unhelpful.

With this close, neighbourhood life of the men went a 'strictness' which had a Victorian ring about it. These men were masters in their own homes, either demanding that their wives should keep the children in order or holding a stern rule themselves. 'I'll tell you what I think. I think that since t'war the've played up this children job too much and t'children's taken advantage of it. I were brought up wi't'boot and t'fist in my young day, but nowadays you can't touch 'em.' And Mrs. Murgatroyd's husband agreed: 'If he had it to do again he wouldn't send her because he thinks that it made her cheeky.' One son summed up these fathers as 'the hard core of the working class', and certainly—for a type which literature would have us think is dying out—they exhibit a remarkable vitality and tenacity in clinging to older modes of life. The opportunity of state education dragged divisions of sympathy between a working-class man and his wife to the surface. Mrs. Ackroyd's husband had been a handyman, well-known in the district and well-liked, but he had been improvident, both for himself and for his children. His widow's picture of him at a distance of ten years was streaked with bitterness, as she saw more and more clearly the way in which her husband had, as she thought, blocked her children's chances. 'My eldest boy passed to go to grammar school, and I played pop with him because he wouldn't go, but I think it was because of his father. I don't want to say anything about him—he's dead now, died ten years ago—but he didn't show any interest in his children. He were one o'them that were all for himself, and he drank a bit an'all you know, and somehow he didn't seem to help 'em like a father should. Our Margaret passed to go to Ash Grange but she went to Howard Court. That were her father's doing. It were my fault as well. I blame myself a lot now when I see her and see how she's having to work even though she's getting older. I think what a shame it is. As the years go by, I think more and more how she'd have liked to be a teacher.'

It was more than a single clash of personalities. It was a different way of life, the man more in contact with the neighbourhood, more concerned with the immediate, everyday affairs on the estate; perhaps more at ease in the 'local' with his friends than at home with his wife and children. 'I first met him when we were dancing and he were all right then. He were all right for the first few years of our married life until he started drinking. He's more of a one for t'local, but he wouldn't go in a crowded room either. He liked to stand at t'bar. He used to say, "Come down some night. Have an hour," and I used to go once or twice. Anything for a quiet life, but when I got there I'd be sitting in a crowded room and he wouldn't be there. He'd be at t'bar, and I used to wish I'd never gone.' But as Mrs. Ackroyd spoke the harsh outlines of her description were softened. 'Mind he were all right with people outside, my husband. If there was anybody out o'work he'd bring 'em in and give 'em a meal, give 'em a couple o'weeks' work. And he were that way outside, he were t'friendliest man out, but inside he were strict, too strict I thought. I think he ruled 'em too hard. It's no good that, is it? He should have looked after his own. He'd educated himself and he used to like to talk, you know. I remember once he sat up all night arguing about Russia, and what things were like in Russia, and he were interested in astronomy an'all. He used to be leaning out of his bedroom window all hours o't'night wi' Margaret, but somehow he didn't seem to *help*.'

If a child went to grammar school from one of these homes it was almost in a fit of absent-mindedness on the father's part. Mr. Clough let his eldest daughter, Phyllis, slip by. But: 'I wasn't having any more like t'first one. I'd enough wi' one at Ash Grange. You had to give her sixpence to speak to her. I wasn't going to let 'em ruin t'others an'all.' He sent the others to Howard Court. It was only because Mrs. Clough had died that we got to see Mr. Clough. For the first time we met someone who was actively hostile to grammar schools— to the point of refusing to allow his daughters to go to one. About his conversation there was a Victorian distrust of the 'blue stocking'. 'A girl's an unknown quantity tha knows. A girl's a very unstable thing. She might go on until she's 25 and then, like that!—she gets married. Now *you* know that seven out of ten girls, secretly, at t' bottom of 'em want to get married. There might be three out o'that ten that wants to be career women, but tha never can tell. There's Joe Hargreaves down at our place, spent £1,000 on his girl's education and she went straight out when she was 21 and got married. She's never used it a bit. She were a teacher, and he's fair sickened over that job he is. And then you see if she's a career woman she'll go on and she'll go on until she's perhaps 25 and she'll be doing right well, and then all of a sudden she'll realise that she's been left on t'shelf, and she'll get a vinegary outlook on life.'

There was a strictly practical aspect to Mr. Clough's hostility. Grammar school he thought, had given his daughter nothing but an irritating 'middle-class' polish. He preferred the girl as she had or might have been. And from his point of view a grammar school education was a *handicap* since it narrowed the range of possible jobs. His mind naturally turned to well-paid and skilled work in the woollen mills, but this was precisely the range of employment that Ash Grange had taught her she must not consider ('That's all they learn 'em—how to be snobs'). His daughter objected to his swearing and he was quick to taunt her as 'the Ash Grange lady'. He saw more clearly than most parents what an unsettling impact grammar school could have on a child from an estate. 'Tha can't *afford* to send t'lasses to t'grammar schools. Tha sends 'em and when they come back they're no good to y'. They don't want a mucky job even if that's where t'brass is. They won't look at it!' He had not withdrawn Phyllis, who was protected from his scorn by her mother. But Phyllis herself decided to leave grammar school before taking her G.C.E.; for at school she found herself just as disturbed by the atmosphere as her father said—and it is immaterial whether he was being wise after the event here. What emerges is that under the prevailing conditions he was right in thinking that central schools would unsettle his daughters less, and provide them more cheaply with a means of earning their living. Whether the 'unsettling' was valuable in itself is arguable. Mr. Clough had the tenable viewpoint that it was not, and his choice of school for his younger daughters emerges as less self-interested than it appears on the surface.

Politics

The parent's political views reflected markedly these class boundaries and enclosed feelings of impotence in the face of higher powers. There was support for all three parties, and two non-voters, but underlying such differing political attitudes there was the feeling that politics were in a mess. Government was in the hands of the wrong people, and the whole business was so abstract that it was very difficult to know what to do. In these circumstances one might wash ones hands of the whole business and not vote at all, as many of the women and two of the men felt inclined to do. Or, in the mass of puzzling complications, one might cling to the familiar and well-tried.

So the women told us that they voted Labour like their husbands. 'Oh aye, his father were always a Labour man. They're all Labour round here, although I can never weigh politics up. They always say that Labour's for t'working class, but I sometimes wonder whether they are. I don't think they bother much do you?' Mr. Royal voted

Liberal in an attempt to break up the power nexus: most of the men voted Labour in the hope that 'they' would give the power back to 'us'. 'T'only way I can see 'em getting back in is like 1945. They let 'em get in then to clear t'mess up, and then when they'd got things going properly they took things over, took it off 'em.'

There were no floating voters among these parents. Their sense of where the power lay in society was too strong, even though their solutions as to its redistribution were varied. If there was a floating tendency it was a kind of despair with the whole business. Things were in a mess but you *had* to do something. A quasi-religious impulsion drove the professed 'non-voter' in spite of family tensions. 'Well, politics, love, is a thing that my husband and me never discuss. We're not interested and we've not discussed it with anybody. I don't think it's any good do you? And we're not people who vote, my husband and me. We never vote because my husband says that whoever gets in they're both the same—they're only after what they can get for themselves. I'm a Liberal. I work for the W.V.S. and I've been out working for the Liberal women, I go round canvassing sometimes. I think that politics is like religion. It's no good talking to people, because you're not going to change their views and they're not going to change yours. I wouldn't go round again. I only went up to the doors and knocked and asked if they were prepared to give their vote, and if they said no I just said thank you, and I walked away. I wasn't prepared to say anything. One of my neighbours came and we used to put crosses on houses that we hadn't been to. We daren't go. You don't like people to know what you are do you, not in your own district, and some people don't like you knowing what they are, so it's embarrassing.'

Two sunken middle-class families followed the pattern of isolation and Conservative voting described before (chapter 3).

The 'early leavers'

Such then were the homes and parents of the 'early leavers'. Some homes were aspiring, uneasy and intellectually stimulating, with a constant drive outward and upwards from the local community. In others there was only mild encouragement, even hostility, little advice and a strong sense of fixed class boundaries blocking any rise through grammar school. There was, also, a wide range of attainment among the children at primary school. Pamela Royal and the sons of a foreman and a sunken middle-class mother only scraped through to grammar school. All the other children had been in the A class or the group of children who were promoted a term early. They passed without fuss. Yet, with the possible exception of Pamela Royal, the children's school careers were remarkably similar in their unrest and small success. These children were not withdrawn by their parents. Except for the expulsion they decided to leave of their own accord. They all wanted to leave, which is not to say that they would have been allowed to stop on. Where there was encouragement from parents— and we must see what this encouragement meant in practice—the only apparent difference was that children stopped on to take School Certificate or G.C.E., rather than leaving at the minimum legal age. When they insisted on leaving, parents were too weary or disappointed to drive them any further.

Why did these children leave, when their home backgrounds repeated so exactly those of other working-class children who were eventually successful at grammar school? With one voice the 'early leavers', puzzled and resentful, threw out incident after incident which relived that shock of the first impact of grammar school. All the boys from Railway Street, irrespective of family background or chosen grammar school, ran into the same continual clash with the school authorities. Carthorpe children were quieter, easier to handle, and the connecting thread there was fear, loss of confidence, and the inability to recapture the intimate relationship with the teachers which they had enjoyed at Carthorpe. We must be careful here not to repeat experiences which are documented elsewhere in the book. But we might just recall that what characterized the children who rebelled against school authority was a close identification with school *work*, and the parents' backing of the child *against* authority. What we have to trace in the Carthorpe and Railway Street children is why they were unable to pursue their school work in this same spirit.

The children and parents were more a part of their surroundings than they knew. Among themselves they differed, but this was marginal compared with families from around Edgefield and Wood-leigh. Carthorpe and Railway Street mothers tried to keep their children from playing with the 'rougher element' a few streets away, but their ideas of respectability were all contained within local standards which to an outsider would seem rough enough. In part the claim to live in a quiet area of the city centre or estate was an expression of defensive solidarity against outside opinion, an expression of community even—the rough part of any city is never just here, where the interviewer is asking questions. Professor Sprott coined the phrase 'delinquescent society' for these districts where not only the behaviour is different, but the standards by which misbehaviour is judged are themselves very different. Mrs. Stevens spoke from within such standards when she said, 'I'm not saying anything about behaviour. When our Ronnie was little he wasn't an angel by any means, but if anybody came to the door it wasn't about cheek. It was only to collect money for a broken window like any boy does.' The very fact that parents had sent their children to Railway Street, when nearby there was the highly successful Millcross primary school, demonstrated how far they were enclosed by local value judgments. Even after a lapse of 20 years Mrs. Burgess could not see what was wrong with Railway Street where she had sent her sons. 'There's a lot of people round here, they'll send their kids to Edgefield, even though it's an awful trail. I say it's just snobbery is that. It sounds better if they say they go to Edgefield School.'

As the children played in the streets near the estates or in areas which parents had carefully circumscribed, they did come into close contact with neighbours' children. 'I mixed in all right, although they did call me "professor". I could fight. I could meet them on their own terms. I didn't play games but in the sort of language they understood I was on even terms.' On even terms, and yet by virtue of a slightly superior background and intelligence, part of the primary school 'establishment'. By Railway Street and Carthorpe standards they were well behaved, and since they had outstripped the rest of the pupils in their school work they were made into monitors, called upon to do responsible little jobs about the school like filling the aquarium from a local mill dam, or fetching back boys who had run away from school. In the quieter atmosphere of Carthorpe, children had been particularly close to their teachers. This had seemed the ideal school. 'I idolised the teachers there. There was one man especially that all the girls idolised, and there was one woman teacher that all the boys idolised, and we all used to think that these two would get married. We used to talk about it in the yard. Well, you couldn't imagine us being bothered like that about teachers at Ash Grange now, could you?' Unlike the more successful primary schools, Carthorpe and Railway Street were co-educational and largely staffed by women teachers. There was none of that sterner atmosphere of the 'Big Boys' section, where men teachers used the stick freely and the pace of work quickened as strictness of discipline intensified. The 'early leavers' all commented on what good teachers they had. A slower boy who had been kept down after the first year at grammar school said feelingly, 'At primary school if you couldn't understand anything and you were lagging behind the class, the teachers were good enough to come to you and spend the extra time with you and explain things so that you could be up to the standard of the class. Then they'd take the *whole* class along at a faster speed so that you could catch up and they'd keep all together.' What Railway Street boys remembered was the fairness of the discipline. When they spoke of trouble it was as if they had never been aware that there was such a thing until they got to grammar school. 'Trouble' had been a natural part of life. 'I sometimes got into trouble and perhaps I got caned for it, but that was the end of it. It wasn't held against you. You weren't always *expected* to get into trouble like I was later. The teachers down there seemed to know how to handle this kind of children. I don't know whether they'd done it for a long time, or whether they knew the district well or what it was, but they seemed to be able to accept them and to teach them.' The selection examination had approached so quietly that the children had hardly thought about it.

The impact of grammar school

Grammar school brought them into an alien world. 'It seemed to be left foot forward all the time. It was as if they'd got a mould and they were putting all those children into this mould; but me, I seemed independent minded and that created all kinds of bother.' This might not have been as bad if the children had managed to absorb the work at school. But the slow broader pace of primary school had not accustomed them to the speed of the first few months of grammar school. 'I think they should have made allowances, they should have given us time to get adjusted and got used to the new conditions. It was all right for some boys. We got talking when we'd been there for a while and you got us children from Carthorpe and Railway Street, and there were one or two from Woodleigh, and we were comparing notes and it seemed that it wasn't so much different for them. We were talking about schools and they said that the grammar school wasn't much different from their old school, but for us it was completely different. You can't imagine.'

The first plunge into testing and streaming had a demoralising effect. Two of the boys had illnesses which kept them away for trifling periods. 'When I first went to school I was keen on the work. They put me in the B stream and I had some trouble with my ears, and when I came back everybody seemed so far ahead it was a terrific blow to my pride, even in such a short time as three weeks they'd got so far ahead with subjects like algebra, and I didn't seem to know anything. And I think after that I decided that I wasn't going to be in it.' When they emerged from this first shuffling these top children from their primary schools were all in B or C streams. Two of the boys from Carthorpe were kept down at the end of the first year; they noticed that higher up the school the same thing was happening, and all Carthorpe children were a year out of step. One boy worked strenuously at the bottom of his form, struggling with lengthy homework for the first three years at school until he decided to abandon it for outside activities.

The two other boys in B streams clung there by eking out their own homework with copied work from other boys. By this means an intelligent child could hang on and gain sufficient marks in the exams, but he could rise no higher.

The less assertive children suffered a permanent loss of confidence. Mary Adams was typical of Carthorpe. 'The happiest time of my schooldays was that time at Carthorpe. I liked Ash Grange—don't get me wrong—I wasn't unhappy there, but I felt more at home at Carthorpe. I fitted in better. I was always very quiet at Ash Grange. I never offered anything. You know, in some subjects like English where the teacher asks your opinion quite often I knew what I wanted to say, but I'd never speak up and say anything. I seemed to lose all my confidence. It wasn't that I was like that outside. I was all right outside and I'd been all right at Carthorpe. One thing that you noticed at Ash Grange, it was a different class of people that went there. You noticed that as soon as you got there, quite different from Carthorpe. And I didn't seem to get on with the teachers except one. One of them you could laugh and joke with, but the others, I didn't seem to be able to get on with them.' Later on she and Phyllis Clough improved their positions until they were promoted into the A stream after three years, but they were never comfortable at school. Why did these girls in the A stream leave school? Both of them had seen jobs which they would like, one as a typist, the other as a student teacher at an estate school. And, as a tentative suggestion, it could be that the very size of the group which rebels against authority and lasts into the sixth form is an encouragement to the doubtful working-class child to stop on. Ash Grange had no such rebel group, only individuals and Abbeyford was almost too small to contain one. It was only at Marburton College that there were enough like-minded boys to form a supporting group in the sixth form.

Most did not get within striking distance of stopping on. They had too many interests and diversions outside the school and they had never recovered from the first set-backs. The 'cocky' children from Railway Street covered up as best they could. 'I didn't realise it at the time, but it must have been a hell of a psychological step going from Railway Street to grammar school. There were all sorts of things. You found it was easier if you didn't know a thing to let on that you did know. You didn't tell anybody that you didn't know, otherwise you'd have been ridiculed. You'd lose a lot of status. And homework. Well, I never did any homework. That was a big step and after the first year or so I didn't bother with it.' This was obviously a situation which would get worse and worse. And endemic in it were mis-understandings such as the one which, David Burgess said, started his 'inferiority complex'. In one lesson the teacher was a Jewish, half-caste woman. 'We were doing some heavy stuff, you know, some Shakespeare job reading round the class, and all of a sudden we got to a bit, you know how it is when you're lads. Things make you laugh then that don't make you laugh when you're grown up. You hear a lot of dirty jokes and you come across odd words that you think are funny. I can't remember what it was, but in Shakespeare you do get the odd word don't you, sexual words. What comes to mind is "The left pap of Pyramus". Well we came to this bit and I burst out laughing.' From this grew a major incident and the boy was caned for seeming anti-Semitic, although he hardly knew what a Jew was. 'I wouldn't have cried in the normal way. I never did cry when he hit me, but I did cry that time. I'd have told him anything then but he just wouldn't listen.' Ever afterwards he had to stand out in front of the school in assembly, marked out as a potential wrongdoer. He left without taking School Certificate.

Some parents were not even aware that their children were major problems at school since half of them never went to the school. 'We took them to school on the first day and they spoke to us about it and they said that if anything was wrong they'd send us a letter and tell us, and we never had any complaints about Dick.' But there were other parents, over-eager for their children to get on at school. Some of these fathers and mothers were particularly tough, well-equipped for any interviews with school teachers—they did not complain that their children were unknown to the school authorities; Railway Street children made themselves felt in the school. And with one exception, these parents trusted the schools, and in the face of manifest bad behaviour and 'slacking' backed the authorities against the child. What would have happened to Mrs. Ackroyd's son cannot be told, since he was expelled. But in two of the other families the parents' support of the school, paradoxically, tilted the balance and determined their children to leave after School Certificate. Ronnie Stevens, the boy with ear trouble, found himself in B stream and stopped doing homework. But at the same time he was a little ashamed of this attitude and he knew his own abilities. For the first three years at school he had no grammar school friends, and streaming had taken him above the level of the other children from Railway Street. He had friends near home, but when they became apprentices and motor mechanics on leaving school he turned more and more towards working class boys at school who were against authority—the 'non-joiners'. At the turning point 'I was trying to run with the hare and hunt with the hounds and I couldn't do both. I was running with the hare down round home going out with my friends, and at the same time I couldn't be hunting with the hounds doing my homework. When I was 13 or 14 I began to take days off school. I began to play truant for days. Now that was a thing that I'd never have dreamt of doing at Railway Street.' Gradually he broke away from the Railway Street gang, and with a grudging respect for the authoritarian head of the grammar school, he settled down sufficiently to take a School Certificate good enough to base a sixth form career on.

But by the time School Certificate results came out he had left school. 'With everybody telling me that I was a failure, and that I was bound to fail and that I had no chance of passing School Certificate I'd come to believe them.' His mother had bet him ten shillings to a penny that he wouldn't pass. 'I said, "What's the use. It's only a bit of paper, anyway", so ever afterwards when I wanted him to do his homework he used to bring this up.' This parental pressure had been the deciding factor against stopping on. 'It did cross my mind, just for a fleeting moment when I got my School Cert. results, "Shall I go back to school and ask them to take me on again," but I didn't. I'd got a job for the first time in my life. I'd got a bit of independence. Nobody could tell me what to do, and they never have since. Neither bosses nor parents.' The equation of parents with bosses or school authorities illuminates the paradox. The harder the parents tried to get the boys to work by aligning themselves with the school, the more uncomfortable the boys felt. Truancy was a typical child's reaction to such tension, and leaving school provided a release from an intolerable situation. The other boy didn't play truant. He withdrew into himself, so that neither his parents nor the school authorities could make the slightest reason out of his attitudes. They pronounced him an 'introvert'.

Some of the working-class children who had stopped on at grammar school said they would have left if only they could have seen a job to go to. When we have studied this group of 'early leavers' this seems plausible, but probably untrue. Those successful grammar school children required something else to make them leave school—they were too good at their work, and they had too much vested in the school. Even, they enjoyed the clash with authority, and there were enough of them to establish a strong positive cell. The 'early leavers'' school work was not so rewarding, and the upper reaches of grammar school did not look as attractive to them. Ronnie Stevens had been repelled by the a-sexuality of school as part of its middle-class tone. 'While I was at school I used to think I was oversexed because I was thinking too much about girls, and then when I got outside I found that there were other blokes just like me. But at school there were blokes up at the top of the A forms who were almost indifferent to girls. They had almost a monastic view about women. They were celibate in a way, and I think that if I'd stopped at school that would have crossed with my way of thinking.' The fact that some children had jobs to go to and others looked for them after they left was immaterial to the central impulse to get out of school. With little encouragement, and so much uncertainty such children fell easily to any blandishments from employers.

After grammar school

The 'early leavers' had been out of grammar school for between eight and 15 years. When they left grammar school they had experienced a strong sense of relief ('Some people say to me "Weren't you sorry to leave school when you did?", but I wasn't because that was the happiest two years of my life.') They still lived in the small one-up one-down houses, or on the estates near where their primary school friends lived—still the 'real' friends even when they were at grammar school. 'At school you only seemed to get to know the surface of people. You only saw how they were at school between nine o'clock and four o'clock.' But back on the estate it was different. You went into their houses, and you saw their brothers and sisters and fathers and mothers, the lot, and you knew all about them. They were a different kind of friend if you see what I mean.' The 'early leavers' ' fear of the teachers and loneliness at grammar school contrast so harshly with the warmth of friendships around home that leaving school might appear a point of return. Their school work was so bad that further studies seemed out of the question, and the qualifications that they had won at grammar school only equipped them for minor laboratory jobs or clerical posts.

What happened when they left school, and what 'traces' remain of their grammar school education? Although these boys and girls had seemed ready to reject the class shift that education was imposing, their stay at grammar school had bitten too deep. They had come off the education ladder, but like many working-class boys and girls who had been unsuccessful at a higher stage of education, they *knew* this. Ten of them still lived in Marburton. They had a definite sense that Marburton belonged to its grammar schools, of which they were products. Face-to-face with the community into which they had been born, they couldn't 'forget' like the boys and girls who had left the city. Nor could they 'belong'. They rejected the values of Marburton's business class above them, and were unable to merge again into working-class life. They lived in the constriction of Marburton's student population.

The two girls who became teachers moved easily and naturally into the middle class. Training College ironed out any difficulties of manner and accent—although it could not quite remove that last trace of Marburton which helped to keep many local teachers penned in Yorkshire. Both girls married privately educated men, and Mary Adams from a strong Socialist family became a Conservative like her husband: 'I'd always thought that the Conservatives were for the people with money, and then when my father got his pension through Labour I never thought that I should ever vote for anybody else. But times change and you can't go on voting for old ideas.' For the rest of the early leavers there was many a backward glance. As they came nearer to commanding a middle-class position, the internal dialogue became more insistent. They presented in their attitudes the whole spectrum of the progress from grammar school to the 'limited success' class.

Leaving school had not meant a sudden strengthening of friendships with the working-class children they had known up to now. Rather, taking up work had placed the children immediately in different strata of employment from friends who became mill-girls, apprentices, or labourers. The 'early leavers', with two exceptions, went at first into clerical work—the post office, laboratory jobs, the family firm, and office jobs (Table XXVII). They kicked against the more middle-class aspects of the work ('There was all that Mr. and Miss business'), but they left one such job only to take up another similar. Ironically, abandoning grammar school did not mean a less close relationship with other grammar school boys, but a more intense and lasting one. 'Up to about 15 my friends seem to have been the kids who lived round me, but since 15 they've been more the friends that have been to grammar school and they've been a different kind of friendship.' Such friendships flourished through the Technical College, the local jazz or sports clubs, or nebulous groups who drifted round a small number of Marburton's 'classier' public houses. The boys who had done manual work were not content to stay in the same niche all their lives. Their energies turned to building up their own businesses painting and decorating, or a £600 Sunday newspaper round. Or they tried to regain their foothold in education by taking courses at the Technical College for an external degree or professional qualifications.

Further education

Seven of the boys had taken courses for G.C.E., or one of the craft certificates, and these further ventures into education are worth following up. For one boy, the Technical College, with a new range of subjects and a different set of teachers, had been a sudden liberation. 'It was different. I don't know how it was. Perhaps I woke up when

I went to the Tech. Perhaps I sat back one night and thought, "Well it's no bloody good my going to tech, and wasting all my nights a week if I'm going to bugger the whole job up and not pass my exam., is it?". I don't know how, but I was keen. I was very interested, and I stuck it. And look here—there was quite a big class of us when I started, and that's five years ago, and I'm the only one that's finished my Higher National Certificate out of the whole lot. In fact Tech. seems part of my life. It's led on to all kinds of things. It's been more a part of my life than school ever was.' But this was not the general experience, as the remark illustrates. Other boys tried to study, but it was a hard road to follow. And there was an unfortunate tie-up, where the masters who had taught the 'early leavers' at the grammar schools came down to the technical college in the evenings. 'I'd do a piece of work and he'd come round and look at it and he'd shout, "Rubbish!" and scrawl across it. He'd be all right to other people in the class. He'd never say anything to them.' So most of these courses dragged to a halt, or they were abandoned in favour of the correspondence course.

Formal education was by-passed in another way too. One of the markings of the 'anti-authority' group at the grammar school had been a strong assertion of the value of arts subjects, and in particular English. This had always flourished outside and against the school's teaching of the subject. And amongst the 'early leavers' we caught an echo of this, for the new grammar school friendships overlapped with boys still at school and university. 'I used to go and sit in the pub with his friends, and at first I used to be very quiet and sit in the corner and I'd listen to these blokes—great big blokes they'd seem, drinking their pints of beer, with their beards, and their bright red jumpers on—and they used to talk about things. Things like Michaelangelo, Leonardo da Vinci, T. S. Eliot. Well! I used to sit back and gasp. I'd never heard of those things. Imagine the old music master at school. All we ever got was pictures of fiddles and piccolos, and perhaps they might play us a record of Gilbert and Sullivan.' A genuine will to learning was awakened at this late stage after grammar school had apparently closed the 'early leavers' ' minds. But with the failure to train in these children any true critical awareness, or really to indicate what literature, painting and music were about, there were many pitfalls. Dilettantism and sheer eccentricity were rife: the peculiarities of the latest 'Beat' craze found fertile ground. Yet a working-class child might make here the first contact with literature, unimpeded by the middle-class atmosphere surrounding all that grammar school had touched upon: 'I've read *Women in Love, The Rainbow,* and a John Steinbeck novel called *Mice and Men,* and I'm just

247

starting one by a Russian called Dostoievsky. It's called *Crime and Punishment* is this one. Is it a good one?' In their reading was a fresh concern with people and this led to a kind of humane, omniverous interest in books. 'I like science fiction books because they're about humanity. They're about society, our world, about its problems and how we could solve them.' Four of them touched upon such groups, whose existence gives the tone of the 'early leavers' ' search towards a broader 'culture'.

Young men and women moving outwards from estates felt the comfort of groups like this. But older pupils too, coming up to the managerial level of the middle class, felt the same need to relax. 'Yes there was a time when I grew my hair long and had a big moustache and went all tweedy and wore check trousers. Funny, that was my attempt to conform. That was when I believed in business. Take the man next door. He's a nasty sly little jumped-up progress clerk. Well I suppose I'm a jumped-up librarian, but going down to meet the crowd in the *Woolpack* is my attempt to feel different.' More ambitious men deplored their fathers' lack of initiative, but themselves were too nervous to manage that final crossing into the middle class, by taking elocution lessons for example. The only two men who could whole-heartedly accept their move towards the middle class were both still manual workers hardly within striking distance of their aim. This was mirrored in their choice of spouse, for all those who had married, except one, chose a working class girl who had been to grammar school or to one of the public or fee-paying commercial schools.

A footnote—return to the community

What would these gifted working-class children have been like had they not gone through grammar school? Derek Ackroyd, on the 'early leavers' sample, was expelled from grammar school, as he described it, for 'independent mindedness'. He had returned to the estate with a heightened sense of the 'working class' and a determination to fight against 'injustice'. He had returned, in fact, as an unofficial leader; the kind of man who in industry might be a shop steward, or a leader of 'unofficial strikes'. 'They all know me round here. If ever anything goes wrong they're likely to turn to me. I make myself a bit of a nuisance sometimes I know, but you've got to make yourself a bit of a nuisance in an estate like this to get anything done. Like there was a boy I was very friendly with, and there's a mill dam, and he fell down the slope into the water and he was drowned before anybody could get to him. I was only a kid at the time. Then a few years ago there was another accident. Another boy got drowned in the same dam, and I was staggered that nobody had built a fence or a wall or something round that dam, and I found that sometime when I'd been away there'd been *another* child drowned!' His enquiries in this case revealed an official deadlock. 'Well, I wrote more letters to the *Echo* and I got a petition up and went round the estate and got people to sign it. And it's like that; once you start speaking up against something, lots of people start speaking up against it. Before, they haven't the courage, they haven't got the confidence. They've got the rights, and they've got the complaints, but they don't do anything.' The result of all this was a 'damned good wall, big and strong and safe.'

These everyday 'political' activities demonstrated how in his daily living Mr. Ackroyd drew on strengths of community not available to other grammar school pupils. Their political views had a 'bloodlessness' which gave them the character of labels rather than deeply-held beliefs. Political responsibility tended to stop short at the ballot box, where the 'early leavers' followed the voting pattern of the main sample (Table XXVIII). Yet at the same time the freshness and revolt of Mr. Ackroyd's approach—like the 'early leavers' new learning—was vulnerable. And although he attempted to divorce his opinions from present-day power politics, it was to Communism that his sympathies, like those of many other 'unofficial' leaders, turned. 'I'm a Communist. That doesn't mean I can't see anything wrong with Russia or China, or think that everything they do is right. It's not, very often far from it; but the theory of it, the basic ideal, that's what I believe in.

'On this estate you've got more community spirit than you would have, say, down Edgefield—real community spirit. We've got to think first of all of getting this on a local scale; everybody in Marburton being co-operative and community-minded. Then on a national scale. Then on an international scale. I take it that's brotherhood. I take it that's what Christianity is all about.' This statement of his ideals is both a comment on the grammar school concept of 'leadership', and an expression of the failure of grammar schools to enlist potential leaders from the new generation of working class children.

Appendix 2

ADDITIONAL TABLES

TABLE IX

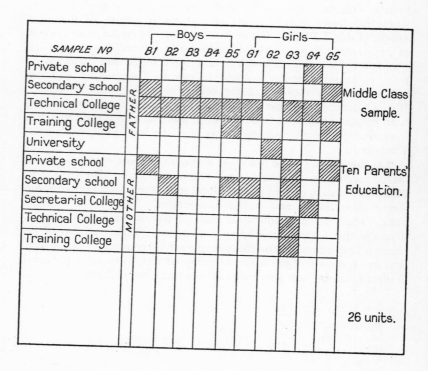

SAMPLE Nº		B1	B2	B3	B4	B5	G1	G2	G3	G4	G5	
		Boys					Girls					
Private school	FATHER									▨		Middle Class Sample.
Secondary school	FATHER	▨		▨				▨			▨	Middle Class Sample.
Technical College	FATHER	▨	▨	▨	▨	▨	▨		▨			Middle Class Sample.
Training College	FATHER					▨				▨		
University	FATHER							▨				
Private school	MOTHER	▨							▨		▨	Ten Parents' Education.
Secondary school	MOTHER		▨			▨	▨					Ten Parents' Education.
Secretarial College	MOTHER									▨		
Technical College	MOTHER								▨			
Training College	MOTHER							▨				
												26 units.

Appendix

TABLE X

SAMPLE NO		Boys — S2 S14 S28 S30 S37	Girls — SG33 SG1 SG3 SG18 SG23	
Private School				Working Class Sample
Secondary school	F A T H E R		▨ (SG33)	
Technical College		▨		Ten Parents' Education
Training College				
University				
Private school				
Secondary school	M O T H E R	▨		
Secretarial College			▨ (SG1)	
Technical College				
Training College				
				4 units

TABLE XI

SOCIAL CLASS OF CHILDREN PASSING A LEVEL 1949-52

	Second Class Grammar Schools	First Class Grammar Schools
Higher Professional	6%	14%
Lower Professional	27%	37%
Clerical	25%	13%
Skilled	34%	28%
Semi-skilled	3%	6%
Unskilled	5%	2%
Total %	100%	100%
Number	64	161

Table XII

The Fifth Form 'C' Stream at Ash Grange

	1929	1930	Year of Birth 1931	1932	1933	1934	Average
	%	%	%	%	%	%	%
Manual	38	40	61	44·5	67	65	54
Doubtful	15	25	13	11	22	17·5	17·5
Clerical	47	35	26	44·5	11	17·5	28·5
Total %	100	100	100	100	100	100	100
Number	13	20	23	18	18	23	115

Notes: (a) This estimate is necessarily rough since it is compiled from school records not designed for sociological analysis. In assigning girls to the class of doubtful occupations, we have been most stringent with those children who might be manual workers' daughters. Probably most of the doubtful families were working class.

(b) The figures are complicated by changes in the naming of the 'C' stream, and subdivision of the classes into 'German' and 'General'. This is too difficult to follow statistically, but it looked as though there was a further concentration of manual workers' children in the 'General' section of the 'C' stream.

Table XIII

Percentage of Manual Workers' Children Leaving from the 'C' Stream
(as a proportion of manual workers' children entering the school)

	1929	1930	Year of Birth 1931	1932	1933	1934	Total
	%	%	%	%	%	%	%
Manual	23–28	33–46	41–57	18–24	22–35	22–35	25–38
Clerical	15–20	21–37	16–26	15–20	5–18	8–18	12–22

Notes: The same limitations apply to this table as to Table XII.

In words, out of the children of different classes entering Ash Grange between 1940 and 1945, 25 to 38% of the manual workers' children finish in the 'C' stream, with 12 to 22% of the clerical workers' children.

There was no reliable record of how many girls subsequently went to training college. The school records gave only one manual workers' daughter, but this is probably on the low side.

Appendix

Chapter 3

TABLE XIV

OCCUPATION OF 86 WORKING-CLASS FATHERS

Occupation	Working-class population of Marburton	Sample
	%	%
Skilled	64	78
Semi-skilled	21	17
Unskilled	15	5
Total	100	100

TABLE XV

SUCCESS OF SIBLINGS IN PASSING THE SELECTION EXAMINATION

(i) 20 families in which a parent had had secondary education

No. of siblings to grammar school etc.	No. of siblings to secondary modern
20	3

(ii) 16 families in which a parent had been unable to take up a secondary school award

No. of siblings to grammar school etc.	No. of siblings to secondary modern
14	3

(iii) 50 families in which neither parent had passed a secondary selection examination

No. of siblings to grammar school etc	No. of siblings to secondary modern
27	20

Appendix

TABLE XVI

PARENTS' POLITICS AND HOME OWNERSHIP

(main sample)

	Conservative	Liberal	Labour
	%	%	%
Tenants	21	11	68
Owners	41	16	39

Chapter 4

Table XVII

Grammar School Streaming: main sample

	Boys	Girls	TOTAL
A Stream	33	33	75%
B Stream	8	4	14%
C Stream	2	0	2%
Unstreamed or unknown	6	2	9%
	49	39	100%

TABLE XVIII

DISTRIBUTION BETWEEN ARTS AND SCIENCE SIXTHS

(main sample)

	Marburton sample	Oxford sample *
	%	%
Arts	47	44·8
Science	48	49·4
Mixed	5	5·8
Per cent	100	100
Nos.	88	2,822

* calculated from *Arts & Science Sides in the Sixth Form*

Chapter 5

TABLE XIX

SOCIAL CLASS OF 88 FORMER WORKING-CLASS CHILDREN

I.	15
II.	67
III.	5
unclassified	1
Total Nos.	88

TABLE XX

PROFESSIONS OF 88 FORMER WORKING-CLASS CHILDREN

Teaching	46
Industrial Management	7
Industrial Research	11
Civil Service	7
Medicine	2
Church	3
Military or police	3
Others	9

TABLE XXI

CONTACTS OF 84 FORMER WORKING-CLASS CHILDREN WITH THEIR PARENTS

	Men	Women	Both
	%	%	%
Daily	18	27	21
At least twice a week	7	10	9
Weekly	7	13	10
Monthly	22	24	22
3 Monthly	20	16	18
6 Monthly	25	10	19
Annually	1	nil	1
Total %	100	100	100
Total Nos.	46	38	84

Appendix

TABLE XXII

EDUCATION OF BOYS' AND GIRLS' BROTHERS AND SISTERS
(Main sample)

Type of School	Boys		Girls		All %
	Brothers	Sisters	Brothers	Sisters	
Secondary modern	6	13	3	1	27
Fee-paying 'commercial'	5	1	1	2	11
Secondary technical	4	3	0	2	11
Grammar school	15	11	9	9	51
Totals	30	28	13	14	85 = 100
Sixth form	5	2	3	4	16
University	1	0	2	1	7

TABLE XXIII

NUMBER OF BROTHERS AND SISTERS
(main sample)

	Boys	Girls	Both %
Only child	13	21	38
One sibling	22	10*	36
Two siblings	8	5	18
Three siblings	5	3*	7
Four siblings	1	0	1
Totals	49	39	100
Total brothers	30	13	43
Total sisters	28	14	42
	58	27	85
Size of family **	2·2 average	1·7 average	1·9 average

* In each of these totals there is a family with two girls on the sample—each girl has been counted separately, so that two families appear twice in these figures.

** The average size of the families in the three groups of manual workers in the Crowther Report 'National Service' survey (vol. 2 p. 125 and 8) ranges from 3·1 to 3·8.

Appendix

Appendix 1.

TABLE XXIV

OCCUPATION OF PARENTS

Railway Street 1943

Former social class
(children at Primary school)

Class II	1	III manual
Class III		
clerical	1	
own acct.	1	
manual	2	
	—	
Total	5	

Carthorpe

Class II	2	III clerical and III manual
Class III		
manual	4	
Class IV	1	
	—	
Total	7	

TABLE XXV

SOCIAL CLASS OF GRANDPARENTS

Parents' Class

II (total 3)

Both sets of G/p class II	1
Mother's parents class II	1
Both sets of G/p manual	1
	—
	3

Clerical
III (total 1)

Both sets of G/p class II	1

III (manual—7)

Both sets of G/p class II	1
Mother's parents only class II	1
Grandparents all manual	5

IV (total 1)

Both sets of G/p manual	1

257

Appendix

TABLE XXVI

PARENTS' EDUCATION

Selective school
Class II (total 3)
  Both parents   1
  Neither   2

Class III clerical (total 1)
  Both parents   1
    manual (total 7)
  Neither   7

Class IV (total 1)
  Neither   1

Passed scholarship, but not allowed to go:
Class III Manual (total 7)
  Both parents   1
  Neither   6

Class IV (total 1)
  Father   1

TABLE XXVII

SOCIAL CLASS OF EARLY LEAVERS

Parents' Class	Child
Railway Street	
II	III clerical
III clerical	II managerial
III manual	Two are III clerical (one girl)
	One is IIIe own account
Carthorpe	
II	Both girls II, teachers
III (4)	A girl IIIc
	A boy II
	A boy IIIc
	A boy IIIe
IV	A boy IIIe

TABLE XXVIII

POLITICAL VIEWS OF EARLY LEAVERS' FAMILIES

Father /mother (No. of families)	*Children's political views*
II	
Labour/Labour	Conservative
Liberal/Liberal	Not seen
Non-voter/Liberal	Liberal (doesn't usually vote)
III *clerical*	
Conservative/Conservative	Conservative
III *manual*	
Labour/Labour (3)	Communist/Labour
	Labour
	Liberal/Conservative
Unknown/Labour	Labour
Labour/Liberal	Labour
Conservative/Conservative	Conservative
Unknown/Unknown	Not seen
IV	
Non-voter/unknown	Labour tendencies

Parents:	Labour 10	Liberal 14	Conservative 4	Unknown 6
Children:	Labour 5	Liberal 1	Conservative 1	Unknown 2

THE DEFINITION OF 'WORKING CLASS' FOR THE SAMPLE

The problem was how to use the Registrar General's Classification of Occupations to give a sample of occupations which most nearly fitted the social facts of the Marburton area. The problem lies nearly all within the range of the class III.

Broadly speaking we were trying to cut down on the number of people who might be doing clerical jobs, and who lived in middle-class districts on a low income—people who have never worked with their hands at a trade.

At the same time, we wanted to exclude those working men who owned businesses (as opposed to the men who were self-employed at a trade).

Shop and business owners are the main cause of confusion in this classification so that this is the code we adopted:

Appendix

Those included in our sample

(1) Owners of businesses which do not sell retail goods, nor employ people, whether other members of the family or not.

(2) Firemen.

(3) Unqualified nurses.

(4) Part owners of businesses employing nobody else (not retail).

Those excluded

(1) Owners of small *retail* businesses, regardless of size. (e.g. chip shop owners, coal merchants, mixed shops).

(2) All owners of businesses employing workmen. This is a departure from the R.G.C.O., which would include employers of fewer than ten men with manual workers.

Procedure for drawing the main 'working class' sample

(1) We visited all the grammar schools and picked out from the Higher School for 1946 to 1954 certificate or G.C.E. pass lists all those children with a H.S.C. pass in any form or its 'equivalent'. Equivalents taken were 3 passes in G.C.E. 'A' level, two 'A' level passes with two 'O' level passes, or two 'A' level passes and one good scholarship pass. This was necessary to allow for mathematics specialists who often only took two 'A' level subjects. We only used the boys results for 1949 to 1952.

(2) All the parents occupations on the school records were classified according to the Registrar General's Classification of Occupations, using the descriptions provided by the parents. These were some inadequate descriptions:

(a) Clerks, cashiers, civil servants, were all assigned to 890, "other clerks", in the absence of any further information. This gives them a grading of IIIc which may be incorrect in some cases. The number involved here is four cashiers, ten clerks, four civil servants and three secretaries.

(b) All parents describing themselves as "small business owners' "master tradesmen", "painter and decorator", "engineer", "electrical/refrigeration engineer", "cobbler", etc. were visited.

(c) All parents with manual occupations, skilled or unskilled, were visited.

The information from these visits enabled us to assign all the manual workers, 'business owners', and those connected with small business to their class on the Registrar General's Classification.

(d) The remaining shop-assistants, shop managers, shop owners, and works and production managers of various kinds were not visited, but were classified according to the description which they gave on the school records.

(Note: This places reliance on the truth of these records, and in no case were they found to be inaccurate. In the cases where the parent had moved to an occupation of a higher social rating while the child was at school, the *highest* classification was adopted.)

(3) All parents having a social grading of I, II, or IIIc (clerks, shop assistants) were excluded from the working class sample.

In addition, all small business owners falling within class IIIe (except those working by themselves, "own account") were excluded.

(4) This gave us a set of manual workers' children. We further excluded all 'late arrivals' in the district—children who had not at least been to local primary schools—and one girl who had been to private school.

(5) Two pupils had died. Three parents had died and two had moved away. We could not contact four pupils who were abroad throughout the survey. We also excluded ourselves and one relative. This left us with the sample set out in the following table—39 girls and 49 boys.

(6) Two girls refused to see us, and the parents of two boys also refused to be interviewed. We failed to contact two boys and two girls, but they filled in elaborate schedules which we sent by post. These were not satisfactory, but they helped to complete the statistics.

Procedure for drawing the 'middle class' sub-sample

The intention, in drawing the middle class sample, was to provide a set of twenty interviews (ten with children and ten with their parents) with people of a social grading markedly different from the main working class sample.

(1) All parents with occupations rated III or below on the Classification were excluded from the middle class list.

(2) All these master tradesmen who were employers but who could not be definitely placed in classes IIIe or class II (for lack of information as to the size of the business) were excluded from the list. There were three of these, who were known to be employers in their own right, who were not visited during the drawing up of the working class sample.

(3) We had no systematic information about the size of the shops listed. (Some of these had been visited during the check on "small business owners".) We grouped all persons connected with shops

CENTRAL SAMPLE

(A sample of working-class children drawn from boys (1949–52) and girls (1946–1954) who passed H.S.C. or G.C.E. at 'A' level.)

	1946	1947	1948	1949	1950
No. of girls passing	27	23	17	20	23
No. of boys passing	**	**	**	40	40
Girls on sample	2	5	2	7	7
Boys on sample	**	**	**	15	12
Total passing				60	63
Total on sample				22	20

	1951	1952	1953	1954
Girls passing	20	20	20	18
Boys passing	24	42	**	**
Girls on sample	5	5	3	3
Boys on sample	11	11	**	**
Total passing	44	62		
Total on sample	15	17		

Total girls passing 188: Total boys passing 146
Girls on sample 39: Boys on sample 49

together, regarding shop assistants and small shop owners, together with branch managers, as similar to the clerks whom we placed in IIIc and the lower part of group II. Licensees and commercial travellers were also excluded at this stage, owing to similar difficulties in determining the status of individuals in those occupations. We retained coal merchants, thinking that the nature of the business necessarily involved a larger amount of capital equipment. Owners of chemists' shops were retained as being, probably, pharmacists differently described.

(4) We excluded Haulage Contractors (rated IIIe by the Registrar General, but possibly class II on a level with "garage owner.") The engineering aspects of the district were already adequately represented on our list.

The final list contains approximately one third of the passes, and after late arrivals, and pupils at private schools had been excluded there were 38 boys and 58 girls drawn from the same years as the main working class sample. We selected our ten families at random from these: three girls from Ash Grange and one from Thorpe Manor; five boys from Marburton College and one from Abbeyford.

Appendix 3
LIST OF REFERENCES

ARNOLD, M. *Culture and Anarchy*. London, Smith & Elder. 1891.

BANKS, O. *Parity and Prestige in English Education*. London, Routledge & Kegan Paul. 1955.

BARTLETT, F. C. *Remembering*. London, Cambridge University Press, 1932.

BENDIX, R. and LIPSET, S. M. (eds.). *Class, Status and Power: A Reader in Social Stratification*. London, Routledge & Kegan Paul. 1954

BERNSTEIN, B. 'Some Sociological Determinants of Perception.' *British Journal of Sociology*. vol. ix. part 2, 1958.

BERNSTEIN, B. 'Language and Social Class.' *British Journal of Sociology*, vol. xi. no. 3. 1960.

BURT, C. 'The Crowther and Albemarle Reports.' *British Journal of Educational Psychology*. Vol. xxx, part 3. 1960.

CLARKE, F. *Education and Social Change*. London, Sheldon Press. 1940.

CLEMENTS, R. V. *The Managers: A Study of their Careers in Industry*. London, Allen & Unwin. 1958.

CONWAY, J. 'Inheritance of Intelligence and its Social Implications.' *British Journal of Statistical Psychology*. Vol. xi. part 2. 1958.

DALE, R. *From School to University*. London, Routledge & Kegan Paul. 1954.

DALE, R. 'Reflections on Research on Allocation to Secondary Education.' *British Journal of Educational Psychology*. Vol. xxx, Part 3. 1960.

DANIELS, J. C. 'The Effects of Streaming in the Primary School.' Unpublished Ph.D. Thesis. University of Nottingham, 1960.

DAVIES, H. 'The Social Effects of the 1944 Act on the Grammar School.' *Bulletin of Education*. No. 23, 1950.

DENNIS, N., HENRIQUES, F. and SLAUGHTER, C. *Coal is our Life*. London, Eyre & Spottiswoode. 1956.

ELIOT, T. S. *Notes Towards The Definition of Culture*. London, Faber and Faber. 1948.

FLOUD, J., HALSEY, A. H. and MARTIN, F. M *Social Class and Educational Opportunity*. London, Heinemann. 1957.

S

FRANKENBERG, R. *Village on the Border*. London, Cohen and West. 1957.

GLUCKMAN, M. 'Man the Social Animal.' *The Listener*. October 22nd, 1959.

HALSEY, A. H. 'Genetics, Social Structure and Intelligence.' *British Journal of Sociology*. Vol. ix. No. 1. 1958.

HALSEY, A. H. 'Class Differences in General Intelligence.' *British Journal of Statistical Psychology*. Vol. xii. Part 1, 1959.

HALSEY, A. H. 'Changing Functions of Universities.' *Harvard Educational Review*. Vol. 30, No. 2. 1960.

HEWITT, E. A. 'The Performance in English at "O" level of a sample of University Students.' *British Journal of Educational Psychology*. Vol. xxx. Part 1, 1960.

HOGBEN, L. *Statistical Theory*. London, Allen & Unwin. 1957.

HOGBEN, L. (ed.). *Political Arithmetic*. London, Allen & Unwin. 1938.

HOGGART, R. *The Uses of Literary*. London, Chatto and Windus. 1957.

KERR, M. *The People of Ship Street*. London, Routledge & Kegan Paul. 1958.

KNIGHTS, L. C. *An Approach to Hamlet*. London, Chatto and Windus. 1960.

LEYBOURNE-WHITE, G. *Education and the Birth Rate*. London, Jonathan Cape. 1940.

LINDSAY, K. *Educational Progress and Social Waste*. London, University of London Studies in Economics and Political Science. No. 88. 1926.

MALINOWSKI, B. 'A Nation-Wide Intelligence Service.'

MADGE, C. and HARRISSON, T. *First Year's Work in Mass Observation*. London, Lindsay Drummond. 1938.

MARRIS, P. *Widows and their Families*. London, Routledge & Kegan Paul, 1958.

McINTOSH, D. M. *Educational Guidance & the Pool of Ability*. London, University of London Press. 1959.

MOGEY, J. M. *Family and Neighbourhood*. London, Oxford University Press. 1956.

NISBETT, J. *Family Environment*. London, Cassell. 1953.

OTTAWAY, A. K. *Education and Society*. London, Routledge & Kegan Paul. 1953.

PAPE. G. V. 'Accident of Birth.' *Education*. November 16th. 1956.

PEDLEY, R. *Comprehensive Education*. London, Gollancz. 1956.

PETERSON, A. D. C. *A Hundred Years of Education*. London, Duckworth. 1952.

REE, H. Letter. *Times Educational Supplement.* October 16th. 1953.

REE, H. *The Essential Grammar School.* London, Harrap. 1956.

SHARP, J. *Educating One Nation.* London, Max Parrish. 1959.

SILBERSTON, D. M. *Youth in a Technical Age.* London, Max Parrish. 1959.

SIMON, B. *The Common Secondary School.* London, Lawrence & Wishart. 1955.

SIMON, B. *Studies in the History of Education.* London, Lawrence & Wishart. 1960.

SIMON, S. 'Refusal Rates in Manchester.' *Education.* September 1936.

STEVENS, F. *The Living Tradition.* London, Hutchinson. 1961.

TANNER, J. M. *Growth at Adolescence.* London, Blackwell. 1955.

TOWNSEND, P. *The Family Life of Old People.* London, Routledge & Kegan Paul. 1957.

TOWNSEND, P. 'The Institution and The Individual.' *The Listener.* June 23rd, 1960.

TURNER, M. *Forgotten Men.* London, National Council of Social Service. 1960.

TYLECOTE, M. *The Mechanics' Institutes of Lancashire and Yorkshire.* Manchester, Manchester University Press. 1957.

VAIZEY, J. *The Costs of Education.* London, Allen & Unwin. 1958.

WARNER, W. L., HAVINGHURST, R. J. and LOEB, M. B. *Who Shall be Educated?* New York, Harper & Bros. 1946.

WATTS, A. F. *The Language and Mental Development of Children.* London, Harrap. 1944.

WHITE, R. C. *These Will Go To College.* Cleveland, Ohio. Western Reserve University. 1952.

WILLIAMS, W. M. *The Sociology of an English Village: Gosforth.* London, Routledge & Kegan Paul. 1956.

WOLFLE, D. *America's Resources of Specialized Talent.* New York, Harper & Bros. 1954.

YOUNG, M. and WILLMOTT, P. *Family and Kinship in East London.* London, Routledge & Kegan Paul. 1957.

Annual Report on the Derbyshire School Health Service. Derbyshire County Council. 1959.

Arts and Science Sides in the Sixth Form. Oxford University Department of Education. 1960.

Census 1951. England and Wales. Occupation Tables. London, H.M.S.O. 1956.

Census 1951. Classification of Occupations. London, H.M.S.O. 1956.

Appendix

Central Advisory Council for Education (England): *Early Leaving*. London, H.M.S.O. 1954.

Central Advisory Council for Education, (England): 15 *to* 18. London, H.M.S.O. Vol. 1, 1959. Vol. 2, 1960.

The best selective bibliography of work in educational sociology is to be found in *Current Sociology* Vol. vii. No. 3, 1958. (FLOUD, J. and HALSEY, A. H. 'The Sociology of Education: A Trend Report'.)

INDEX